SONOMA COUNTY LIBRARY
3 7565 0271 50795

The African Slave Trade

Books about Africa by Basil Davidson

HISTORY

THE AFRICAN GENIUS

THE LOST CITIES OF AFRICA

BLACK MOTHER: THE AFRICAN SLAVE TRADE

THE AFRICAN PAST: CHRONICLES FROM ANTIQUITY TO MODERN TIMES

THE GROWTH OF AFRICAN CIVILIZATION: A HISTORY OF WEST AFRICA 1000–1800, with F. K. Buah

A HISTORY OF EAST AND CENTRAL AFRICA TO THE LATE NINETEENTH CENTURY, with J. E. F. Mhina

GUIDE TO AFRICAN HISTORY

AFRICAN KINGDOMS (with the editors of Time-Life Books)

AFRICA IN HISTORY: THEMES AND OUTLINES

LET FREEDOM COME: AFRICA IN MODERN HISTORY

CURRENT AFFAIRS

CAN AFRICA SURVIVE? ARGUMENTS AGAINST GROWTH WITHOUT DEVELOPMENT

REPORT ON SOUTHERN AFRICA

THE AFRICAN AWAKENING

WHICH WAY AFRICA? THE SEARCH FOR A NEW SOCIETY

THE LIBERATION OF GUINE: ASPECTS OF AN AFRICAN REVOLUTION

IN THE EYE OF THE STORM: ANGOLA'S PEOPLE

BLACK STAR: A VIEW OF THE LIFE AND TIMES OF KWAME NKRUMAH

FICTION

THE RAPIDS

THE AFRICAN SLAVE TRADE

a revised and expanded edition

BASIL DAVIDSON

an atlantic monthly press book
little, brown and company
boston / toronto

LIBRARY OF CONGRESS CATALOG CARD NO. 81–65588

A

The African Slave Trade was originally entitled *Black Mother* in hardcover.

ATLANTIC-LITTLE, BROWN BOOKS
ARE PUBLISHED BY
LITTLE, BROWN AND COMPANY
IN ASSOCIATION WITH
THE ATLANTIC MONTHLY PRESS

BP

PRINTED IN THE UNITED STATES OF AMERICA

To the Memory of
William Adlington Cadbury
February 17, 1867 – July 8, 1957

Contents

PART FIVE: EAST COAST FORTUNES

PART SIX: FRONTIER OF OPPORTUNITY

PART SEVEN: FOUR CENTURIES: A SUMMING UP

MAPS

INTRODUCTION

Only the wholly other can inspire the deepest love and the profoundest desire to learn.

JOSEPH NEEDHAM

Introduction

MORE than five hundred years have passed since Europe and Africa – continental Africa, the land of the blacks – first made acquaintance and began their trading intercourse.

After this early discovery of one another, Africans and Europeans knew four centuries of varied friendship and hostility, good and evil, profit and loss; and the fortunes of Africa and Europe, through all these years, were caught and woven ever more tightly together. Then came the onset of European conquest and now, in our own day, an end to the colonial system and the rise of an Africa which has regained or is fast regaining its independence. And so the cycle is rounded and complete. The relations of equality and self-respect that were known in the early years of this long connection are reforged or once again are in the making.

But why did history take this course? Why was European conquest so much delayed; and why, after that delay and often lengthy experience of one another, did so large a part of Africa collapse into rapid and unrelieved subjection to Europe? We know that the Spanish occupied Central America; the Portuguese seized Brazil; the French and British spread across the seaboard lands of North America, and all of them flew conquering flags in the eastern world. Yet Africa, bating small footholds here and there, remained inviolate until late in the nineteenth century. Then, almost from one decade to the next, wide areas of Africa became colonies of Europe.

One can ask the question in other ways. Why did Europe tremendously expand and grow in power and wealth, and yet Africa fail to do the same? How was it that early European captains and their backers could treat Africans with the respect that was due to equals, and yet a later world, setting this aside or else forgetting it altogether, could regard Africans as naturally inferior?

Some of the answers lie in purely European history. They can be found in a thousand books, telling the story of commercial growth, industrial revolution, empire and expansion. But other answers lie in Africa. And of these, I think, the most potent and illuminating are provided by the curious tale of Europe's dealings with Africa, and Africa's with Europe, in the period between the middle of the fifteenth and the middle of the nineteenth centuries: between, let us say, 1450 and 1850.

This book is therefore an attempt to explain the nature of the European-African connection in pre-colonial times, and its peculiar and special impact on Africa. No such attempt can hope to be definitive at this early stage in the recovery and rediscovery of African history; nor could it ever be comprehensive within the limits of one short book. Yet something useful can be done, it seems to me, even within these limits. So I have taken three important areas of Africa – those of the old Congo kingdoms, of the city-states of the East Coast, and of some of the strong societies of the Guinea Coast – and examined these against a general background of their time and circumstance.

Inevitably this means a fresh look at the oversea slave trade, the steady year-by-year export of African labour to the West Indies and the Americas that marked the greatest and most fateful migration – forced migration – in the history of man. Many writers have investigated the European and American side of the slaving experience, but little or nothing has been written on the consequences of the slave trade for Africa itself. Yet slaving rapidly engulfed the whole connection. Its influence bore heavily, perhaps decisively, on the destiny of many African societies. Nothing in their history during these centuries can be understood without a cool appraisal of the slaving impact. What I have tried to offer here, accordingly, is an unsentimental inquiry into some characteristic aspects of African history in several regions where slaving was of major importance.

One comes at once against a difficulty. The records are copious, but mainly they are European records and they are coloured indelibly by the myth and prejudice which the trade itself did so much to promote. Through long years the 'Black Mother' of

Africa would populate the Americas with millions of her sons and daughters, and Europe would pile up libraries of comment on the nature of these victims and of the Africa that could yield them. But where in the multitude of these opinions – philanthropic or cynical, sincere, self-interested or merely superstitious – may one safely draw the line between illusion and reality? Perhaps it is only now, when the bitter memories of slaving are assuaged by time, when the old servitudes of Africa begin to be dispelled by a new freedom, and when there is no longer any point in the beating of breasts or the apportioning of blame, that one can usefully look for the truth of those astounding years.

But to set the scene and indicate its special flavour – so vigorous and obstinately hopeful in spite of all its misery and death – let us begin with some contrasts.

* * *

There was misery, unending misery. There was so much death in the Americas that whole slave populations had to be renewed every few years. The records are eloquent enough . . .

In 1829 an Englishman called Walsh took passage from Brazil in a British frigate, the *North Star*. Somewhere in the South Atlantic they chased and stopped a slaver. Walsh went on board and afterwards described what he saw – the familiar horrors of the Middle Passage. The slaving ship's cargo was of five hundred and five men and women – the crew had thrown fifty-five overboard during their seventeen days at sea – and these slaves

> were all enclosed under grated hatchways, between decks. The space was so low that they sat between each others' legs, and stowed so close together, that there was no possibility of lying down, or at all changing their position, by night or by day. As they belonged to, and were shipped on account of different individuals, they were all branded like sheep, with the owners' marks of different forms. These were impressed under their breasts, or on their arms, and, as the mate informed me with perfect indifference, burnt with a red hot iron . . .

Many of these branded chattels, Walsh found, had no more than ·09 square metres, or one square foot, of sitting space, with no chance of standing up, and all suffered from a deadly shortage of water. Walsh was shocked, but his naval companions, 'who had passed so long a time on the coast of Africa, and visited so many ships' in the course of their anti-slaving patrols, said that this slaver was 'one of the best they had seen'. Headroom for slaves was as much as one metre whereas sometimes, Walsh was told, headroom was no more than forty-five centimetres and slaves were generally chained, as these were not, by the neck and legs during their crossing of the Atlantic.

Such scenes were not rare. They had occurred month after month for nearly three hundred years by the time that Walsh took passage from Brazil. This was the physical degradation of the trade.

There was also a moral degradation: of the slaves, and of the slavers. Through enslaving Africans, Europeans abused their own humanity as well. They came to believe that Africa was indeed cast away in savage chaos, that Africans had never known any reasonable social order of their own, and that African slaves deserved no better than they got. The slavers justified their work by such beliefs.

'Africans being the most lascivious of all human beings', declared a Liverpool pamphlet of 1792, 'may it not be imagined, that the cries they let forth at being torn from their wives, proceed from the dread that they will never have the opportunity of indulging their passions in the country to which they are embarking?'

Often the arguments were less coarse and brutal. Sometimes they verged on the 'scientific'. Writing of the Guinea Coast in the late eighteenth century, a German named Soemmering observed that the people there 'are more insensible than others towards pain and natural evils, as well as towards injurious and unjust treatment. In short, there are none so well adapted to be the slaves of others, and who therefore have been armed with so much passive obedience.'

What could be the value of such captive trash? The spirit of the times awarded them no value: even the achievements of their toil and sweat were denied them. African slaves had fertilized great regions of the New World by the nineteenth century, but their part in all this was ignored or forgotten. 'Before the West Indies could grow a pumpkin for any Negro,' Thomas Carlyle was declaring, and without irony, in 1849, 'how much European heroism had to spend itself in obscure battle; to sink, in mortal agony, before the jungles, the putrescences and waste savageries could become arable, and the Devils be in some measure chained up!' Thus was history stood upon its head.

* * *

There was another side to the story: surprisingly, one of hope and courage and survival. Here too the records are eloquent.

Consider the epic, or such as is known of it, of Jacintha de Siqueira, an African woman of Brazil. Brief but intriguing fragments of her biography were collected by Luis Pinto, a diligent clerk of the inland province of Minas Gerais: Gilberto Freyre has presented them in his book about Brazilian beginnings, *The Masters and the Slaves.*

Pinto was an obscure archivist whose task was the ordering and arrangement of official papers in a small Brazilian town. Yet Pinto was also something of a local historian. He enlivened his daily round by collecting facts about the early settlers of his province; and these facts were anything but dull and dreary, for the province of Minas had lately been – indeed, still was – the wild *sertão*, the lawless badlands of the far interior that settlers along the Brazilian coast held cautiously in awe. Even today the men and women who trekked inland to the conquest and settlement of the *sertão* are famous in memory as bold heroes, flaming and flamboyant in their grip on life, turbulent and reckless, enterprising and ambitious.

These pioneers pressed inland from the coast in small companies, *bandeiras*, that were soon legendary in the seaports and plantations for their courage and endurance. They climbed to the unknown hills with their pack-mules and pack-horses wending up behind them, perhaps a dozen or twenty men and women in leather jerkins and trousers or long cotton gowns, wide-brimmed hats of straw, red and blue and yellow blankets rolled tight at their saddles or wound upon their shoulders against the upland wind, flourishing their whips, the muzzles of their strange old guns like clumsy banners prodding the South American sky. It was they who took the challenge of this new country and opened up the mineral-rich interior.

Few saw them go, for among these *bandeirantes* were many on the run from slave plantations. Once clear of the coast-long tyranny they made their own law, just as other pioneers would do on other frontiers. This unwritten law was as strong as armed daring could devise or care to enforce. Some of it had to do with the taking of the land and the enslavement of the indigenous peoples, who were called 'Indians'. Some of it was concerned with the staking out of mining claims or the establishment of tented camps. However much they might prey on one another, these *bandeirantes* were not really bandits. They were intending settlers.

Their aim was to build a new life for themselves beyond the reach of colonial law, and to search for the gold and silver, diamonds and emeralds that were said to lie in this fabulous but utterly unknown *sertão*; and to these ambitions they brought, each of them, whatever skills and knowledge they might have. When they were fortunate they built their camps into towns: some of these towns are the cities of modern Brazil. They married or took mistresses and begat as many children as might be, brown and black and white and all the shades between: among these children were many who became the active makers of the Brazil we know today.

So it was that the memoirs gathered by Luis Pinto or others like him, and put together by their inquisitive forgotten hands, were the tales of a frontier folk of unusual daring and accomplishment. They were the gossip of a thousand meetings and disputes, squalid or amazing, which come about when a land is settled and a nation is born.

Somewhere round the year 1700, records Pinto, a company of pioneers of this sort departed on the inland trail from the port of Bahia – Bahia of All the Saints, greatest of the ports of old Brazil – and made their way into the remote wilderness that would one day be the province of Minas Gerais. They were, says Pinto, 'various *bandeirantes*'. Among them was Jacintha de Siqueira.

Jacintha became famous. To her 'is due the credit for the discovery of gold in the Quatro Vintens ravine and the founding of the settlement of Villa Novo do Principe in 1714'. To her, as well, is due the credit of founding not one family, but many families. Women were few and the land cried out for settlement. 'The fathers of all the sons of Jacintha de Siqueira were rich and important individuals,' says the record, 'and many of them were prominent in the government.'

What manner of woman was Jacintha, this founding mother of the richest of all the provinces of Brazil? Pinto offers one fundamental fact: he calls her 'the celebrated African woman'. Jacintha, that is to say, was a woman either brought in slavery from Africa or born into slavery in Brazil. She would have had her origins somewhere on the Guinea Coast or in Angola – a woman, one may well imagine, of large and splendid frame, strong and confident, tough in mind and morals: just such a woman as any traveller will meet today, without much searching, in the villages and towns of western Africa.

This Jacintha, founder of Villa Novo do Principe, was typical, in being an African, of many of the *bandeirantes* who settled the interior. It is because of this that the settlement of inland Brazil (as of some other parts of Central and South America) has left a unique and often astonishing body of evidence on the kind of men and women these African slaves really were, and on the nature of the African cultures from which they came.

Here in their regained freedom these Africans applied the skills and knowledge they had brought from their homeland. Already, as workers in the coast-long plantations, they had made a success of cultivation under climatic conditions that were new to their European masters, but not to them. Now in the interior they applied their arts of cattle-breeding, learned in the African savannahs, and their old skills in mining for metal and in smelting ore and in forging tools. Strange though it may seem, it was the Africans – whether bond or free – who often led the way.

In 1818 a Swedish engineer, von Eschwege, lately returned from service in Brazil, published a book of memoirs. 'The Captaincy of Minas Gerais', he observes, 'seems to have been the last in which the usability of iron ore and the extraction of iron was learnt from African negro slaves.' The equipment used by these Africans included the small furnace and the hand-blown bellows that were the traditional equipment of Africa.

'The search for gold in the Brazilian highlands', comments Lowrie, 'depended largely upon Negro labour, and the mineral industries of colonial Columbia would have been impossible without Negro slaves.' Roberto Simonsen, in a standard work, has estimated the total number of Africans employed in Brazilian mining throughout the eighteenth century as not fewer than six hundred thousand men. Even as late as 1856 Ewbank could note in Rio de Janeiro that 'the modes of working copper are very similar to ours ... In one shop twenty blacks were at work, and not a white face among the blacks.' Yet for the most part these skills had not been learned from Europeans: they had come with the slaving ships from Africa.

One could multiply the evidence. What went for metals was also true for precious stones. The very folk-customs of the country proved it. 'When a Negro is so fortunate as to find a diamond of the weight of an octavo (17½ carats), much ceremony takes place; he is crowned with a wreath of flowers and carried in procession to the administrator, who gives him his freedom, by paying his owner for it. He also receives a present of new clothes, and is permitted to work on his own account ...'

Africans were thus the 'technological element' in early Brazilian society. 'I have now seen', Ewbank wrote in the middle of the nineteenth century, 'slaves working as carpenters, masons, pavers, printers, sign and ornamental painters, carriage and cabinet workers, fabricators of military ornaments, lamp-makers, silversmiths, jewellers and lithographers.' No fewer than a million African slaves laboured in the Brazilian sugar plantations towards the end of the eighteenth century; but as well as providing field work Africans also provided the arts and crafts and the foundations of Brazilian industry. They tilled and bred cattle and mined and gathered wealth, for others if not for themselves. Far from showing 'passive obedience', they rebelled time and again. They built free republics of their own. They added their own culture to the cultures of Europe and of aboriginal South America, for along with their strength and experience they had brought with them their songs and arts and various beliefs. They were, said Freyre, himself no kind of revolutionary, 'an active, creative and, one might almost add, a noble element in the colonization of Brazil'.

* * *

An astounding contrast ... that glimpse of human cattle in the slaving ships compared with this other scene of bold and skilful pioneering. But it is also, I hope, a useful introduction to what follows here; for it suggests how widely the reputation of peoples can stand apart from their ability.

Many African peoples escaped the oversea slave trade and even the less important but long enduring overland slave trade. Anthropologists and historians are able to give an increasingly clear account of them, since much of their traditional culture survived into recent years. But many other African peoples failed to escape the trade, and some were overwhelmed by it. Even for those who were able to fight off its worst effects the trade grew often into a dominant influence on their life and development or failure of development. And it is precisely of these populations, coastal and near-coastal for the larger part, that the European records mainly tell: slaving became the main regulator of their lives. But slaving also became, as a matter of fact or a matter of myth, the great conditioning factor of most European ideas about Africa; and this is where myth and fact about Africans have become most confounded.

Modern research has made it possible to distinguish more closely between illusion and reality. The trade now dwindles to its true proportions and may be seen for what it was, an episode in African history, though a major episode that was huge in its consequences. This remains a complicated story. But the plan of this book, at any rate, is simple. To place the European-African connection in its historical perspective it is first of all necessary, even at the risk of over-simplifying complex traits, to consider how matters stood in Africa before the trade got into its stride, and how far the structure of leading states in Africa differed from that of contemporary states in Europe. This is the aim of Part One.

Then what were the course and growth of the trade, why did it rely so enormously on slaving, and how did it end? That is the subject of Part Two, the 'years of trial'. Part Three fills in this outline with some of the vivid and densely personal experience of the old trading partnership, its manners and morals, attitudes, customs and ambitions.

But in what ways did all this affect Africa? Here is the main question of my book. In answering it, Parts Four, Five and Six are concerned with three regions that were renowned during the trade, and where the coming of Europe had profound and often decisive influence on Africans, on the way they lived, and on what they believed or hoped of the outside world. Part Seven, finally, offers some general thoughts and conclusions on this epoch in African history.

PART ONE

FACT AND FABLE

Lang heff I maed of ladyes quhytt,
  Nou of ane blak I will indytt,
That landet furth of the last schippis;
  Quhou fain wald I descryve perfytt,
My ladye with the mekle lippis.

WILLIAM DUNBAR
Edinburgh,
in about 1509

1. Before the Trade Began

EUROPEAN ideas about Africa, before the years of discovery, varied remarkably with time and place. In southern Europe, face to face with North African power and commerce, there was beginning to be a good deal of solid information by the year 1500. Some knowledge of the scope and wealth of the lands beyond the Sahara was getting through to influential men. Yet even the well-informed ports of the Mediterranean could yield extraordinary fluctuations of judgement; and the facts they had to go on were encased, all too often, in a lavish covering of imaginative legend.

Much of this legend was learned from the Moors – Berbers and Arabs of the Moorish states of North Africa. Seldom could Christians penetrate the African interior, and only a handful of those who did have left any trace in the records. The earliest known European traveller's memoir from 'inner Africa' – and it would stand alone for many years to come – dates from 1447, and was written by an Italian called Antonio Malfante in Tuat, an oasis of the northern Sahara. Tuat in those days was an important staging-post for trans-Saharan caravans which had come from the south with African slaves, whether as victims or as porters, since times beyond recall.

Malfante picked up the caravan gossip of Tuat, and already it was rich with strange misunderstandings. He explains to a friend in Genoa that to the south of Tuat and the Great Desert there are black peoples who have 'innumerable great cities and territories'. But these peoples of the south 'are in carnal acts like the beasts: the father has knowledge of his daughter, the son of his sister. They breed greatly, for a woman bears up to five at a birth. Nor can it be doubted that they are eaters of human flesh.' Already the image of Black Africa is beginning to be the image of Caliban.

Elsewhere in Europe, especially in northern Europe where the trade with Africa was virtually unknown, opinions could be interestingly different. Northern Europe might understand Africa no more than Africa understood northern Europe: 'Scotland', an Andalusian Arab writer had declared in 1154, 'has neither dwellings, nor towns, nor villages', a considerable exaggeration even in those 'undeveloped' times. Yet even in remote Scotland a little was beginning to be known and thought of Africa by late medieval years; and the Scots by the beginning of the sixteenth century had also welcomed a few visitors from Africa. Such rare 'travellers' were evidently men and women taken out of Portuguese slaving ships by Scottish privateers. One or two of these visitors from the far south became famous in Edinburgh society, and not least of these was that 'black lady with the fulsome lips' of whom the poet Dunbar, who was born in about 1460, wrote some memorable verses.

This black lady had her moment of fame. The occasion was a royal jousting at Edinburgh in 1508 or perhaps 1509 – 'the justing of the wild knycht for the black ladye'. Fourteen men, it is recorded, carried her from Edinburgh Castle, where she was lodged, to the 'barres and syne to the Abbey'. The 'wild knight' who was the challenger seems to have been a Frenchman; but it was the king himself, brawny James IV, who carried off the day and the prize. It was just as well for James that he acquitted himself well because the award for valour was as enviable as the penalty for cowardice was not. At least, according to Dunbar:

Quhai for hir saik, with speir and scheld,
Preiffis maist mychtelė in the feld
  Sall kiss, and withe her go to grippis;
And fra thyne furth his luff sall weld
  My ladye with the mekle lippis.

The gallant who stained his knightly name had less to hope for:

And quhai in feld receawes schame,
And tynis thair his knychtlie name,
  Sall cum behind and kiss her hippis,
And neivir to other comfort claime:
  My ladye with the mekle lippis.

The times were broad, but at any rate they were not condescending.

And if European attitudes to Africans in those early times displayed a wide range of contrast, they were generally uniform in one important respect. They supposed no natural inferiority in Africans, no inherent failure to develop and mature. That was to be the great myth of later years: the central myth of European expansion that first took shape on the deck of a slaving ship. Race contempt crept in when free men could justify their material interests by the scorn they had for slaves – for men, that is, to whom an unnatural inferiority had given every appearance of a natural inferiority. How otherwise would so intelligent a man as Thomas Jefferson have reached the conclusion that he did?

'Comparing them [Negroes in North America] by their faculties of memory, reason and imagination,' Jefferson was writing after more than a century of intensive slaving had passed by, 'it appears to me that in memory they are equal to the whites; in reason much inferior, as I think one could scarcely be found capable of tracing and comprehending the investigations of Euclid; and that in imagination they are dull, tasteless, and anomalous.'

An American contemporary, as it happened, gave the answer to Jefferson. 'Now I beg to know', wrote Imlay White in reply, 'what can be more uncertain and false than estimating and comparing the intellect and talents of two descriptions of men: one enslaved, degraded and fettered in all their acts of volition ... the other free, independent and with the advantage of appropriating the reason and science which have been the result of the study and labours of the philosophers and sensible men for centuries back?'

Was the charge of inferiority altogether a myth? To be treated as an inferior is often to become an inferior, and it is precisely because the judgements of Europe were applied, so persistently and repeatedly, to Africans who were slaves that the writing of African history for this period must involve an analysis of the European state of mind as well as of the African condition. If we keep that in view we shall still not arrive at any final truth because history is not an exact science, susceptible of clear and completely objective categorization, but a more or less fallible means of explaining the present in terms of the past. It will be better or worse history according to the supply and use of fact. Propaganda, one may note, aims at just the opposite, explaining the past in terms of the present; a great deal of historical writing is propaganda. But Africa stands in dire need not of propaganda but of historical explanation.

And here one may take good heart, for in the matter of African history the supply of fact has immensely broadened and improved over recent years. Yet the task of getting to grips with this exciting and elusive theme will none the less remain a problem – and race contempt and its reactions define the reasons why – of getting to grips with oneself and with the limits of one's own formation.

In the early days of discovery, men in Europe believed they had found partners and allies and equals in Africa. 'Let them go and do business with the King of Timbuktu and Mali', Ramusio, secretary to the rulers in Venice, was urging the merchants of Italy in 1563, 'and there is no doubt they will be well received there with their ships and their goods and treated well, and granted the favours that they ask ...'

Three hundred years afterwards other men in Europe were sure that Africans had never so much as known the rudiments of political organization, let alone the means of building powerful states and operating central governments: Africans, it would be commonly said, simply lacked the faculty for growing up. 'Their inherent mental inferiority, almost more marked than their physical characters,' Professor Keane was writing with assured Victorian complacency in 1896, 'depends on physiological causes ...' Once an African grew beyond childhood, Richard Burton had decided a little earlier, 'his mental development is arrested, and thenceforth he grows backwards instead of forwards'.

If earlier Europeans had been closer to the truth, though having less information, they too were astray in their judgement. They avoided the crass absurdity of opinions such as those of Keane and Burton. They were right in thinking that their captains and caravels were discovering powerful states and potent commercial partners. But they were wrong in imagining that this Africa of lord and vassal and willing merchant was passing through the same political development as the states of Europe.

Looking back now, we can see that appearances were double-faced. On the one side it was true that the 'cultural gap' between the European discoverers and the Africans they found was narrow and was often felt to be non-existent. On the other side it was false that these appearances reflected a similar experience and potential of society in Africa and Europe. For the African states, evolving their governments and empires in lands remotely muffled from the heat and clash of European or Mediterranean competition, had reached a phase of relative stability. They could and would continue at much the same level of power and organization for a long time to come. But the states of Europe were anything but stable. On the contrary, they were about to trip the springs of all those piled-up tensions and turbulent contradictions that a restless and much-invaded past had compressed in their inheritance. Unlike the states of Africa, they were about to enter a time of fast and furious growth and change. They stood on the threshold of revolutions both economic and political.

It was in these peculiar circumstances of likeness and unlikeness that the African-European connection began. And it was out of this equivocation that much of the confusion and misunderstanding of later years would grow.

2. The Old States of Africa

ONE outstanding fact about the old states of black Africa, well understood in earlier times but afterwards forgotten, is that they were seldom or never conquered from outside the continent. They resisted invasion. They remained inviolate. Only here and there along the coast could European men-at-arms gain foothold even when they tried to win more. The Arabo-Berber states of northern Africa had little luck with their overland invasions of the south, and were in the end frustrated and forced to withdraw.

Writers of the colonial period were prone to explain this fact of successful African resistance by reference to the climate and the mosquito. Certainly, malaria and the sun were grim discouragers of foreign invasion. Yet the early records indicate another and more persuasive safeguard against conquest. They point to the striking-power of African armies. They show that it was the military factor, time and again, which proved decisive.

Even in the fifteenth century the Portuguese, then feeling their way round the long western coast, were vaguely aware of powers and principalities beyond the shoreward skyline whose alliance was desirable. 'The King', wrote De Barros, 'began cautiously to send agents with messages to the important chiefs, and to involve himself as a close and powerful friend in their affairs and their wars.' In the last quarter of the fifteenth century he sent 'Pedro de Evora and Gonsalo Eannes to the prince of Takrur' – inland from the coast of Senegal – 'and to the lord of Timbuktu'. From further to the south, the Portuguese also despatched a mission up the Gambia river 'to Mansa Mundi, one of the most powerful chiefs of the province of the Mandingo', who also was, in fact, the lord of the very extensive empire of Mali.

In 1482 they built their first fort on the Gold Coast, at a place they named El Mina, 'the mine', believing that from here they could best tap the sources of African gold. Yet they had to build this fort by agreement with the chief of the people of the region, and not after conquest. At the close of a long plea by Diogo de Azambuja, who commanded the Portuguese expedition, the chief in question consented to the building of a fort, but only on condition that 'peace and truth must be kept'. And one of the earliest actions that followed on the building of the castle at El Mina was not a military expedition to 'the mines' of the interior, but a diplomatic mission of friendship and alliance. Messengers had come from Mamadu, lord of Mali. King John of Portugal ordered that these messengers should be accompanied back to their country by eight Portuguese emissaries, including two knights of the royal court, 'with gifts of horses and mules and arms and other things prized in that country'.

El Mina was no disappointment. It delivered the gold of Africa; and in quantity through many years. But neither the Portuguese nor the Dutch nor any other European power ever secured access to the 'land of gold' until the British fought their way into Asante (Ashanti) at the end of the nineteenth century. Forts were built, but they were never secure. Garrisons were placed in them and repeatedly replenished from Europe; time and again they were besieged and overwhelmed. Governors were installed; yet they were obliged to live in close agreement with their African neighbours or else lose their power.

Opinion in Europe none the less grew common that European power held sway over the interior. 'There is no small number of men in Europe', a Dutch factor on the Gold Coast wrote back to his employers in the year 1700, 'who believe that the gold mines are in our power; that we ... have no more to do but to work them by our slaves: though you perfectly know we have no manner of access to these treasures.' By this time men in Europe were accustomed to seeing Africans only as men in chains, captives without power, and they transferred their impressions to Africa and the states from which these slaves had come. The belief in African inferiority was already in full bloom.

Those who actually travelled in Africa knew better. 'With nauseating presumption', complained Father Cavazzi of northern Angola in 1687, 'these nations think themselves the foremost men in the world, and nothing will persuade them to the contrary ... They imagine that Africa is not only the greatest part of the world, but also the happiest and most agreeable.' The ruling lords, he found, were even more arrogant. 'Similar opinions are held by the king himself, but in a manner still more remarkable. For he is persuaded that there is no other monarch in the world who is his equal, or exceeds him in power or the abundance of wealth ...'

The reasons for this African self-confidence were not really obscure. They were the fruit of a long social development. The steady growth of Iron Age productive power and an improving command of environment; the evolution of new forms of self-government; the formation of kingships, the raising of armies, the swearing-in of vassals: all these and much else had signalled the processes of this development over many previous centuries. Increasingly, states had emerged. Now, often enough, they had become strong states whose central power rested on taut structures of lord-and-vassal dependence.

3. Similarities

It would be an illusion to see the institutional structures of African society, even where strong kingships existed, as being in any way strictly comparable with those of post-medieval Europe in these opening decades of discovery. There were large differences of history, technology, class crystallization, much else. Yet there were similarities which can make comparisons instructive; and the similarities were often strikingly close. They are worth dwelling on because nothing but strong political organization can properly explain the political and military strength of many African states that were found by Europe in the fifteenth and sixteenth centuries, and respected by Europe (at any rate in the beginning) as allies and equals.

To get at the true position one must look at the nature of society as it had evolved in the maturity of Africa's Iron Age: the 'age' beginning around 2200 years ago that launched and promoted Africa's historical development. One useful approach, especially in the light of what was to come, is from the standpoint of who was bond and who was free. In Western Europe during the Dark Ages, the formative period of European feudalism, there had come a gradual transformation of slave into serf; and this change was accelerated in feudal times until 'old slave' and 'old freeman' were little by little merged together into 'new vassal'. In Africa, meanwhile, wherever strong states and empires shook and changed the old framework of tribal equality, there emerged the new phenomenon of mass subjugation of one people by another. This was not slavery as Europe understood the word – chattel slavery, the stripping of a man of all his rights and property – but serfdom, vassalship, 'domestic slavery'. Degrees of servility and obligation would immensely vary with time and place, as they would elsewhere; but this vassalship in Africa would have many institutional parallels with that of Europe.

One arresting parallel may be seen in land rights. 'The Ashanti, under certain conditions not unlike those that existed [in England] at the time of the Norman conquest, seem to have evolved an almost exactly similar land code.' This parallel of Rattray's must be taken with caution. But the titles and the rights of great lords, the obligations of the common people, the custom of trade and tribute, the swearing of fealty, the manners of war – all these and a hundred other manifestations have seemed to speak an institutional language that Europeans could recognize from their own experience.

Not much more than a hundred years ago the little army of Amadou Hammadi, founder of the Fulani empire in the Macina lands of the Middle Niger, faced their much more powerful assailants in a battle for survival. They took the field in doubt and great anxiety. Amadou gave the command of his army to his henchman Usman and bestowed on him the title of Amirou Mangal, great chief. Then tradition makes Amadou say to Usman: 'Great chief, raise your eyes and look about you and tell me what signs you see.' Amirou Mangal does as he is bid and replies: 'Verily, I see on every hand the signs of our victory. I see that God is with us.' At this point there enters the herald of the 'invincible' king of Segu. He rides up with his entourage in a grand flurry of horses and banners and demands that Amadou Hammadi should at once surrender, admit homage to the king of Segu, pay tribute and be gone. 'For otherwise the vultures shall tear your flesh.'

Calm of heart, Amadou answers with a mocking smile and says to the herald: 'A messenger can meet no evil. Be welcome here, bold herald, and you shall have refreshment.' As for submitting to the king of Segu, 'let him know that my submission is already to God and will be made to no man'.

That is one example among many; and completely African. Yet King Henry V before the battle of Agincourt said nothing different to the herald of King Louis of France, although he may have said it, thanks to Shakespeare, somewhat better –

> There's for thy labour, Mountjoy.
> Go, bid thy master well advise himself:
> If we may pass, we will; if we be hinder'd,
> We shall your tawny ground with your red blood
> Discolour: and so, Mountjoy, fare you well.

The medieval states of the Western Sudan repeatedly show how closely the condition of subjugated peoples – commonly referred to, alike by Arabs and Europeans, as 'slaves' – resembled that of feudal vassals. In the Songhay kingdom of the fifteenth century along the Middle Niger, 'slaves' from the non-Muslim peoples of the forest verge were extensively used in agriculture. They were settled on the land and tied to it. In return for this livelihood they paid tribute to their masters both in crops and in personal services. Their bondage was relative: time and custom gave them new liberties. Yet being generally restricted by custom and convenience in the varieties of work they might undertake and the peoples among whom they might seek wives, these 'slaves' tended to form occupational castes. They became blacksmiths, boatbuilders, stablemen, makers of songs, bodyguards of their sovereign lord. Along with the 'free peasants' – whose social condition was really little different – these 'vassal peasants' and 'vassal artisans' formed a large part of the population.

Contrasts in status between the freeman who belonged to a conquering people and the 'slave' who came of a conquered people would grow narrower as time went by and the system grew stronger; and in this too, there was a broad parallel with medieval Europe. Caste and even class divisions might emerge and sharpen among the mass of 'commoners': the dominant factor in society increasingly became the difference in power which separated prince and lords from the people, from all the people. This stratification occurred among the strong nations of the forest belt, behind the coast, just as it appeared among the Muslim peoples of the northern plains. It was narrowly limited by the nature of West Africa's own economy, which remained largely one of subsistence and barter; and it differed essentially from European feudalism in the crucial matter of land tenure. It was further modified by the electoral principle of chiefdom and the checks and balance of customary rule. But the lord-and-vassal stratification none the less grew sharper among the groups who held power. There are many examples.

Early in the nineteenth century the old Hausa states of northern Nigeria were taken over by an invading army of Fulani. All the captains and leaders under Usman dan Fodio, the great Fulani leader, were then endowed with large land-holdings seized from the defeated Hausa lords (except where these, as occasionally happened, had thrown in their lot with the new régime). The old Hausa royal title of *sarki* was perpetuated, and the whole titular structure was bound directly to the newly created *fiefs* and regions of command. And this oligarchy came with time to exercise rights of life and death over the common people, and could call on them for labour in the fields or the building of houses or the maintenance of roads and river fords.

It is a case with many instructive aspects, not the least of these lying in what may be called the mechanism of this change. Like other such changes before and since, it eventually turned its own propaganda upside-down. At least some of the origins of this Fulani rising, and rise to power in Hausaland, had lain in revolt against social inequalities. Explaining 'the reasons for our holy war with the Hausa Sultans', a contemporary Fulani document, written some four years before Europe heard news of the Battle of Waterloo, says that in the beginning Usman dan Fodio 'did not address himself to the kings. After a time his people grew and became famous, till they were known in Hausaland as "*The People*". Men kept leaving their countries and coming to them. Of the ruling classes some repented' – for Usman preached a purified Islam, calling on the rich to abandon their wealth and the poor to put their trust in God – 'and came to him with all they possessed, leaving their [Hausa] Sultans. Then the Sultans became angry, till there ensued between them and their chiefs the war we remember.'

Yet in freeing the people of the Hausa states from their old bondage, the Fulani reformers soon found themselves binding on a new one. However egalitarian Usman dan Fodio might be, his henchmen were ambitious men whose reforming zeal was tempered by a healthy territorial ambition. Besides, they were rulers of their time. They soon found they must either forfeit their new-found power and wealth, or else revert to those very methods of extortionate government that they had set themselves to overthrow. And little by little, there being in any event no alternative but abdication, the new Fulani structure had to be built on the old Hausa one. Being intrusive, it was probably still heavier in its oppressive weight on the common man.

Usman himself resisted the trend towards self-enrichment.

Many vivid stories tell of his shrewd prevarications when faced with the urgent pleas of his commanders. One day they came to him and said they must be allowed to sell land, as the Hausa lords had done before them, for otherwise they could not discipline the people. Usman had always laid it down that the land belonged to God and was not for anyone to sell. Now, faced with this new demand, he asked for a cupful of earth and sent it to the market place for sale; after a few days he inquired of his servants whether anyone had bid for it. They replied that none had made an offer. Whereupon Usman, calling his commanders together, declared that there could be no sense in giving them the right to sell land, since none desired to buy.

But self-enrichment continued. The early reforming vows were forgotten. The ruling emirs claimed more and more power. And in this increasingly stratified society, just as earlier in medieval Europe, the dividing line between bond and free among the common people became ever more hard to trace. The degree of freedom or unfreedom that distinguished the 'free peasants' (*talakawa*) from the 'serfs' (*cucenawa*) narrowed or was blurred in practice: all were embraced as subjects, and perhaps the most that one can say about their difference in status was that some were more subjected than others.

Naturally, the process varied with circumstance. In nineteenth-century Bornu, heir to the ancient state of Kanem in the region of Lake Chad, custom seems to have recognized three social groups beneath the noble families: the *kambe*, who were freemen drawn from the ranks of freed slaves and the children of freemen married to slaves; the *kalia*, who were slaves, whether foreigners or men and women captured in war; and the *zusanna*, the descendants of slaves, who also provided the rank-and-file footsloggers of the army of Bornu. Yet the differences between the *kambe* and the *kalia* and the *zusanna* were undoubtedly less important, so far as the distribution of social power was concerned, than the differences between all these three on one hand and the nobles on the other. Here, once again, was a system recognizably hierarchical if not properly feudal: a system, moreover, which had grown with Iron Age development from the earliest beginnings of the old pastoral empire of Kanem, forerunner of Bornu, during a period that was contemporary with the beginnings of European feudalism.

Such systems continued into modern times. One other example may be useful from another part of Africa, the kingdom of Ruanda, lying in a small country of tall mountains between the Congo and the East African lands of Uganda and Tanzania. Ruanda possessed a close-knit social order that persists in large measure even today, so that anthropologists have been able to make direct reports about it.

This society was divided into three kinds of people. Foremost were the Tutsi – of late years much photographed for their splendid dancing – who number about one-tenth of the population. They, says Maquet, 'do no manual work and have leisure to cultivate eloquence, poetry, refined manners'. Beneath them were the Hutu who 'do not enjoy such gracious living', because 'they have to produce for themselves and for the Tutsi'. And beneath the Hutu in the third rank, were the Twa – 'so low in the social hierarchy and ... considered so irresponsible, that they have had a greater independence of action'.

In Ruanda, accordingly, nobody was 'free' in the modern sense of the word, for even the Tutsi were wedded to their labourers by a formal code of interwoven duties. Moreover, it was better for a Tutsi to become the vassal of a stronger man than to remain 'on his own'. 'We desire,' Maquet's Tutsi informants told him, 'to become the vassals of great chiefs, or even of the king, because we are then under the protection of somebody very important, we get more cows, and that allows us to have more "clients"' – that is, more Hutu workers who will labour in their turn so as to gain 'protection'.

Compare this 'ladder of duty-and-obligation' with that of feudal Europe. Many European slaves were liberated – 'manumitted' in the language of the times – but few were then able or desired to remain on their own. They found it better and safer to bind themselves to a master, and they chose the most powerful lord they could find. 'The manumitter', Bloch has written of medieval France, 'even if he agreed to give up a slave, wished to conserve a dependant. The manumitted himself, not daring to live without a protector, thus found the protection he desired.' In Europe as in Africa, like causes produce like effects.

Next to Ruanda, in the neighbouring Ugandan kingdom of Ankole, there was until recent times much the same system of rulers and ruled: Hima nobles, in this case, and Iru vassals. Such as were chattel slaves – genuine slaves without rights or claims – consisted, Oberg reports, 'entirely of Iru captured in raids made upon neighbouring kingdoms, [but] there is nothing to indicate that slaves were sold or exchanged, although chiefs gave each other slaves as presents . . . [and] from all accounts, slavery was restricted to the very wealthy, and slaves were restricted in numbers'.

With the actual institutions of kingship, Afro-European parallels become closer still. Here it seems very much a case where like needs produced like results, however different the material or ideological circumstances might otherwise be. In Ruanda, to continue with the same example, a king could not be held to be bad. Being a ruler sanctified and fortified by spiritual authority, deriving from God, he was above criticism. If, nonetheless, he behaved badly, bringing ruin by his kingship, this could not be his fault; it had to be the fault of bad counsellors. In all this and much else, kingships such as that of Ruanda (and there were many, however various their circumstances) were thought to operate on principles no different from, for example, the kingship of England. In their essential 'rules for operation' they were at one with English constitutional law in holding, with Blackstone in 1765, that the king 'is not only incapable of doing wrong, but even of thinking wrong: he can never do an improper thing: in him is no folly or weakness'. Nor does it seem that the ideas governing the 'divinity of kingship' were essentially different in Europe from those of Africa.* This was the broad type of centralized social organization in Africa that would prove, time and again in the coastal regions, too strong for challenge from outside.

A history of this period could also pay much attention to those states and polities which evolved without kingships or other centralizing institutions of political or economic power. Sometimes called 'states without rulers', these were many and important, and in certain ways their part in African history has been more important than that of the 'states with rulers'. But it happened that the dominant societies along the western seaboard,

*For a detailed treatment, see my *The Africans* (Longman, 1969), esp. chs. 20 and 21 (U.S. edn: *The African Genius*, Atlantic, 1969).

where Europeans first made their landfalls and long conducted the bulk of their African trade, were of the centralizing type. Here there had emerged or would continue to emerge states and empires which European venturers had to respect as being superior in power to themselves: Benin, Oyo, Denkyira, Akwamu and others. And society had become increasingly divided into rulers and ruled, base and noble, bond and free, with weaker clans or even whole tribes reduced to this or that productive position in the social system of the stronger peoples.

Europeans of a somewhat later day often misunderstood the essentially vassal nature of this African subjection. Such slavery, argued the defenders of the slave trade, was no different from any other. This argument they used repeatedly in their eighteenth-century battles against those who wished to abolish the trade. Do not prevent us from taking these poor savages away from Africa, the slavers urged, for otherwise you will condemn them to a fate much worse. Confirm us in our right to carry them off to America, and you will encourage 'a great accession of happiness to Africa'. The British Privy Council of Enquiry into the slave trade, which sat in 1788, was doubtfully impressed. One may note that other men would afterwards urge a continuance of the colonial system with much the same argument. Do not ask us to abandon our responsibilities for governing Africans, for you must otherwise confirm these people in a savage fate . . . Support us in our powers of dominion, and you will ensure rich benefits for Africa . . .

Yet the 'slave' peoples of the hierarchical or 'centralizing' states, whether near the coast or inland across the Sudanese grasslands, were in truth serfs and 'clients', often with valued individual rights. Their status was altogether different from the human cattle of the slave ships and the American plantations. Early European traders on the Coast, though freely misusing the word 'slave', repeatedly drew attention to this. 'Those who come from the inward part of the country to traffick with us', Bosman reports of the Guinea Coast round the year 1700, 'are chiefly slaves: one of which, on whom the master reposes the greatest trust, is appointed the chief of the caravan. But when he comes to us he is not treated as a slave, but as a very great merchant whom we take all possible care to oblige . . . Indeed, I have observed that some of these slaves have more authority than their masters;

for having long exercised command over their masters' dependants, by their own trading they are become possessors of some slaves themselves, and in process of time are grown so powerful, that their patrons are obliged to see with their eyes only . . .'

One could multiply such observations, and for every part of Africa where the outside world had contact. Sometimes they were casual and inconclusive, mere traders' gossip of strange people and exotic countries. Now and then they were more than that. An early American Negro explorer of Southern Nigeria, Martin Delany, spoke in sharper tones. 'It is simply preposterous to talk about slavery, as that term is understood, either being legalized or existing in this part of Africa', he wrote. 'It is nonsense. The system is a patriarchal one, there being no actual difference, socially, between the slave (called by their protector son or daughter) and the children of the person with whom they live. Such persons intermarry and frequently become the heads of state . . . And were this not the case, it either arises from some innovation among them or those exceptional cases of despotism to be found in every country . . .'*

What was true of southern Nigeria was true of other 'forest' peoples. In Ashante (Ashanti), Rattray found, 'a slave might marry; own property; himself own a slave; swear an oath; be a competent witness; and ultimately become heir to his master . . . Such briefly were the rights of an Ashanti slave. They seemed in many cases practically the ordinary privileges of an Ashanti free man . . . An Ashanti slave, in nine cases out of ten, possibly became an adopted member of the family, and in time his descendants so merged and intermarried with the owner's kinsmen that only a few would know their origin . . .' Captives, that is to say, became vassals; vassals became free men; free men became chiefs.

Set this highly mobile social order alongside the slave system of the North American States, and the vital and enormous difference becomes immediately clear. There the slaves were entirely a class

*I am indebted for this quotation to Professor George Shepperson: it comes from the official report of the Niger Valley Exploring Party, published in New York, 1861, page 40. Delany was a serious observer who travelled in West Africa between July 1859 and August 1860. See, e.g., A. C. Hill and M. Kilson, *Apropos of Africa* (Cass, London, 1969), p. 69.

apart, labelled by their colour, doomed to accept an absolute servitude: in Tannenbaum's words, 'the mere fact of being a Negro was presumptive of a slave status'. And slave status was for ever. Manumission became increasingly difficult: often it became impossible. An early law of Maryland, dating from 1663, declared that: 'All Negroes or other slaves within the province, all Negroes to be hereafter imported, shall serve *durante vita*': but their children were to serve likewise. A few free Negroes there might be; yet they were tolerated with the utmost difficulty. A South Carolina law of 1740 provided that any free Negro should be sold at public auction if he had harboured a runaway slave, or was charged 'with any criminal matter'. A Negro or mulatto in Mississippi could be sold as a slave unless he were able to show himself a free man. As late as 1801 a Georgia law imposed a fine of two hundred dollars on any master who freed a slave without previous consent of the legislature. Seventeen years later the law-makers of Georgia went even further. They imposed a fine of one thousand dollars on anyone who gave effect to a last will and testament freeing a slave or allowing him to work on his own account.

This is not to suggest that the life of an African 'client' or vassal was one of unalloyed bliss, but that the condition he suffered was in no way the same as plantation or mining slavery in the Americas. His status, often, was comparable to that of the bulk of men and women in Western Europe throughout medieval times. In this respect Africa and Europe, at the beginning of their connection, traded and met as equals. And it was this acceptance of equality, based on the strength and flexibility of systems of state organization on one side as on the other, which long continued to govern relations between Africa and Europe. Even in the matter of slaving their attitudes were much the same.

4. Slaves and Slaving

WHEN the traders of Europe first began their traffic with the empire of Benin, not far from the coast of Nigeria, they found that captives could be purchased there without much difficulty.

'The trade one can conduct here', Pacheco was writing in about 1505, some thirty years after Portugal's earliest contact with Benin, 'is the trade in slaves . . . and in elephant's tusks.' But the traders also found that objection was taken at Benin to the enslavement of the natives of the country – of men and women, that is, who were within the protection of the *Oba* of Benin, a monarch whose power derived from God. By custom and by moral law, slaves ought to be men and women captured from neighbouring peoples. They ought to be 'outsiders', 'unbelievers'. This rule was often broken; but it was very widely admitted.

Turn to the European records, and one finds the leaders of Christianity busy endeavouring to apply precisely the same rule – and with about as much success. Slaves being a highly perishable commodity, the supply was always running short. Where possible the European merchants who dealt in chattel slaves were accustomed to buy infidels or Jews: otherwise they simply did as the Benin traders would do in somewhat later times. They bought 'believers'. They sold their 'fellow-natives'. Papal records show the Vatican repeatedly inveighing against this practice.

All the great city states of medieval Italy appear to have dealt in Christian slaves. The Venetians and the Genoese were deep in the trade as early as the tenth and eleventh centuries. They continued in it, together with the Pisans and the Florentines and the merchants and mariners of ports as far apart as Lucca and Amalfi, until as late as the middle of the fifteenth century. Throughout the thirteenth century European slaves were being carried in European ships to the Sultanate of Egypt despite all ecclesiastical rebukes and threats. 'The excesses of the traders', Scelle records, 'were such that Pope Clement V excommunicated the Venetians and authorized all Christian peoples to reduce them in turn to slavery.'

Little more than half a century before the launching of the oversea slave trade from Africa, Pope Martin V published a bull of excommunication against the Genoese merchants of Caffa, Genoese city-state on the Black Sea, for their persistence in buying and selling Christians. This was as ineffectual as the earlier excommunication of the Venetians, and in 1441 the laws of Gazaria (as the Genoese called their little trading 'empire' on the Black Sea coast) expressly provided for the sale and purchase of Christian as well as Muslim slaves.

Another aspect of this early equality between Europe and Africa, in respect of slaves and slaving, lies in the treatment of those who were captured. In Africa, as we have seen, slaves could almost at once begin climbing the ladder of liberation from their right-less condition. And it was not much different for the captives who were brought from Africa into fifteenth-century Portugal and Spain. The many African slaves of Andalusia enjoyed a special code of law awarded by royal authority; and their principal judge, who was one of their own folk and represented them, was known as the 'Negro count'. With the passing of the years they mingled with their 'free neighbours' and lost their ethnic identity.

Or consider the attitude of the fifteenth-century Portuguese to the Negroes who were beginning to arrive in the earliest slaving ships. Azurara has described this in his famous chronicle of 1453. Finding these captives prepared to become Christians and 'not hardened in the belief of the other Moors' – the Muslims of North Africa – the Portuguese 'made no difference between them and their free servants, born in our own country. But those they took while still young, they caused to be instructed in the mechanical arts. But those whom they saw fitted for managing property, they set free and married to women who were natives of the land – making with them a division of their property, as if they had been bestowed on those who married them by the will of their own fathers ...

'Yes, and some widows of good family who bought some of these female slaves, either adopted them or left them a portion of their estate by will; so that in the future they married right well; treating them as entirely free ...' Even if the good Azurara was looking on the bright side, and many African slaves failed to fare as well as this, we are evidently still a long way from chattel slavery.

As in Africa, so in Europe: the medieval slave, in one as in the other, was a captive who could win access to a system of mutual duty and obligation that bound noble and commoner together. And what went for the manners of society went for the morals of the merchants too – whether in Europe or Africa. European traders sold their fellow-countrymen to the oversea states of Egypt and North Africa. Pressured by the need for European goods, the lords of Africa began to sell their own folk to the mariners who came from Europe.

It is important to establish this point. For it was the ground of departure on which the whole connection between Europe and Africa was firmly set. Out of this common acceptance of bondage in a given situation there would flow, in post-medieval times, a common acceptance of the slave trade between the two continents. Thus the African notion that Europe altogether imposed the slave trade on Africa is without any foundation in history. This idea is as baseless as the comparable European notion that institutions of bondage were in any way peculiar to Africa.

Africa and Europe were jointly involved. Yet it is also true that Europe dominated the connection, vastly enlarged the slave trade, and continually turned it to European advantage and to African loss. And when one begins to examine why this was so one sees how the similarities between European and African structures and institutions concealed differences that were more important – and were decisive.

5. Differences

MUCH has remained obscure about those early years of contact. One of the certainties, however, is that it was only from the north that discovery came. The little ships of that heroic enterprise came always from the ports of Western Europe, from Lisbon and Seville, Nantes and Boulogne and Plymouth, and never from the harbours of the Guinea Coast. Why was this? If leading peoples in Africa and Europe lived within systems of centralizing kingship, structures of 'lord-and-vassal' dependence, and broadly corresponding modes of labour exploitation, why were the technological initiatives always European? Or, to put the matter in a nutshell, why were the seaborne discoverers always European? It is an old question, and has been met by many different answers. Different parts of the world seem always to have developed, culturally and technologically, at different periods of history and at different speeds. Emerging from the Middle Ages, western and southern Europe owed their primacy to a specially fortunate combination of circumstances. Much else has been argued to the same effect.

No part of the answer, in any case, has to do with differences in 'racial talent', intellectual or cultural potential, or any other manner of supposedly inherent superiority or inferiority. It has to be sought in the strictly objective differences that lay beneath the apparent (or even real) similarities between systems in Africa and in Europe. There is no space here for a prolonged discussion of this fascinating topic, upon which, in any case, the last word will always remain to be said. But a few thoughts on the subject may still be useful.

By the period of oversea discovery, Africa had reached a social equilibrium and evolved a society that was largely balanced in itself, any 'overflow of discontent' being allowed to disperse across the endless lands. African growth and development went easily together, neither pressing on the other. Yet Europe was in a very different situation. Europe had already jumped from feudal equilibrium into the tumult of social progress through acquisitive advance. Spinning on its money-driven axis, heir to the peculiar pressures of its past and impelled by a marvellous curiosity and will to know, Europe now moved across the threshold of a new age. Beyond that threshold lay new worlds to discover, loot, exploit, conquer or else trade with. Though still using silver as its means of monetary exchange, this age became the 'age of gold' even if, in almost every other sense, it was nothing like a golden age. The prizes now were for bold initiative. Within eighteen years of Portuguese arrival at Benin, Columbus had found land across the Atlantic. Within another seven years, Vasco da Gama had reached the golden East.

In this comparison of Africa and Europe in the fifteenth

century, the equivocation between appearance and reality was the fruit of complex differences. The old system of society in Iron Age Europe had worked on the basis of a chattel slavery wherein men and women who were slaves had enjoyed no rights and held no property. This was the slavery of the Ancient World, of Greece and Rome and the empires of the Near East before them. It was a vital part of the social foundation of all those Iron Age concentrations of wealth and power which had given Europe its high civilizations of antiquity.

Then 'tribal Europe' intervened. The nomad peoples of the north conquered Rome, assumed Roman civilization, were in turn absorbed in it, and yet destroyed the old and clear distinction between freeman and slave. And men in Europe, notably in Western Europe, became fused increasingly into a unified society, but a society in which the old divisions reappeared in another and more strictly hierarchical form. The feudal idea was enthroned.

Gradually, the chattel slaves of Roman Europe disappeared. The liberation, of course, was relative. Chattel slaves were transformed into tied labourers whose rights were few: even their old name, *servi*, being perpetuated in their new name, serfs. And as the slaves came up a little, so the freemen also went down, until the two classes came gradually to occupy positions that were not essentially different. However imperfectly, feudalism may thus be said to have enclosed Western Europe in a framework of social service, ideal of the medieval world. Only when the system broke down, as the cities grew and the barons and the princes ruined each other in endless wars, was the way to be made clear for another unification – this time in terms of social equality, ideal of a later world.

The point here is that the system did break down. It broke down throughout medieval times, continuously if erratically, and gave way little by little, confusedly, obscurely, to the capitalism that would dominate the future of Europe. And it may well be – extending a parallel of Needham's – that the key component in this tortuous and onward-shifting machinery of social movement lay precisely in the industrial slavery of Roman Europe.* For it

*Cf. J. Needham: 'Science and Society in Ancient China', a paper prepared for the Conway Memorial Lecture Committee of the South Place Ethical Society.

was this mass slavery – acid solvent of the old relations of 'tribal equality' – which first 'detribalized' large numbers of Europeans, concentrated wealth in the hands of a few men who were not necessarily kings and rulers, enabled these men to discover new ways of using and accumulating money, and created the mass of 'masterless wights' who increasingly found a new life in towns and cities. And it was these cities and towns that were the makers of commerce, the gatherers of capital, the champions of individual liberty and promoters of inquiry, the sources of new thought and the powerful levers that switched the whole of Europe into new directions. It was here that the banker and merchant and *entrepreneur* were born and had their being and rose to power.

This explanation telescopes much history. Yet it may contain a good part of the reason why Africa and Europe, at the time of their early confrontation, were both living under systems that contained servile institutions of a broadly comparable character, and yet had reached sharply different stages of social growth.

There were towns in black Africa before the coming of Europe, even large towns, but they were only another type of settlement for communities which continued, for the most part, to live by the old rules of traditional loyalty and custom. Their inhabitants were seldom or never opposed to their rulers in the way that opposed London to the barons, or the cities of the Holy Roman Empire to their kings and emperors. They were not the refuge of large numbers of men who sought to fashion a new society out of a new concept of freedom. They were powerless to impel Africa into new directions.

Exceptions to this there undoubtedly were, notably in the Western Sudan and along the East Coast: Djenne and Timbuktu, Malindi and Kilwa; but these exceptional cities were of marginal importance to the situation in continental Africa as a whole. The capitalist techniques they began to evolve – banking, lending, the use of currency – had little impact outside the relatively narrow limits of their mercantile connections across the Sahara and the Indian Ocean.

Why this contrast with Europe? There was, to begin with, the absence in black Africa of any direct and steady influence from the old civilizations of the Mediterranean and the Middle East. Beyond its seas of sand and salt water, continental Africa was left to work out its own destiny. In fact, Africa worked out many destinies. Some African societies, their contact with the outside world muffled by immense forests and daunting plains, carried their traditional structures and cultures into very recent times. Even today, after half a century of incessant pressure for change, the loyalties and attitudes of ancient custom and morality often remain powerful and even decisive, and give life here a special quality and accent.

Other African societies, differently placed in terms of internal or external stimulus, embarked on processes of social and economic change which testify to a long development before any Europeans came upon the scene. They evolved new cultures, fashioned new systems of government, developed hierarchies of power and influence, and often extended their states by the conquest or absorption of neighbours.

Islam infused in certain regions something of the same organizing and centralizing – even, from certain standpoints, levelling – influences as those that Christianity supplied in Europe. And often enough, as I have suggested, African systems could look very much like those of feudal Europe (at least in its continental and less rigid versions); and the appearance was not always misleading. Yet it often was. At least one 'key component' of European feudalism was missing in Africa, aside from the major difference arising from altogether different concepts and usages of land ownership. There lay in the heritage of these ancient systems in Africa no large period of chattel slavery, no far-reaching process of 'de-ruralization' – or, as it has been called, 'de-tribalization'.

More often than not, the lineage systems of this or that people or population held firm even when long overlaid, politically, by the power of large enclosing states. The Mali and Songhay systems were among the largest constellations of political and state power of the fifteenth and sixteenth centuries. But when they broke down it was found that their constituent lineage systems could survive them; and only the memory of their power and prestige survived. Built from an assemblage of lineage systems, these great states never succeeded in welding those systems into a coherent whole. That is why I proposed, in the first edition of this book, that African lord-and-vassal systems might reasonably be labelled as 'tribal feudalism'. The term was attacked at the time; but lately I have found it used by African analysts.*

Perhaps this term, 'tribal feudalism', is open to ambiguities that may rob it of durable value. Its usefulness lies in the fact that it indicates that these lord-and-vassal systems did not crystallize in societies which rested on slave labour, but in societies whose labour relations (whose productive systems) were those of lineage-conceived communities, or, in common parlance, 'tribal' communities. From this standpoint they may be seen as standing closer to the systems of pre-Roman Gaul or pre-Saxon England than to those of European feudalism, even if the parallel is otherwise remote. When the Portuguese arrived in West Africa in times of European autocracy, they thought they found there the same stiff hierarchies of rule and precedence as those they knew at home. They hastened to interpret Africa in terms of fifteenth-century Portugal. Vercingetorix and Boadicea, chiefs in Gaul and Britain long before, might have understood the situation better. The thegns and earldormen of Alfred's England would certainly have done so.

Another explanation as to why the kings and emperors of medieval Africa never developed the same autocracy and tyranny as their contemporaries in Europe may be found in the balance of weapon power. The European knight in steel from head to foot, riding a great horse, was immensely more powerful than the mass of freemen and serfs, at least until the coming of the long bow and later of the gun. And there were comparable cases in Africa wherever centralized states were able to develop the force of cavalry, as notably across Western and Central Sudan and in some of the states of the forest fringe. Even so, the class stratifications of this Africa remained far less clear and conscious than in Europe. Rigid autocracies were hard to build, and harder still to sustain.

A third reason why African structures remained closely tied to the development of systems of lineage and kinship may lie in the far-ranging movement of African peoples. This was the ever-freshened impulse of migration that took them across the

*E.g. Central Committee of FRELIMO in its analysis of structures: report to third congress, Maputo, February 1977, ch. 1.

continent from north to south throughout the centuries of an Iron Age which began, for Africa, at about the same time as Europe knew the decline of Greece and the rise of the Roman Republic. There is scarcely a modern African people without a more or less vivid tradition that speaks of movement from another place. Younger sons of paramount chiefs would hive off with their followers, and become paramount themselves in a new land. Stronger peoples would conquer those who were weaker, marry their women, merge with them, weave yet another strand in the fabric of African life.

But this wandering of peoples clearly acted as a powerful preserver of the old system of 'tribal-feudal' relationships, for it gave play to an elasticity and tolerance that could absorb and eliminate strains and stresses which must otherwise have forced a social crisis. Hence, to a large extent, the enduring stability of the general pattern of society in Iron Age Africa. Hence its appearance of immobility, often misleading though that appearance really is. For this continual making and weaving of new threads and strands strengthened rather than weakened the total fabric.

When Europeans first entered on their trading and political missions in Africa, here and there along the coast, it seemed for a time that their coming must provide the 'break and change' whereby African society would move into a new form, mercantile and capitalist. The outcome was different. There were many shifts of power and many innovations; yet African society generally failed to undergo any radical and basic change of productive system or structure. What happened instead was a change, small at first but steadily growing larger, in the balance of power between African societies on one hand, and European societies – or certain European societies, those most influenced by technological progress – on the other.

This is the change, onwards from about 1650, that increasingly dominates the scene. So large does it become, by 1850, that these European societies can come to feel that they possess some prescriptive right, and even a 'moral duty', to control and govern African societies now seen as 'hopelessly backward'. So large does it continue to become, by 1950, that European societies are commonly referred to as 'developed' and African societies as 'undeveloped' – rather as though the whole growth and evolution of mankind in Africa since the most remote Stone Age times had never been.

In promoting this change in the 'technological balance', many factors had their place. But the greatest of them, overall, was probably the Atlantic slave trade. This trade had stood there, in the Afro-European relationship, from the very first. But then the cloud had been no bigger than a man's hand.

PART TWO

THE YEARS OF TRIAL

Car, comme ont dict les vieux proverbiaux,
  Tousjours Aphrique apporte cas nouveaux.

JEAN TEMPORAL

1. At First a Trickle

In the year 1441, just half a century before Christopher Columbus crossed the Atlantic, there sailed from Portugal 'a little ship' under the command of one Antam Gonçalvez. The orders of this 'very young man', as he was called by Azurara, the Portuguese chronicler, were to steer southward along the western shore of Africa as other captains had done for several years before him. He was not yet to try for new discoveries but to prove his worth by shipping a cargo of skins and the oil of those 'sea wolves' – sea lions – whose acquaintance the Portuguese had lately made on the Atlantic coast of Africa.

Gonçalvez and his crew took their cockleshell as far as the southern seaboard of what became Morocco or the Spanish colony of Rio de Oro. This was a considerable achievement, for it was only seven years since the long-feared Cape Bojador had been doubled by a Portuguese ship which had managed to return in safety. In this southward sailing it was not the going that was difficult beyond Bojador but the returning: on that coast the winds blow always from the north. Only with their recent adaptation of the lateen sail of the Eastern Mediterranean did it become possible for the Portuguese – and then for others – to sail close enough to the wind to enable them to count on getting safely back again.

Having persevered southward for as far as he judged it wise or useful to the winning of a reputation, the youthful Gonçalvez conceived the idea of pleasing his royal master, Prince Henry of Portugal, by capturing some of the inhabitants of this unknown southern land. 'O how fair a thing it would be,' Azurara makes him say to his crew, 'if we, who have come to this land for a cargo of such petty merchandise, were to meet with the good luck to bring the first captives before the face of our Prince.'

On the following night Gonçalvez went ashore with nine of his men. 'When they were about a league distant from the sea they came on a path which they kept, thinking some man or woman might come by there whom they could capture; but it happened otherwise.' They pushed on for another three leagues and there they 'found the footmarks of men and youths, the number of whom, according to their estimate, would be from forty to fifty, and these led the opposite way from where our men were going'.

Should they persist or go back? Heat, fatigue and thirst discouraged the raiders. They decided to give up. But while returning over the sand-warm dunes to the sea, 'they saw a naked man following a camel, with two assegais in his hand, and as our men pursued him there was not one who felt aught of his great fatigue. But though he was only one, and saw the others that they were many, yet [this African] had a mind to prove those arms of his right worthily and began to defend himself as best he could, shewing a bolder front than his strength warranted.

'But Affonso Goterres wounded him with a javelin, and this put the Moor in such fear that he threw down his arms like a beaten man.' The Portuguese took him prisoner and then, 'as they were going on their way, they saw a Black Mooress come along' and so they seized her too.

Spear to spear: such is the first-recorded skirmish of Europeans and Africans south of the Sahara. The Moor was probably a Berber of the Sanhaja of the far western desert while the woman may have been a black slave in Sanhaja keeping. And this capture was otherwise no different from countless other episodes of the time, except that it was made by men from Europe; since the first thought of all such raiders was to seize prisoners who might tell them the nature of the land and its people.

This need for information merged in Europe, as in Africa, with the commercial and social advantages of capturing persons who could be sold as slaves. Portugal was full of Moorish captives, but the market was still a good one. The taking of prisoners for information led to kidnapping for profit. Luck had it that another Portuguese venturer, Nuño Tristão, was also on the coast. Tristão joined the little ship of Gonçalvez and, thanks again to Azurara, we have an almost direct and altogether dramatic record of what these raiders did together. The newcomer, 'a youthful knight very valiant and ardent', was captain of an armed caravel with orders both to explore the coast and to take captives 'as best he could'. The two captains decided on a joint enterprise.

'And so it chanced that in the night' – after their landing together – 'they came to where the natives lay scattered in two encampments . . . And when our men had come nigh to them, they attacked [the natives] very lustily, shouting at the tops of their voices "Portugal" and "Santiago", the fright of which so abashed the enemy that it threw them all into disorder.

'And so, all in confusion, [the natives] began to fly without any order or carefulness. Except indeed that the men made some show of defending themselves with their assegais (for they knew not the use of any other weapon), especially one of them who fought face to face with Nuño Tristão, defending himself till he received his death. And besides this one, whom Nuño Tristão slew by himself, the others killed three and took ten prisoners, what of men, women and boys. And it is not to be doubted that they would have slain and taken many more, if they had all fallen on together at the first onslaught.'

These twelve captives they carried back with them to Lisbon, and one of the Africans, a man who claimed chiefly birth, explained to the Portuguese what manner of land he had come from. Much encouraged, Prince Henry thereupon sent a special embassy to the Pope, explaining his plans for further raids and even conquest; and the Pope, welcoming this new crusade, granted 'to all of those who shall be engaged in the said war, complete forgiveness of all their sins'. In Christianity as in Islam, after all, the heathen were expendable.

The prisoner of chiefly birth 'greatly desired to be free, and often asked Gonçalvez to take him back to his country, where he declared he would give for himself five or six Black Moors'. In the end he had his way. Gonçalvez sailed once more to the south and ransomed this prisoner and another for 'ten blacks, male and female, from various countries' – African slaves, that is, of the Berbers of Mauretania; and these in turn he brought back to Lisbon.

So far the score was only twenty. Now it rose by leaps and bounds. In 1443–4 Nuño Tristão, again far down the western coast, reached the island of Arguim, soon to become famous in Portuguese slaving annals, and seized twenty-nine men and women from canoes in which they were paddling near the shore. And now the critics at home were confounded. Many had blamed the Prince for incurring the expense of sending ships where nothing seemed more likely than their total loss. 'And the worst of it was that besides what the vulgar said among themselves, people of more importance talked about it in a mocking manner, declaring that no profit would result from all this toil and expense.

'But when they saw the first Moorish captives brought home' from the African coast, 'and the second cargo that followed these, they became already somewhat doubtful about the opinion they had at first expressed; and altogether renounced it when they saw the third consignment that Nuño Tristão brought home, captured in so short a time, and with so little trouble . . .'

Such was the effect that so small a cargo as twenty-nine slaves could have on medieval Lisbon. The critics changed their tune, 'and their covetousness now began to wax greater. And as they saw the houses of others full to overflowing of male and female slaves, and their property increasing, they thought about the whole matter and began to talk among themselves'. The outcome of their talking was financial support for a large expedition of six ships under Lançarote and Gil Eannes (he who had first passed southward beyond Cape Bojador in 1434), and a small-scale war on the western coast in which one hundred and sixty-five men, women and children were taken captive 'besides those that perished and were killed'.

Beating northward, Lançarote and Eannes looked for still more captives. Fifteen Portuguese were ordered to 'march along the land, and look if they could see any Moors, or find any trace of them'. The ships stood off from the flat coastline while boats were launched to row along the shore within sight of the marching men. 'And on their way they saw the Moors flying as fast as they could; for they had already caught sight of [the Portuguese]; and at once all our men leaped on shore and began to run after them. But as yet they could not overtake the Moor men, but only the women and little children, not able to run so fast, of whom they caught seventeen or eighteen.' The whole expedition reached Lagos in southern Portugal with two hundred and thirty-five captives. With this pathetic triumph the oversea slave trade may really be said to have begun.

It spread with the daunting speed of a plague. As proof of that, there are the memoirs of another early voyager from Europe, a Venetian in Portuguese service called Ca' da Mosto who sailed in 1456 as far as the estuary of the Gambia River, where the great western bulge of Africa begins to bend eastward. Already the early raiding of Tristão and Lançarote, a dozen years before, had given way to regular trading.

'Note that before this traffic was organized', Ca' da Mosto wrote, 'the Portuguese caravels – sometimes four, sometimes more – were wont to come armed to the Gulf of Arguim, and descending on the land at night would assail the fisher villages and so ravage the land. Thus they took of these Arabs [they were not Arabs, of course, but Berbers and other Africans] both men and women, and carried them to Portugal for sale: behaving in a like manner along all the rest of the coast . . . But for some time past all have been at peace and engaged in trade.'

The chiefs of the Sanhaja and of neighbouring peoples had in fact quickly shown the Portuguese that slaving was easier by trade than by war. Hitherto the slaving chieftains of the southern Sahara had acted only as intermediaries in the overland slave trade from West Africa to the Mediterranean and Europe. Now they began to sell slaves directly to Europe; and Arguim became an important market. The Portuguese had thus triumphed in one of their main objectives. They had broken the monopoly on African trade that the Muslim states of Mediterranean Africa had possessed for many centuries. They had turned the Muslim flank at last.

'These Arabs', observed Ca' da Mosto, but once again he meant the Berber chieftains of the southern Sahara and the fringes of the Sudanese savannah, 'have many Berber horses, which they trade and take to the land of the Blacks, exchanging them with the rulers for slaves. Ten or fifteen slaves are usually given [by the rulers of the Blacks] for one of these horses, according to their quality.' These rulers of the Blacks would have been tributaries, for the most part, of great Negro states such as Mali and Songhay. Their need of horses, which they found difficult to breed efficiently for themselves, had previously been met from North Africa.

Other luxury goods were also in demand at African courts. 'The Arabs likewise take articles of Moorish silk, made in Granada' – in southern Spain – 'and in Tunis of Barbary, silver and other goods, obtaining in exchange any number of slaves and some gold. These slaves are brought to the market and town of Hoden: there they are divided. Some go to the mountains of Barcha and thence to Sicily, [others to Tunis . . . and others again are sold to the Portuguese leaseholders of Arguim]. As a result, every year the Portuguese carry away from Arguim a thousand slaves.'

The trade prospered, though still on a tiny scale compared with what was now to come. From the first it was essentially a royal trade. A year after Ca' da Mosto's voyage to the Gambia the records show Diogo Gomes taking ten horses to Arguim, and finding there another Portuguese called Gonçalo Ferreira, as well as a Genoese in Portuguese service, Antonio da Noli. Both were in the business of trading horses for slaves. But Gomes, having the king's commission, took their horses from these other two at the rate of seven slaves each, while himself obtaining from the African dealers as many as fourteen or fifteen slaves for a horse. In this early incident one may see at work the principle of royal monopoly that would later on prove fatal to the whole Portuguese trading venture in Africa, India and beyond.

Another encounter on this same voyage of Gomes casts light on the mind and temper of the times. Gomes came up with a caravel commanded by a fellow-countryman called De Prado, went aboard and found that De Prado was carrying arms for the Moorish enemies of Portugal and Christendom. De Prado was handed over to royal punishment. 'The King ordered that they should martyrise him in a cart, and that they should make a furnace of fire and throw him into it with his sword and his gold.'

Under the eager influence of the court at Lisbon, slaving was pushed vigorously on. By about 1506 Duarte Pacheco Pereira is reporting that the goods exchanged at Arguim and elsewhere consist of gold, black slaves, oryx leather for shields and other items, against Portuguese red and blue stuffs and various textiles, of both poor and good quality, as well as horses. More than fifty years had passed since Lançarote had brought back that first great cargo of slaves to an astonished Portugal, and the trade by now was extended far to the south.

'When trade was good here', Pereira could report of the estuary of the Senegal river, 'as many as four hundred slaves could be had in this river . . . in exchange for horses and other merchandise.' For the whole trade from the estuary of Senegal 'on the frontier of the kingdom of the Joloffs, where are the first Negroes', as far as Sierra Leone on the Guinea Coast, Pereira's estimate was that 'when the trade of the country was well ordered, it yielded 3,500 slaves and more, many tusks of ivory, gold, fine cotton cloths and much other merchandise'. The European slave trade from Africa had trebled in size during its first fifty years.

2. Gold and Elephant's Teeth

RAPIDLY though slaving grew, it yet remained within the bounds of a trading system in which other goods were valued and were often more important. Thus far, the trade of the Portuguese differed little from the trans-Saharan trade of the Moors or the trans-ocean trade between East Africa and the lands of India and beyond. It was found that Africa, whether in east or west, had much to offer Europe and Asia – gold, wrought iron, ivory, tortoiseshell, even textiles – while there was much that the states of Africa (or at any rate their chiefs and notables) desired to buy in exchange. Slaving was merely a part of the trade from Africa, just as it was merely a part of the trade from Europe.

With the advent of the Portuguese, slaving undoubtedly became a larger part of the whole trade, since slaves were increasingly important for the Portuguese economy; but men in Lisbon were even more interested in gold, and gold soon became the lodestar of their enterprise. Gradually, too, their ships began to act as maritime carriers for African states along the coast. 'Our people who are sent out by the Most Serene King in his ships', Pereira reported, 'buy slaves two hundred leagues beyond the Castle [of Elmina in modern Ghana] by a river where there is a very large city called Beny [Benin] . . . and from there the slaves are brought to the castle of San Jorge da Mina [Elmina] where they are sold for gold.'

Portuguese and Spanish demand for slaves was limited: other European countries had no demand at all. In the sixteenth century neither France nor England had any significant interest in slaves. Neither possessed or had sufficient use for the large slave reserves which Christian reconquest had conserved in Portugal and Spain. Both were moving into a mercantile economy which would soon give them primacy through the western world. Their early expeditions to the Guinea Coast accordingly concentrated on gold and ivory and pepper.

Thus the first English voyage to West Africa, that of William Hawkins in 1530, yielded a cargo of ivory; and the next, that of John Landye, a captain in Hawkins's service, did the same ten years later. Its bill of lading shows 'one dozen elephants' teeth weighing one cwt'. Thirteen years later Thomas Windham sailed from Plymouth to the Gold Coast and Benin, where he bargained successfully for gold and ivory and pepper but showed no interest in slaves. Lok followed with still greater success. Where Windham's voyage had yielded 150 lb of gold, Lok came home with more than twice as much.

'They brought with them', says a contemporary account, 'foure hundred pound weight and odde of gold, of two and twentie carats and one graine in finenesse: also sixe and thirtie buts of pepper graines, and about 250 elephants' teeth of all quantities . . .' Lok also returned with 'certaine blacke slaves, whereof some were tall and strong'; but it appears that these captives, actually five in number, were acquired more or less haphazardly, and somewhat later they were taken home again.

Rules for trading were already firmly established. These African merchants of the Guinea Coast, runs the account of Lok's voyage, 'are very wary people in their bargaining, and will not lose one sparke of golde of any value. They use weights and measures, and are very circumspect in occupying the same. They that shall have trade with them must use them gently: for they will not traffique or bring in any wares if they be evill used.' When an English sailor stole 'a muske cat', the Africans in that place brought all trading to a stop until restitution was made.

And so it continued for a while. Towerson made three voyages between 1555 and 1557, returning with various goods but no slaves. Rutter did the same in 1562. Even as late as 1623 an English captain called Jobson could describe how he was offered slaves on the Coast but refused them. A Mandingo (Mandinka) trader 'showed unto me certain young black women who were standing by themselves . . . which he told me were slaves, brought for me to buy. I made answer, We were a people who did not deal in any such commodities, neither did we buy or sell one another, or any that had our own shapes'.

Besides, the profit on other goods was more than satisfactory. Lok's voyage of 1554 is thought to have shown a return amounting to about ten times the capital that was risked. True enough, Lok's was a more than averagely successful voyage, but others could always hope to copy it. Towerson's voyages proved that a copper basin on the Guinea Coast could be exchanged for gold worth some thirty pounds in the sterling of the time, a fabulous return. By 1561, if not before, Queen Elizabeth had taken a leaf out of the King of Portugal's book and engaged royal money in the Guinea trade. Her share in the voyage of 1561 was £1,000 in the money of the time, or about a third of the total investment, and the profits were about sixty per cent.* The next year's expedition, that of 1563, had to fight the Portuguese but in spite of this both ships, the *Minion* and the *Primrose* with Lok in command, came home with 155 tusks and 22 butts of pepper, commodities of great value; and an undated document which may refer to this voyage says that it also yielded three hundredweight of gold.

If the profits were great, so also were the risks. In the expedition of 1564, Williamson writes, the *Minion* 'was reported lost, but she was an ill ship to beat. At midsummer, 1564, an Englishman coming from the Azores declared that he had seen her there, her victuals finished, most of her crew dead, and the few survivors refitting for the voyage home.' Again she was given up for lost. Again she fooled the prophets. On July 5th that summer she 'came into the Thames, with a great haul of gold, ivory, and other wares'.

French crews and captains had much the same experience and

*These profits were paid over to the Treasurer of the Navy for the use of his department.

ambitions; and their country, unlike England, specifically condemned the trade in slaves. A royal declaration of 1571 had declared that 'France, mother of liberty, permits no slaves'; and a famous legal dictum of 1607 confirmed this with the words: 'All persons are free in this kingdom: as soon as a slave has reached these frontiers, and become baptised, he is free.' Not for another century and a half would any judgement in England echo sentiments of that kind.

Up to this point, then, the picture is one of a profitable and developing exchange between the thriving maritime nations of western Europe and some of the coastal states of western Africa. Neither the French nor the English (nor the Dutch, hard on their heels) engaged in slaving; while the Portuguese and Spanish were interested in slaving only to the limited extent of their domestic slave markets. Had matters continued in this way, the slave trade to Portugal and Spain must have dwindled to an insignificant size, and finally ceased altogether as the economies of Spain and Portugal merged with the mercantile system then expanding throughout Europe. The history of the oversea slave trade would have remained as little more than a relatively small if painful incident in the enlarging connection between Africa and Europe. The coastal states of Africa would have found themselves pressed and stimulated to deliver not more slaves but more pepper and palm-oil, gold and ivory. There might then have arisen on the West African coast the same commercial civilization in trade with Europe as had already developed on the East African coast in trade with Asia. The old equality of status might have broadened into a new equality.

It fell out differently. No more than twenty years after the first Portuguese landing in the Bight of Benin – that of Ruy de Siqueira in 1472 – Columbus sighted the West Indies. Another eight years, and Pedro Alvares Cabral had made a landfall on Brazil while steering far west of Guinea during a voyage to India. Another thirteen, and Balboa climbed his peak in Darien and saw the Pacific. The course of history was abruptly changed: for Europe and America, but also for Africa.

Up to this time the trade may have delivered to Europe a few tens of thousands of slaves. But from then until late into the nineteenth century, a period of nearly four hundred years, millions of captives were to suffer transportation in the ships of Portugal and Spain, and afterwards in those of England, France, Holland, Prussia, Denmark, Sweden, Brazil and the United States of America. The early nature of the African-European connection was to be utterly deformed.

3. And Then a Flood

THE slave trade to the Americas began, at least in rudimentary form, with the earliest ships that crossed the Atlantic; but it was not at first a specially African trade. Domestic hands were needed, and these could also be found in Europe.

Yet the demand for labour in the West Indies and the mines of Central America grew with frantic speed. The conquerors began by enslaving the populations they had found, the 'Indians'; but death robbed them of these. Next they turned back again to Europe, and attempted to fill the ranks with 'indentured' or near-slave workers from home. When this would not suffice they applied to Africa; and there at last they saw their problem solved.

By as early as 1501, only nine years after the first voyage of Columbus, the Spanish throne had issued its initial proclamation on laws for the export of slaves to America: mainly, as yet, to the island of Hispaniola, which later became Haiti and San Domingo. These slaves were white – whether from Spain or from North Africa – more often than black; for the black slaves, it was early found, were turbulent and hard to tame. How poorly grounded in fact was the old legend of 'African docility' may be seen from the events of 1503. In that year the Spanish governor of Hispaniola, Ovando, complained to the Spanish Court that fugitive African slaves among the Indians were teaching disobedience, and that it was impossible to recapture them. Ovando asked for an end to the export of African slaves, and Queen Isabella consented. She seems to have decided to allow the export to the Indies only of white slaves, although her motive was no doubt different from Ovando's: she hoped that Christian slaves would help in the work of converting the heathen, not knowing, of course, that most of the heathen would soon be dead.

Export of European slaves continued, though in small numbers, until the end of the seventeenth century; generally they were women, and they were for use but not for sale. Thus in 1526 a licence was granted to a certain Bartolomeo Conejo for the opening of a brothel at Porto Rico, and to Sanchez Sarmento for the establishment of another in San Domingo; and white girls were needed for these. A few years later the Spanish Governor of Peru secured a licence through his brother Fernando Pizarro for the import from Spain of four girls who, the licence stipulated, 'must be born in Castile and Christians baptised before the age of ten' – not, that is to say, converted Moorish or other African women. This early white slave traffic dwindled after the middle of the sixteenth century; yet as late as 1692 there is record of a permit issued for the export of four girls to Vera Cruz in Mexico.

The trade in African captives became important as early as 1510. Before that there had been sporadic shipments whenever the need for labour was especially acute. Ovando in Hispaniola had soon been forced to change his mind about suppression of the African trade: already in 1505, thirteen years after Columbus had made his crossing, the Spanish archives mention a caravel sailing from Seville with seventeen African slaves and some mining equipment. Soon Ovando was asking for many more African workers. And in 1510 there came the beginning of the African slave trade in its massive and special form: royal orders were given for the transport first of fifty and then two hundred slaves for *sale* in the Indies. Throughout the years that followed it was to be the searing brand of this trade that it would consider its victims not as servants or domestic slaves who deserved respect in spite of their servile condition, but as chattel slaves, commodities that could and should be sold at whim or will.

From its earliest growth this trade bore the marks of an exceptional cruelty and waste. Yet these were not peculiar to the African trade, European slaves and near-slaves were treated little or no better. Irish and other prisoners transported to the West Indies in Cromwellian and later times – all those, in the slang of the period, who were 'barbadoe'd' – suffered appalling conditions. A petition to Parliament in 1659 described how seventy-two unfortunates from England had been locked up below deck during the whole passage of five and a half weeks, 'amongst horses, that their souls through heat and steam under the tropic, fainted in them'.

Transport conditions for slaves from Africa were generally worse: witness a well-known letter of the Spanish king to a certain Sampier, in Hispaniola, in the year 1511, in which the king complains that 'I cannot understand why so many Negroes die'. Yet the intolerable and special aspect of African slavery was its very permanence: even though manumission of slaves was sometimes less resisted in the Caribbean and South America than in the states of North America, Africans were everywhere intended to occupy the lowest ranks of society and to stay there.

This the African slaves resisted. They escaped when they could. They rose in bloody rebellion. They fought for their lives. The first notable African slave revolt in Hispaniola broke out as early as 1522. Five years later there was another in Porto Rico. A third at Santa Marta in 1529. A fourth in Panama in 1531. By 1532 the Spanish had established a special police for chasing fugitive slaves.

Yet nothing could stop the trade. There was too much money in it for the courts of Europe. The Spanish king was probably in receipt of cash from slaving taxes even before 1510, the date of the first big 'licence' for Negro slaves. In 1513 a royal tax was promulgated which made every licence cost two ducats, a licence being understood as the permit for shipping a single slave; on top of this there was an export tax. These taxes immediately provoked smuggling; and it appears that the earliest African slaves sent from Portugal to the Indies were sent out clandestinely by tax-evaders.

In 1515 there came the first Spanish shipment of slave-grown West Indian sugar and in 1518, as though by the sheer logic of the thing, the first cargo of African slaves shipped directly from Africa to the West Indies. Royal authority was given for the transport of four thousand black slaves. These were to be obtained directly from the Guinea Coast to obviate any danger that North African captivity might have tainted them with Muslim loyalties; but it is quite clear, of course, that so large a number could not possibly have been got from anywhere except the Guinea Coast. The 'Black Mother' had already shown how fertile she could be, and how blind to the consequences.

After 1518 the trade became increasingly an institution, a part of the Spanish economy, an absolutely essential aspect of the whole Spanish-American enterprise. The kings of Spain lived off the trade. Even the licences they authorized and sold became, with time, saleable property in themselves, shares in the great process of colonial pilfering and pillage that were exchanged in the money markets of Spain just as government stock is bought and sold today.

As with other economic enterprises, the right to collect and deal in slaves remained a royal property. The kings themselves took no direct part in the business, but farmed it out to wealthy merchants and mariners. This method of 'farming out' the right to buy slaves in Africa and sell them in the Americas was that of the *assiento*, in essence a royal permit carrying strict conditions of time and price. So far as slaving was concerned, the *assiento* system applied only to Guinea slaves, since Christianity forbade the sale (though not the use) of Christian slaves, and discouraged the export of North African slaves because they were Muslims and might make anti-Christian propaganda.

There were *assientos* for every branch of business that royalty could lay its hands on, but the slaving *assiento* overtopped them all. The system really began to show its value in 1592. Before that, the king had generally granted licences for small numbers of captives and on few occasions. But in 1592, trying to meet a demand for slaves that was rendered practically inexhaustible by the holocausts of those who died, the court spewed up a monster of an *assiento*. No longer was it a question of delivering a few hundred African captives to the Americas: the new licence was for the transport of 38,250 slaves. Gomes Reynal, who bought this licence, was to deliver his captives over nine years at the rate of 4,250 a year: of these, it was stipulated, at least 3,500 a year must be landed alive. Reynal had to pay nearly a million ducats for this concession and agreed to forfeit ten ducats for every slave short of 3,500 a year. The captives were to be fresh from the Guinea Coast and were to include 'no mulattoes, nor mestizos, nor Turks, nor Moors'. (They would have included many Negro Muslims, of course, but nobody in Spain would have known of this, and perhaps nobody would much have cared.)

How far Reynal managed to honour his monstrous contract is not entirely clear, but the profits of slaving and of using slave labour came in any case from many regions. A report of 1520 shows that Portuguese planters were already producing sugar by slave labour in the South Atlantic island of São Tomé, off the coast of Angola. Yet the main profits were always in the Americas. By 1540 the annual rate of direct shipment from Africa to the other side of the Atlantic was possibly running at as many as several thousand captives, although fewer than fifty years had passed since the discovery of America.

Other maritime nations watched with gathering interest. Though formally debarred from any part in this promising commerce, English and French interlopers soon took a hand. Nothing more clearly shows how things were moving than the contrast between most of the early English and French voyages to the Guinea Coast, whose object was gold and pepper and ivory, and the slaving ventures of John Hawkins at about the same time.

Son to that old William Hawkins of Plymouth in whose service Landye had sailed to Guinea many years before, John Hawkins began his oversea trading with the Canaries. 'There', says the record, 'by his good and upright dealing being growen in love and favour with the people, he informed himselfe amongst them by diligent inquisition, of the state of the West India . . . And being amongst other particulars assured, that Negroes were very good merchandise in Hispaniola, and that store of Negroes might easily bee had upon the coast of Guinea, resolved with himselfe to make triall thereof . . .'

Merchants in London liked the scheme and backed Hawkins with 'three good ships', the *Salomon*, the *Swallow* and the *Jonas*. With crews totalling a hundred, Hawkins 'put off and departed from the coast of England in the moneth of October 1562 and . . . passed to the coast of Guinea . . . where he stayed some time and got into his possession, partly by the sword and partly by other meanes, to the number of three hundred Negroes at the least . . .' This is all that the English documents have to say; but the Portuguese, who suffered from Hawkins's large-handed piracy, add something to the tale. Their records complain that Hawkins seized a Portuguese slaver with two hundred Negroes aboard, three other vessels with seventy apiece, and a fifth with five hundred. But these numbers seem much exaggerated, for Hawkins's ships were small.

'With this praye', whatever its true dimensions, Hawkins 'sayled over the ocean sea unto the iland of Hispaniola ... and there hee had reasonable utterance of his English commodities, as also of some part of his Negroes ...' Thence he went on from port to port, 'standing alwaies upon his guard', and finally disposed of all his cargoes. For these he received 'such quantities of merchandise, that hee did not onely lade his owne three shippes with hides, ginger, sugars, and some quantities of pearles, but he fraighted also two other hulkes with hides and the like commodities, which hee sent into Spain'. (Why he should have risked sending his goods to Spain remains obscure: they were seized on arrival, along with the crews of the ships that carried them, and Hawkins estimated his loss at £20,000 in the money of the time.)

Thus began the 'Great Circuit' trade that was to dominate much of the commerce of the western world for long years thereafter. This circuit consisted in the export of cheap manufactured goods from Europe to Africa; the purchase or seizure of slaves on the Guinea Coast and their transport across the Atlantic; the exchange of these slaves for minerals and foodstuffs in the West Indies and Americas; and, lastly, the sale of these raw materials and foods in Europe.

By this triangular system three separate profits were taken, and all in Europe: the first profit was that of selling consumer goods to the slavers; the second derived from selling slaves to the planters and mineowners of the Americas; while the third (and biggest) was realized on the sale of American and West Indian cargoes in Europe.

The actual size of these profits has been much discussed and partially researched over the past twenty years. Each, of course, varied through time. Few merchants at the beginning had the capital or commercial power to benefit from more than one 'side' of the triangle. Only the biggest merchants or groups of merchants, even at the zenith of the trade, could manage to benefit from all three 'sides', or even from two of them. Broadly and increasingly, as it appears, the largest source of profit came not from selling consumer goods to slavers, nor from selling slaves to planters, but from marketing slave-grown American and West Indian products in Europe, especially cargoes of sugar. That became very big business. In building the commercial supremacy of England and France, during the eighteenth century, this sugar business undoubtedly played a leading part. But this is looking ahead. Profits at the beginning were very much a matter of luck.

Hawkins sailed again in 1564 and a third time in 1567; on both occasions he went mainly for slaves, and with like success. He financed at least one other slaving voyage on which he did not sail himself, that of Lovell in 1566. The king of Spain was furious but as yet unprepared to act: not for another twenty years would the Armada sail for England. Meanwhile, Queen Elizabeth returned soft misleading answers to the protests of Guzman de Silva, Philip's ambassador at the Court of St James; and so did Cecil, her principal minister.

'I have spoken to the queen about the six ships that are being fitted out for Hawkins', de Silva wrote to his master on the eve of the third voyage. 'She says she has had the merchants' – the London backers of the venture – 'into her presence and made them swear that they are not going to any place prohibited by your Majesty ... Cecil also says they are not going to your Majesty's dominions but still I am doubtful, because what they seek in Guinea most are slaves to take to the West Indies. I will use all efforts to prevent their going, but the greed of these people is great and they are not only merchants who have shares in these adventures but secretly many of the queen's Council ...' Philip might grieve for his slaving taxes. So much the worse for him. The gentlemen of England wanted their share as well.

Yet the slave trade of the sixteenth century, despite these occasional raids from the north, was essentially a Spanish-Portuguese monopoly. The French and English, early on the Guinea Coast in the wake of the Portuguese and Spanish, sometimes worked together against a common enemy, and sometimes fell out and fought. Their interest in any case was not in slaving. Towerson on his second voyage, that of 1566–7, both worked with the French and came to blows with them: his dramatic story illustrates the ruthless competition that was to accompany the Guinea trade to the very threshold of the twentieth century.

Returning westward, Towerson says, 'we had sight of a shippe in the weather of us, which was a Frenchman of ninety tunne who came with us as stoutly and as desperately as might be, and coming neere us, perceived that we had bene upon a long voyage, and judging us to be weake, as indeed we were, came neerer to us and thought to have layed us aboard.

'And there stept up some of his men in armour and commanded us to strike saile; whereupon we sent them some of our stuffe, crossebarres and chainshot and arrowes, so thick that it made the upper worke of the shippe flie about their eares, and we spoiled him with all his men, and toare his shippe miserably with our great ordinance, and then he began to fall asterne of us, and to packe on his sailes, and get away.

'And we, seeing that, gave him four or five good pieces more for his farewell; and thus we were rid of this Frenchman, who did us no harme at all. We had aboord us a Frenchman, a trumpetter, who, being sicke and lying in his bed, tooke his trumpet notwithstanding, and sounded till he could sound no more, and so died . . .'

Out of these grim rivalries, in small ships and with small crews, attacked by fevers and the furies of the sea, wrecked and ruined by one another in sudden battles from the coast of Senegal to the Bight of Benin and far beyond, there none the less emerged a pattern of commercial exchange and, little by little, a recognized order of behaviour.

4. Battle for the Coast

NEW competitors appeared. The French and English grew bolder and were joined by Dutchmen and Danes and Swedes, and afterwards by Prussians. Tactics changed. The English and French had generally contented themselves with mere 'interloping trade': their method was to anchor offshore, having slipped out of the way of large Portuguese fleets or fought their way through small Portuguese fleets, and stay just long enough to sell their goods and buy ivory and gold or – as now increasingly – a number of captives for enslavement. But the Dutch proceeded otherwise.

Commercially more efficient than the English or the French, the Dutch in the early seventeenth century perceived that the key to a command of this rapidly developing trade was to copy Portuguese example, and establish permanent settlements and strong points on shore. They were helped on the Gold Coast by the exertions of a coastal people living near Commenda and known to the records as the Fetu. This people saw that Dutch wares would be preferable to Portuguese if only the Portuguese monopoly could be systematically broken, and not merely evaded from time to time. They accordingly rose against the Portuguese and drove them from all their settlements on the Gold Coast except Axim and Elmina, which the Dutch had already, though unsuccessfully, assaulted.

Taking advantage of this, the Dutch built a Gold Coast base of their own at Mowree (or Mouri) in 1611 or 1612, and named it Fort Nassau. Five years later, much further to the west, they obtained from its local ruler a small island lying within the lee of Cape Verde, called Gorée. There they built two forts; and opposite Gorée, on the mainland at Rio Fresco (Rufisque) they ran up store-houses and established a 'factory' – which meant a trading post, of course, and not a place where goods were manufactured. Finally they seized Elmina Castle from the Portuguese in 1637, one hundred and fifty-five years after its construction, and put an end to Portuguese presence on the Gold Coast by taking their last remaining fort of Axim in 1642.

Whether Dutch or not, these enterprises were set in train partly by the European governments concerned and partly by investing merchants. The usual procedure was for a government or king in Europe to grant a national monopoly of trade with the Guinea Coast to a company of merchants. Such ventures were among the earliest experiments in company formation. Thus the first genuine incorporation of English investors for the Guinea trade occurred in 1618, when James I gave a charter of monopoly to thirty London merchants, the Company of Adventurers of London Trading into Parts of Africa. Other companies followed, some successful and others not.

The Dutch were soon ahead of their rivals. They knew more about commerce and were less hampered by royal prerogatives. Their West India Company – joining trade to Guinea with settlement in the West Indies – was formed in 1621, only a few years after their first appearance in West Africa. This company prospered. It did so well that rival Dutch merchants found its monopolist claims intolerable and gave their backing in 1647 to a

Swedish African Company, formed under Swedish royal patronage. On behalf of this Dutch-financed Swedish company, a Danish captain called Carloff founded four settlements on the Gold Coast. He then quarrelled with his employers and transferred his service to the government and merchants of his own country. So Denmark appeared on the Coast. Later in the same century the Danes were followed by the Germans of expanding Prussia.

Almost from the first, then, the coastal peoples were presented with the spectacle of intense and warring rivalry between these newcomers from oversea. They could seldom know exactly what the motives and methods of these European rivals might be, nor how the profits were realized and shared; but their own experience of trade was an old one, and they soon came to terms with the strangers. Between them these various and assorted partners worked out an intricate system of business habits, taxes, currencies and trading jargon. This widely accepted system, one should note, had come into existence many years before slaving dominated the whole trade. The slave trade, in short, was grafted little by little into a living nexus of commercial needs and appetites and habits.

Many letters of the period throw light on the manners of this system. Rivalry was the great driving force. 'The Dutch', writes an English agent at the famous trading point of Cormantin on the Gold Coast in 1663, 'give daily great presents to the King of Futton and the *cabesheers* [the African chief's trading agents] to exclude their honours [the English Royal African Company] from the trade, and to the King of Fantyn and his *cabesheers*, to make war on the English castle of Cormantin, saying that if they could but get that place never Englishman more should have trading upon that coast . . .'

In the same year another English agent, Captain Stokes at Ardra in modern Dahomey (now the Republic of Benin, not to be confused with the city of the same name in Nigeria), is complaining that: 'The Dutch told the King of Ardra that they had conquered the Portugals, the potentest nation that ever was in those countries, and turned out the Dane and Swede, and in a short time should do the same to the English, and by these discourses hindered the Company's factors from trade . . .'

Still in this same year of 1663, with English-Dutch rivalries coming to a peak, the English agent at Commenda on the Gold Coast, a Mr Brett, reports how he 'came to the place on the 21st [August], and the Dutch man-of-war told them they must not go ashore; in two days more the *Amsterdam* came from Castle de Myne [Elmina, then in Dutch hands], and sent two men on board to see if they belonged to the Royal Company, pretending if they had been interlopers that they [the Dutch] had power to take them. Next day the Dutch manned out three long boats, and continued firing at all canoes that would have traded with the English, and those canoes that were made fast to the English ship the Dutch cut from the ship's side, which one of the seamen endeavouring to prevent, a Dutchman cut him in the leg. So the English boat weighed anchor, the long boat's men giving us such base language as was not to be endured ...'

These brawling manners on the Coast were to have their effect on the opinions about each other of Europeans and Africans. Both sides tended to generalize from their own experiences; and both reached some surprisingly odd conclusions.

It became common belief among Europeans that Africans habitually ate men from taste and preference. But it became just as common belief among Africans that Europeans did the same. 'Among the many slaves we carry thence to America', an agent of the French Royal African Company, John Barbot, was noting around 1683, 'there are many ... who are positively prepossessed with the opinion that we transport them into our country in order to kill and eat them ...' Such reports were not rare. About fifty years later a British slaving ship's surgeon, John Atkins, warning of the risks of insurrection, remarked that: 'When we are slaved and out at sea, it is commonly imagined that the Negroes' Ignorance of Navigation will always be a safeguard; yet, as many of them think themselves bought to eat, and more, that Death will send them into their own country, there has not been wanting Examples of rising and killing a Ship's Company, distant from Land, though not so often as on the Coast.' Nobody talked as yet of any 'civilizing mission'.

And as yet there was little talk of conquest, either. The coastal peoples were far too strong. European captains and traders went ashore, whether for trade or warlike expedition against rivals, in agreement with this or that coastal chief. More often than not, the two sides still dealt with each other as equals unless, as happened frequently, the Europeans sued for favours, bribed for preferences, bought the use of land for forts, or simply talked their way ashore. Gradually, as time went on and European striking power increased, this early equality would be altogether lost. Many of the smaller kings along the Coast would become the clients or protected agents of this or that European fortress. Later again the bigger kings would be picked off one by one or else subjected by force of arms. But all that lay in the future. The nineteenth-century world that maritime Europe would dominate by war and conquest was still in the making.

That world was partly made by European penetration into the rich lands of the East. Yet penetration into the West Indies and the Americas was perhaps even more important. In this seventeenth century when Portugal lost its command of the West African Coast, Spain also lost its primacy across the Atlantic. Spanish monopoly of the West Indies foundered and sank. The armed ships of England, France, Holland and Denmark sailed there as they wished, went ashore and made new settlements, and entered the West Indian enterprise on their own account.

In 1609 the English established themselves in the Bermudas. In St Christopher in 1623. In Barbados in 1625; and thence onward to the Leeward Islands. The French came hard behind them, founding settlements on Guadaloupe in 1626, on Martinique in 1635, and elsewhere in following years. The Dutch, for their part, took the southern Caribbean islands of Curaçao, St Eustatius and Tobago during the 1630s. The Danes occupied St Thomas in 1671.

The coastlands of North America saw the process of step-by-step settlement and occupation. By about the middle of the seventeenth century the French were firmly established along the valley of the St Lawrence river and in the island of Nova Scotia; the English were strong in New England, several hundred miles to the southward; and beyond that again there was the Dutch settlement of New Amsterdam which would afterwards become New York. Continuing southward, there were the English settlements of Maryland and Virginia. Finally, in the extreme south, there was the Spanish colony of St Augustine in Florida.

With this far-reaching spread of European settlement across the Atlantic, there came a fresh and potent encouragement to the Guinea slave trade. Up to now the 'interloping nations' had seen their interest solely in conveying African slaves from West Africa to the Spanish possessions in the Caribbean or to Brazil. They continued to supply the Spanish colonies and Brazil. Cuba, for the West Indies, became their principal 'point of exchange and distribution'. But now they met with a new demand for slaves from their newly-settled fellow-countrymen. Not much of a demand at first, since these early colonists in the West Indies and North America could furnish their slave needs from the Cuba market. By about 1640, though, the settlements had grown and prospered to the point where an enormous extension in the slave trade became necessary. At this point the slaving tide became a flood.

The explanations were two: sugar and tobacco planting. Sugar had been rare in Europe. Now it became big business. For many European merchants the rest of the seventeenth century was almost literally 'the century of sugar'. Tobacco became important, and so did rum and West Indian coffee and cotton; but the grand consumer of slaves in the new lands across the Atlantic, and the great maker of profits for Europe, was 'King Sugar'.

Neither sugar nor tobacco could be grown without abundant field labour. Planters depended directly on the African slave trade. And they used their labour with such wasteful folly that whole slave populations had to be replenished time after time. A British eye-witness in the Dutch West Indian colony of Surinam at the end of the eighteenth century made an observation that applied to many other places. Plantation mortality was so high, he found, that 'the whole race of healthy slaves, consisting of 50,000 are totally extinct once every twenty years'. Did he exaggerate? Perhaps. But the substance of what he said was true.

France and England were the principal agents of this new commercial system. Sugar was introduced into the French West Indies in 1640. It soon outrivalled tobacco as the main product and source of profit. Less than twenty-five years later France was importing so much West Indian 'raw sugar' and had founded so many refineries that she was even able to sell processed sugar to the rest of Europe. And so consuming was the new need for slave labour that the French Government found itself obliged to break the slaving monopoly of the French West Indian Company. A royal order of 1670 threw open the slave trade to any Frenchman who wished to engage in it. The king's desire, declared this order, was to promote in every way possible 'the trade in Negroes from Guinea to the Islands [of the Caribbean]... There is nothing that does more to help the growth of those colonies... than the labour of Negroes.'

The effects were immediate. Like its English counterpart, French slaving grew by leaps and bounds of furious enterprise. From 1670 to 1672, it would appear, French vessels carried slaves across the Atlantic at the rate of more than three thousand a year. This was far more than ever before. But it was still far fewer than during the years of tremendous commercial expansion that now began.

5. The Trade Pays Off

SPECULATION was the particular fury of that time. Great fortunes were made – and sometimes lost – in new colonial enterprise. Money in Europe not only talked: perhaps for the first time on any massive scale, it was also seen to talk. Parliament and posts of influence and favour were repeatedly stormed and won by little men who climbed to power on the profits of sugar, tobacco and slaves. 'As wealthy as a West Indian' was the eighteenth-century forerunner of phrases that would later celebrate the potent riches of oil barons and steel tycoons.

In those racketing years a man like William Miles could walk into the port of Bristol with three ha'pence in his pocket and make a fortune. The story of Miles was certainly not unique. He worked as an unskilled labourer until he had saved fifteen pounds. Then he signed as ship's carpenter for a voyage to Jamaica, where he bought 'a cask or two of sugar' with his savings and sailed back to Bristol, there selling his sugar at the usual fat profit. His next operation was fully in the old Bristol 'circuit'. Miles now bought a consignment of English manufactured goods, sold them against sugar in Jamaica, and re-sold the sugar in Bristol. After that he simply repeated the operation until strong enough to launch out on his own. When his son died in 1848 the Miles estate was valued at more than half a million pounds.

Everyone was doing it. 'Almost every man in Liverpool is a merchant', runs a description of that city in the 1790s, 'and he who cannot send a bale will send a band-box.' In 1720 England had imported just over half a million tons of sugar: by the end of the century the average annual import was about five times as large. In Britain's rising accumulation of capital, the West Indies was now more important even than India. 'There were comparatively few big merchants in Great Britain in 1761', Namier would comment in 1929, 'who in one connection or another did not trade with the West Indies, and a considerable number of gentry families had interests in the Sugar Islands, just as vast numbers of Englishmen now hold shares in Asiatic rubber or tea plantations or oil fields.'

The big men carried off the prizes. In 1753 the Cunliffes of Liverpool fitted out four ships for the transport from Africa to the West Indies of 1,210 slaves. These ships made two or three voyages a year on the regular circuit – England to West Africa, thence to the West Indies and North America, and so back again to England – and brought the Cunliffe family enough return on their investment to stock another dozen vessels in the Caribbean with rum, sugar and other articles for highly profitable sale in England. In 1719 the port of Liverpool had 18,371 tons of registered shipping. By 1792 this rose to 260,382 tons. And it was the 'Great Circuit' trade in consumer goods, slaves, sugar and tobacco and rum that commissioned most of the new tonnage.

Later imperial expansion would make people forget this early importance of the West Indies to the growing wealth of England and France. But no one forgot it then. They saw the fabulous mansions of the West Indiamen, their glittering displays of wealth, their careless influence on affairs; and drew appropriate conclusions. 'Sugar, sugar, eh – all *that* sugar! How are the duties, eh, Pitt, how are the duties?' Such was the King of England's disgruntled comment to his Prime Minister when confronted with the lavish spectacle of a West India merchant in the pleasure resort of Weymouth, driving in state with liveried outriders and every sign of gilded wealth, towards the end of the eighteenth century.

By that time the value of British incomes derived from trade with the West Indies was said to be four times greater than the value of British incomes derived from trade with the rest of the world. And this West India trade was in many respects the ideal colonial system: for unlike the trade with the East Indies, which required the export of bullion and threatened Europe with the import of cheap Eastern textiles, the trade with the West Indies consisted in simple exchange of cheap manufactured goods for African slaves; of African slaves for West India foodstuffs and tobacco; and of these products, once brought to Europe, for a high return in cash.

Out of this rapid expansion there flowed some of the circumstances that enabled England to achieve an industrial revolution. Among these, the stimulus of the 'Great Circuit' trade was undoubtedly a driving factor. It was not only that relatively small amounts of capital invested in this trade could show big returns, for direct re-investment by 'West Indians' went often into mere consumption and display. More important, the trade brought an ever-growing demand for cheap manufactured goods to fill the slave ships on their outward journey. 'What the building of ships for the transport of slaves did for eighteenth-century Liverpool', notes Eric Williams, 'the manufacture of cotton goods for the purchase of slaves did for eighteenth-century Manchester.'

It was the same in France. To merchants in the Atlantic ports the Great Circuit trade was returning a regular profit of three hundred per cent on their investment. 'The founding of industries, private fortunes, public opulence, the rebuilding of towns, the social glories of a new class: great merchants eager for public office that should reflect their economic importance and impatient to be rid of what they called, with careless exaggeration, "the shame of servitude"; such', writes Gaston-Martin, 'were the sum of the essential consequences for eighteenth-century France of the African slave trade.'

On a different scale the East India trade was doing the same work. Import from the East of expensive consumer goods – silks, calicoes, china – stimulated the manufacture of cheaper copies in

England and France: just as, later on, the East would take its revenge, and would in turn manufacture still cheaper copies from European examples. Porcelain from China was expensive; but Josiah Wedgwood showed how glazed earthenware could offer a native substitute within reach of many pockets. Silks and calicoes were costly; but Lancashire led the way in spinning cottons that were not. These factory-made goods spread across the world. Lancashire textiles soon began to oust the home-made cottons of West Africa and elsewhere.

These were years of great industrial invention. More coal, for example, was needed for the new factories: 'the demand for coal was so great', says Plumb, 'that it is almost possible to speak of a coal rush.' But the demand could be met only if better methods were devised for pumping water from ever-deepening mines. The solution was the steam pump. Newcomen and Savery found it as early as 1712. Watt went a step further in 1776. By 1803 Trevithick was building a steam locomotive to run on iron rails; and in 1830 Stephenson's 'Rocket' pulled thirty passengers from Stockton to Darlington at thirty miles an hour.

Growth and innovation in the textile industry showed the same movement. In 1733 Kay invented a mechanical shuttle to displace the hand-thrown shuttle. Five years later Paul came out with a means of spinning by rollers. In 1768 Hargreaves combined various inventions into his 'spinning jenny'. At first an operator could work eight spindles on the 'jenny'; later, as many as eighty or more. Arkwright followed almost at once with the 'throstle' for spinning by use of animal or water power. By 1774 there were thirty thousand cotton workers in or near Manchester, and by 1811 Britain had more than three hundred thousand spindles working on Arkwright's principle.

These inventions were the work of craftsmen struggling to meet an apparently inexhaustible demand for cheap consumer goods. The mere export figures suggest what this demand did for the accumulation of capital in Britain: in 1701 the value of British exports of cotton goods and yarns stood at little more than £23,000, yet in 1800 the total was nearly £5½ millions. Industrialism was born, and it was the West Africa trade in all its ramifications that helped to preside over the event.

For the vast majority of those involved, it was not a happy

event. If the birth was bitter for Africans, it was scarcely less painful for the new workers of Britain. Slave labour on the one side, factory labour on the other: there was little in the manner of the times to distinguish the one from the other. The old England of farming comfort and small merchant cities was hemmed around or swallowed up entirely by a new land of huge and hungry manufacturing towns where poverty and squalor sank to depths not touched before. This was the England Shelley remembered: 'Such starvation cannot be, as in England now we see.'

At this time, whatever may have happened later, there was no social spreading within Britain of the wealth of industrialism. The pyramid of money was hard to climb, and it remained so. One of the greatest West Indians, William Beckford, a Member of Parliament and Lord Mayor of London, declared in 1770 that his son's fortune would be '£40,000 a year, besides many thousands in cash'. Another London merchant-politician, Sir Samuel Fludyer, amassed a fortune that was valued in 1767 at about £900,000. Labour was dirt cheap and income tax unheard of: no one before had ever possessed such wealth in cash.

Rivalry for seats in Parliament – straight road to influence for the common man in a Britain still ruled by aristocracy – expressed the spirit of the times. For money could talk to better effect here than anywhere else in social life. The electorate was tiny, and purchase and intimidation were the order of the day. 'Taking England as a whole,' Namier observes of 1761, 'probably not more than one in every twenty voters at county elections could freely exercise his statutory rights'. Polling was a public affair; and votes were 'usually even recorded in print in the so-called poll books'.

Here was an open field for the self-made man, whether city merchant or planter returned from the Islands. He and his kind lost no time in tilling it. The price of seats rose to fantastic levels. In 1761 as much as £2,000 in the money of the day had to be paid for a 'pocket borough'; and the records swell with aristocratic complaint against West Indian and other merchants for pushing up the price. And although the actual number of oversea merchants who sat in these Parliaments was small – only twelve

West Indians in that of 1761, two East Indian 'nabobs', and nine or ten merchants with Eastern interests – they represented a most puissant concentration of wealth.

A few bare facts are enough to show the central and indispensable part that was played in all this by the African trade, now almost exclusively a trade in slaves. From a casual bargain or 'trading accident', the business of slaving had become a matter of colonial policy, an important affair of state. Gaston-Martin remarks of the French West African trade that after about 1715 it was involved primarily and overwhelmingly in slaving: the purchase of gold, ivory and other goods had fallen to a secondary consideration of dwindling importance. The comment is true for the trade of the British and other nations.

By the beginning of the eighteenth century the Dutch were falling behind. In 1702 the French Guinea Company acquired the Spanish *assiento*, and actually changed its name to the Assiento Company. Its contract called for the delivery of 38,000 Negro slaves to the Spanish colonies, or 48,000 if the war between France and England should meanwhile come to an end, over ten or twelve years. The slaving revenue of the Spanish king was fixed at 33⅓ silver crowns for each *pièce d'Inde*, a reckoning which might mean several slaves or only one, according to quality; and the company was required to pay the greater part of this in advance.

Britain got hold of the slaving *assiento* in 1713; and the trade to the Spanish colonies now became officially British. The terms were much the same as before: the British were to provide 144,000 slaves over thirty years or an average of 4,800 a year. This monopoly they purchased from the Spanish king for 200,000 crowns and agreed to pay a duty of 33⅓ crowns for each slave landed alive. Of their trading profits the merchants were to pay the Spanish royal treasury one quarter, and the English royal treasury another quarter.

But slaving for the Spanish colonies was now only a small part of the business. The British and the French (and the Dutch to a much lesser extent) were also slaving for their own colonies. After 1713, for one reason or another, the business in slaves became increasingly valuable. The English slavers alone probably carried as many as 15,000 captives a year in the period immediately after 1713, or three times the number required by their contract with Spain.

In England the ports of Liverpool, Bristol and London led the way. Records for 1744, a typical mid-century year, show one hundred and four ships as having cleared from those three ports, and a further thirteen from Lancaster, Glasgow, Chester and Plymouth. As the years passed and the new industrial and mercantile system gathered strength, slaving totals continued to swell and multiply. What appears to have been a reasonably reliable estimate for the years 1795–1804, when the trade was at its height, gave the following clearances of ships from the three main English ports:

Port	*Slaves Allowed by Regulations*	*Number of Ships*
Liverpool	323,770	1,099
London	46,505	155
Bristol	10,718	29

The profits of the slaving aspect of the circuit trade were seldom a major interest; and they do not seem, in themselves, to have founded great fortunes. The reason for this was that the risk of loss was always great with a cargo as perishable as sardine-packed slaves. But slaves were a vital factor in the system, which could not be worked without them; and large profits were undoubtedly extracted from 'fortunate' voyages. Liverpool records for the years 1795–1804 suggest that such voyages were by no means rare. The *Lottery* took three hundred and five slaves to Jamaica at a net profit of £11,039 or about £36 a head. The *Enterprise* took three hundred and ninety-two slaves to Cuba at a net profit of £6,428, or about £16 a head. The *Fortune* made a net profit of £1,847 on three hundred and forty-three slaves, or about £5 9*s*. a head. For ten earlier years – 1783–93 – a contemporary writer estimated that Liverpool slavers had made a profit of about £2,360,000 on the conveyance of about 303,000 slaves.

These few examples indicate the scale of the business. It was significant from quite early times; after 1700 it became enormous.

But when one tries to identify the general scale of its profit the matter is difficult. This is partly for lack of information. Not many slaving investors kept their accounts as neatly as the Dutch Middleburg Company, whose records for the last forty years of the eighteenth century were remarkably complete, and have apparently survived intact. Much more of a problem is the fact that many investors in the second 'side' of the Great Circuit trade – the slave-carrying and slave-selling 'side' – became investors in exporting goods to Africa with which to buy captives for enslavement, as well as importers of slave-produced crops from the Americas into Western Europe; at least, later on.

So it is often difficult, and quite often impossible, to separate the *carrying* profits from the whole export–import enterprise. Some useful conclusions have even so been reached; and more may be. These conclusions confirm that the carrying profits were seldom large. 'As to profitability,' Anstey concludes for the period 1769–1810, 'it seems clear that neither the French nor the Dutch, the only two other carriers in respect of whom evidence is available, could attain the British profit level of just under 10 per cent.' One should of course take this conclusion for exactly what it says, and not more. Profits of the slave-carrying trade at an earlier period may have been higher. And the profits of the carrying trade have to be seen only as an integral part of the whole three-sided Circuit trade.

For if the profits of the slave-carrying trade were by no means exceptional in the commerce of those times, the profits of the whole Circuit trade were evidently another matter. They were large and they were continuous. So important were they, indeed, that there appears no reasonable doubt but that the overall profits of the whole Circuit trade became a major factor in the accumulation of English and French capital; and, secondly, that this accumulation was a large, and at certain points probably decisive, contribution to the whole process of industrialization.

This view was first argued clearly and directly by Dr Eric Williams (since Prime Minister of Trinidad and Tobago) in a seminal book, *Capitalism and Slavery*, written during the Second World War. In spite of much largely irrelevant controversy, it is a view that has not been overturned. 'The commercial capitalism of the eighteenth century', Williams affirmed, 'developed the wealth of Europe by means of slavery and monopoly. But in so doing it helped to create the industrial capitalism of the nineteenth century, which turned round and destroyed the power of commercial capitalism, slavery, and all its works.'

This upset the traditionally comfortable view, much held at the time of Williams's book, that the abolitionists around 1800 were able to succeed thanks to a general and godly change of heart, and that this, rather than any shift of economic interest, was the essence of the matter. Williams, in fact, in no way denied the value of the work of the abolitionists whose efforts, undoubtedly, brought the slave trade to an end long before what might otherwise have been the case. On the contrary he regarded the efforts of the abolitionists as 'one of the greatest propaganda movements of all time', for it was the 'humanitarians [who] were the spearhead of the onslaught which destroyed the West Indian system and freed the Negro'. But their opportunity for doing this, he argued, came from underlying changes of economic interest and balance.

These changes he attributed to a diminution in the relative importance of the West Indian system as against the new factory system then in full evolution inside Britain. He may have overstated or mis-stated his case here and there – his, after all, was very much a pioneering study – as for example in holding that the West Indian system had entered a crisis of profitability; but his general proposition appears unassailable. The abolitionists carried the day; but they carried it because they could appeal to the feelings and interests of all those new groups and classes, responding often to a puritan or humanitarian morality, who were hauling the commercial capitalism of the eighteenth century into the industrial capitalism of the nineteenth.

Things changed, as Professor John Hargreaves well remarked in 1965, 'to such an extent as to *permit* the development of an effective movement to abolish the slave trade, rather than to *require* such a movement as an economic necessity'. It was with the emergence of this situation that the abolitionists jumped in and applied their decisive pressures.

What one is saying, in other words, is not that the work of the abolitionists was of little importance: on the contrary, it was crucial. But it could be crucial only because the abolitionists were able to address an audience whose interests and attitudes were no longer the same as those that had prevailed in earlier years. So much ink has been spilt on the 'Williams controversy' that a modern parallel, partial but still instructive, may be permissible here. It is that of South Africa in the twentieth century. For much of this century the exploitation of cheap black labour in the gold and other mines of South Africa, labour organized on what has not unreasonably been called a semi-slave system, has appeared of such importance to British and other foreign investors as to nullify all protest against it. Humanitarians and radicals might condemn the inhumanity of this South African system. For a very long time their words had no more influence than those of the early slave-trade abolitionists of the 1780s.

Late in the 1970s, however, this situation also began to change. This shift in interests and attitudes did not come about because foreign investment in South Africa fell seriously away, or because the South African system entered an endemic crisis of profitability. On the contrary, investment continued to grow, and a temporary crisis of the middle 1970s was overcome. Yet the interests and attitudes invested in this highly profitable system none the less began to be counter-balanced by different interests and attitudes which had not existed earlier. New sources of profitable trade and investment began to be found in the rest of Africa, and these sources, it began to be seen, could be threatened by a continued support for the South African system. New moral and political attitudes, critical of the South African system, gained strength at the same time. None of this *required* decisive action against the South African system. But it began to *permit* such action to become effective: even though any such action, only a score of years earlier, had appeared perfectly 'utopian'.

So it was with the British slave trade. The early 'voices in the wilderness', preaching the immorality of the trade, began to thunder from parliamentary benches and influential pulpits. The time was ripe for change. Bravely, the abolitionists took time by the forelock and pulled hard; and not in vain.

Though no longer a specifically African scene, the drama they unfolded calls for more attention here.

6. Abolition

ENGLAND'S economy was no longer that of a hundred years earlier. Then it had rested in its imperialist aspect on the import of raw sugar and cotton, rum and tobacco; and on the sale of these, whether processed or not, at regularly higher prices. Now it was based, more and more, on export of the finished products of a manufacturing industry that drew its strength from accumulated capital, from mechanical methods of work, and from England's fortunate command of large deposits of coal and iron ore.

These new industries, fruit of new skills and new investment, needed raw materials and foreign markets – not slaves in the Caribbean. They had created their own labour force at home. They had brought into being their own native system of productive coercion. They were strong enough to stand on their own feet; and their owners, the new industrialists, felt themselves less and less dependent on the planters and merchants and slavers of the 'Great Circuit' trade. West Indian interests might rail and rage; but their day, even if not yet their prosperity, was really over.

Early in the nineteenth century Britain abolished the oversea slave trade by means of British ships, and actively sought to prevent slaves being carried by any other ships. And the coercion of slave labour in the Caribbean, as industrialism in Britain gathered force, was gradually transferred and transformed to the new coercion of factory labour in Britain: just as, in later days, the same coercion would be once again transferred and extended to cheap mining and plantation labour in the African colonies. Today, looking back across the years, the process can be seen well enough; yet it remains a strange irony that early British industrialism, bitter curse to its victims, should thus have helped to pave the way for abolition of the slave trade.

The full impact of the change still lay ahead. Growing demands for cheap raw materials and for security of foreign markets would eventually trace the outlines of territorial conquest, of the colonial system of the twentieth century; and Africa, when this came about, would register the full consequences of the slave trade that had gone before. But it was the campaign against oversea slaving that now held all attention.

To say that economic changes underlay the abolition of the slave trade is not, one should perhaps repeat, to deny the great work of the humanitarian abolitionists. They were brave and devoted men, and it was thanks to them that abolition came in the first years of the nineteenth century and not later, perhaps much later. It was they who mobilized opinion, attacked the slavers, exposed the horrors of the Middle Passage, spoke for the victims and drew the whole question of slavery into the train of liberal thought and political action. Even today there is no one, I imagine, or no one with a heart that beats, who can read the story of Thomas Clarkson riding into Bristol, without a thrill of pride and admiration for a bold unself-regarding man.

On that day, still many years before the Parliamentary triumph of 1806, it was David challenging Goliath. Clarkson tells in his memorable book how he first came within sight of Bristol, then one of the greatest slaving ports in Western Europe, 'on turning a corner' of the road. 'The weather was rather hazy, which occasioned Bristol to look of unusual dimensions ... I began now to tremble, for the first time, at the arduous task I had undertaken, of attempting to subvert one of the branches of the commerce of the great place which was before me ... I anticipated much persecution in it, also; and I questioned whether I should even get out of it alive ...'

But Clarkson did get out of it alive; and the noble work of subversion, thanks to his friends and himself, went boldly forward. Much that they did was important for the future of liberal protest in England: they pamphleteered, lobbied, pressured, stumped the country in speaking campaigns which set a precedent for other protesters in the future. They played on the hopes and ambitions of Members of Parliament as well as on their sense of humanity. They engineered debates, promoted commissions of inquiry, drew up 'bodies of evidence'. They sent men out to the West Coast to report the facts that really lay behind the smooth denials of the slaving interest. They tapped the gathering tide of humanitarian liberalism that flowed through those years.

The first sharp notes of criticism began to be heard in Europe.

'Although Europeans have carried on a trade with the natives of the western coast of Africa for three centuries,' wrote Dr Thomas Winterbottom after a visit to the Guinea Coast in about 1796, 'the latter have no cause to rejoice in the intercourse. Instead of introducing among [the Africans] what [the Europeans] pride themselves in possessing, the boasted arts of civilised life, to say nothing of the slave trade, the natural effects of which in degrading and brutalising the human character are sufficiently apparent, Europeans have brought them only the vices of their own countries.' Such comments were grist to the mill of Clarkson and his friends.

For using such evidence and for daring to draw the obvious conclusions, the abolitionists were denounced, pilloried and vilified by the slaving lobby, still powerful in Parliament and high places. They were accused of plotting the ruin of society and the State. Many respectable people found it utterly incomprehensible that honesty should drive other men to radical opinions; and, as usual in such cases, they also found it intolerable. When the ferments of the French Revolution blew their gusty challenge across the Channel, the fears of the respectable became witch-hunting hysteria.

Clarkson recalls of the year 1790 that the publication of Tom Paine's *Rights of Man*, and the new liberties proclaimed by the Jacobins in France, 'had the effect of producing dissatisfaction among thousands; and this dissatisfaction was growing so as to alarm a great number of persons of property in the kingdom [of Britain], as well as the government itself . . .' The slaving lobby saw their chance and took it. 'Their cry', says Clarkson, 'succeeded. The very book of the abridgement of the evidence' – a potted version of evidence against the slave trade presented to Parliament by the abolitionists – 'was considered by many Members as poisonous as that of the *Rights of Man*. It was too profane for many of them to touch; and they who discarded it, discarded the cause also . . .' There began that great retreat from the revolutionary ideas of the end of the eighteenth century that was eventually captained by the kings and emperors of the Holy Alliance, ruling Europe in the name of the past, and presiding in their crass charade of dignity over the long years of bitter reaction that were to follow.

Nevertheless, the abolitionists succeeded in Britain and soon afterwards in France. They had the new industrialism to help them, and another ally in the greedy foolishness of West Indian planters. These men cared little or nothing for any general future: their idea was to enrich themselves as quickly as they could, regardless of the consequences, and return to England where they could build huge mansions and go into Parliament or rot away the remainder of their lives in careless splendour. But it happened that the French sugar islands, for a number of reasons, were better managed. By the middle of the eighteenth century, 'the French were selling their sugar in the West Indies from thirty to forty per cent cheaper than the British planters'.

Long before abolition, in other words, this French-produced sugar had begun to undersell the British product in Europe. When this continued, thoughtful investors in England saw that their immediate interest must lie in cutting down the supply of slave labour to the French islands. Yet it was difficult to do this without cutting the supply to the British islands as well. The wars between England and France broke out and continued and were settled, and broke out again: the slave trade persisted.

Unable to stifle French competition, the British next turned their attention towards safeguarding the monopoly of their trade with the North American colonies. These were now rapidly expanding with the aggressive vigour of their settlers and the increasing wealth of their slave-grown tobacco and other products. But here the British monopolists ran into another difficulty. The North American colonies had begun to feel themselves a new nation of their own, a distinctive unit whose interests were not necessarily the same as those of the home country. What these colonies increasingly wanted was free trade. The British monopoly worked against them. They found it irksome; and eventually unbearable. They were producing more lumber and food stuffs for the hungry and often treeless Caribbean than the British islands needed or could pay for; and yet they were barred by British order from free trade with the French islands.

The British held to their monopoly. Their principal motive was simple. Questions of prestige apart, free trade between the North American colonies and *all* the Caribbean sugar islands would have driven down the price of British-produced sugar. It was here that the West Indian interest, applied in London through a powerful and ruthless lobby, made its second enduring contribution to history: having swollen the oversea slave trade into an all-consuming appetite, the 'West Indians' now helped to thrust Britain into war with the American colonies.

The turning point was probably the Molasses Act of 1733. This measure, promoted by the West Indian planter-slaving lobby, clapped a duty on rum-treacle imported by the North American colonies from the non-British islands. This meant that the colonists were supposed to pay through the nose for their needs so that a handful of men in England and the Caribbean might continue to prosper. They had not populated a new continent to suffer treatment of this sort and they responded at once with contraband trade between themselves and the non-British islands. Not only that: they decided to sell their fish and lumber to the British islands only against cash. Hitherto they had accepted payment in sugar: now they demanded bullion while at the same time buying cheaper sugar from the French islands.

There followed the foolish and eventually futile reprisals of a British Government under the influence of West Indian planters and their friends. The Stamp Act of 1764 applied prohibitively high duties on the import into North America of all non-British sugar, rum or molasses; and there began a stiff British attempt to insist on rigid payment of such duties. But by now the Americans had had enough. For this and for other reasons, they replied with revolutionary war and won their independence.

Thus the British sugar interest not only lost the greater part of their market in Europe: they lost their precious monopoly in North America as well. By the last quarter of the eighteenth century their influence in London had shrunk to a mere shadow of its former power; and proved too weak in the event to withstand the onslaught of the anti-slavery campaign. If the consequences of this loss and defeat were not economically disastrous to Britain, it was precisely because the new industrial system was already far advanced. And the new industrial system, as we have seen, had no need of slaves from Africa.

Often by indirect and subtle moves, by no means always widely perceived at the time, the way was thus made clear for abolition of the British trade in slaves. That came about after memorable campaigns and parliamentary debates which culminated in 1806 and 1807. The abolitionists could rightly rejoice, for they had triumphed over much inveterate prejudice and powerful vested interests. Without their campaign, no doubt, the British slave trade would eventually have come to an end in any case. Yet we may well conclude that it was thanks to their campaign, and to the moral courage and political ingenuity of those who led it, that the end was not long delayed. But the British were not the only slavers in the world. There were many others; and these others were in a different economic situation. They persisted. Even when some years later the trade was abolished by the French, it continued to the Spanish colonies and to Brazil, being promoted by many tough and vigorous operators. It would seem that no fewer than one million slaves were put ashore in Cuba in the years between 1791 and 1840. British parliamentary records suggest that as many as 50,000 slaves were landed in Brazil during the year 1812 alone; and Brazil was evidently taking an even higher number as late as 1839, though the Brazilian total seems then to have fallen to about 14,000 for some years after that. Thus the main period of the European slave trade from Africa ran from about 1550 until about 1850, or three full centuries. In this time it helped to work a massive change in the leading countries of Western Europe.

On many parts of America the influence of slaving was even more revolutionary. By 1798, says Ramos, one half of the population of Brazil was Negro – some 400,000 free Negroes and 1,350,000 Negro slaves, not counting mulattoes, in the coastal regions alone. Peru, Ecuador, Chile, Central America, all were filled with sons and daughters of the 'Black Mother'. By 1810, according to the Colombian historian José Manuel Restrepo, Negroes and free 'men of colour' in New Granada – which included the Isthmus of Panama – numbered 210,000 out of a total population of 1,400,000. In the Captaincy of Venezuela, a total population of 900,000 included 493,000 Negroes and part-Negroes. There were large Negro populations in several of the States of North America, and in every island of the Caribbean.

Against this wider background, we can now look more closely into the consequences of the trade for Africa itself. In the wake of the trade and all its ravages, the European visitor to the West

Coast could observe little but ruin. His typical comment was that of a British naval officer on anti-slaving patrol in the year 1850. These African countries, he wrote with comfortable self-assurance, 'are now in the same state of barbarism as when they were first discovered . . . Altogether, the vast project of civilising and christianising Africa has ended in a melancholy failure . . .' But what were the facts?

PART THREE

MANNER OF THE TRADE

The trade of slaves is the business of kings, rich men, and prime merchants.

JOHN BARBOT
in about 1683

He that is shipped with the Devil must sail with the Devil.

DEFOE: *Captain Singleton,*
1720

1. How Many?

I AM going to look at two questions here. Both are of great historical interest, but neither can be answered in any exact or finally satisfactory way. First, how many African captives were landed alive in the Americas from the beginning of this huge forced emigration, somewhere round the middle of the fifteenth century, until its final termination in the 1880s? Secondly, how many Africans were lost to their native lands during these centuries? The difference between the two totals will consist of those who died in Africa because of the slave trade, and those who died on the 'Middle Passage', crossing the Atlantic.

Before modern slave-trade studies got into their stride, around 1960, the general tendency was to guess at very big totals. Tens of millions were said to have been landed in the Americas; other tens of millions were said to have died before being put aboard the slaving ships or during the 'Middle Passage'. But a figure very generally supported was about fifteen millions for those landed alive. It was another guess, as Professor Philip Curtin has shown in his important analysis of 1969, *The Atlantic Slave Trade: A Census*; but it was still a remarkably intelligent one, as will be seen, considering that it could be based on no study of the archival records.

Another tendency developed during the 1960s, reacting away from 'big figures': a tendency to diminish the totals, as the late Jean Mettas remarked in 1975, that now became very general. Some of this was guessing; but not in Curtin's case. Curtin was not guessing when he reduced the overall total of those landed alive from fifteen millions. He did this only after painstaking labour in shipping registers and in reassessment of secondary materials. He came to the reasoned view that the total landed alive was of the order of nine and a half millions between 1451 and 1870, but with a possible range of error of 20 per cent. This gives, at the 'top' of the range of possible error, a total of some twelve millions.

Curtin's work set up a milestone in the study of the whole subject, and will remain a central point of reference. It gave a sharp clear look at what was known or thought to be known, and it urged others to go further and do better. The conclusion of most of those who followed him through the 1970s was that although he was substantially right in reducing the previously accepted total of those landed alive in the Americas, a preferred estimate of nine and a half millions was too small. But not much too small. In Professor Fage's words, written in 1978, 'even if the researches of the "dig-deepers"', inspired by Professor Curtin, 'are beginning to suggest that his calculations from the printed sources alone may tend to produce under-estimates rather than over-estimates, the difference still seems likely to be well within his own margin of error of 20 per cent'.

This seems right; and just how well Curtin worked has since been shown once more by Fraginals in his masterly study of the Cuban sugar economy, published in Havana in 1964 and in an enlarged edition of 1978. In estimating the number of captive Africans sold into Cuban slavery, the great difficulty begins in 1821 with the ending of the legal slave trade a year earlier and the beginning of more than forty years of the semi-clandestine or smuggling slave trade. Curtin and Fraginals worked partly from the same official sources, but Fraginals also drew on more than a thousand detailed reports of slaves owned by Cuban sugar and coffee plantations, as well as on other local materials. And although neither seems to have known of each other's relevant book, they reach remarkably like conclusions. Thus for the period 1817–60 (inclusive), Curtin accepts an estimate of slaves landed in Cuba of 450,900, while Fraginals, again stressing the uncertainty of all figures after 1820, thinks that 'at least' 442,000 were landed alive in those years.

Archival research will still have more to say on this matter of numbers, as the late Jean Mettas' researches into the French registers began to demonstrate in 1978. What we may perhaps conclude at this stage is that Curtin's 'working total' of nine and a half millions landed alive was certainly not an over-estimate, but an under-estimate by at least about 10 per cent. Perhaps the true total landed alive throughout the period of the Atlantic slave trade was closer to eleven or even twelve millions.

Then what was the total lost to Africa because of the trade and its consequences?

A fairly close answer seems possible to the first part of an answer to this question: to the proportion, that is, of those who died on embarkation or during the Atlantic passage.

Out of 146,799 slaves carried from Africa to the Americas on 541 voyages between 1742 and 1782 out of the port of Nantes (which was then carrying about half the captives exported in French ships), 127,133 were actually sold. The difference is 13 per cent, and most of this difference must have been caused by death on embarkation (for sailing delays on the coast could be long and lethal) or during the ocean passage. On 196 voyages in the last forty years of the eighteenth century, the Dutch Middleburg Company recorded an average loss of 12.3 per cent. Other runs of figures for major carriers show a considerably higher average loss; others again show a lower. Generally, the recorded losses are likely to be conservative, since captains and supercargoes had a natural interest in cooking their returns so as to make them look better, in so far as this was possible, than they actually were.

If fortunate voyages lost 10 per cent or fewer, the worst voyages lost terribly more. And the latter scarcely dwindled in number as ships were improved so as to be able to sail less slowly, or methods became more 'scientific'; for these changes were off-set by profit considerations which induced a crowding of the holds seldom practised in the earliest decades. Especially in the half century or more of the illegal trade, what became known as 'close packing' wiped out huge numbers of captives. The early pages of this book have given one example of what 'close packing' really meant. Fraginals in his work on the Cuban sugar economy offers another. Such examples were common enough; and they need some emphasis. A Spanish frigate ludicrously called the *Amistad*, the *Friendship*, loaded 733 captives on the West African coast and disembarked in Havana, fifty-two days later, only 188; all the rest had died during the voyage. A doctor who examined the frigate on its arrival found that its captain must have 'packed' his captives so 'close' as to allow each of them, on departure from Africa, just over one-third of a square metre. Such horrors multiplied during the decades of the illegal trade.

Taking all this into account, we may not be far from the truth if we say that overall shipboard losses throughout the trade were of the order of 13 per cent of all those taken on board. Supposing that about eleven millions were landed alive, about one and a half millions died on shipboard. It may have been more.

To this approximate total of twelve and a half millions put on board ship, we must now add all those who died in Africa because of the trade, but before embarkation. How many were these? To this question there are no statistical answers, even wildly approximate ones. All that appears certain is that the total number of lives lost before embarkation, as a consequence of one or other aspect of the hunt for captives or the transport of captives to places of embarkation, was very large in particularly ravaged regions – in those of central Angola, for example – and significantly large in many other regions. It cannot have been less than several millions from first to last. It may have been many millions.

* * *

It seems impossible to get nearer than this. It is barely possible, one may add in passing, to arrive at any responsible totals for the non-Atlantic slave trades: first, for the slave trade conducted overland through the Sahara to North Africa and the Mediterranean; and, secondly, for the pre-European slave trade from East Africa to Arabia and India and China. On this, too, there has remained much uncertainty and controversy. The most that one seems able safely to say is that these trades were smaller.

A number of European writers, perhaps from an understandable if quite unhistorical conviction that 'Europe should bear less of the blame', have tended to equate the Asian-Arab trades with the European trade, or even to portray the first as larger than the second. No doubt these Arab-Asian trades were deplorable and painful, and certainly they endured for centuries. But they were smaller. It may be useful to say a little more about this here.*

*I have rehearsed the arguments at some length in an article in N. J. Huggins, M. Kilson, D. M. Fox (eds.) *Key Issues in the Afro-American Experience* (Harcourt Brace, New York, 1971), pp. 58 ff. For a contrary view, see R. A. Austen, 'The Trans-Saharan Trade: A Tentative Census', in H. A. Gemery and J. S. Hogendorn, *The Uncommon Market* (New York, 1979), pp. 23 ff.

The trans-Saharan trade in African captives sold for enslavement in Mediterranean lands was as old as Rome or Carthage. Sometimes with a reflux of other captives from the north being sold into enslavement south of the Sahara, it continued for many centuries. It persisted throughout the Middle Ages, and indeed for long after. As late as 1352 the notable Moroccan traveller Ibn Battuta returned from a visit to Mali, south of the Sahara, in a northward-wending caravan which included some 600 captives.

But it is quite another matter to suggest that millions were involved: or as many as two millions each century for several centuries, as one French historian has proposed. For what were the economies into which these captives were delivered? Essentially, they were economies within which imported slaves were luxuries, put to domestic or military service, and seldom or never used on any large scale as agricultural producers or as mining labour. Being luxuries, slaves were expensive: only the rich could afford to have more than several, and even one or two were beyond the means of most would-be 'employers'. And being expensive and often used in positions of trust or intimacy, they were cherished as individuals: even if when, as eunuchs, they were first subjected to painful or degrading treatment. These economies could use many thousands of slaves; they could certainly not use millions.

Here we may agree with Professor S. D. Goitein. In the countries surrounding the Mediterranean during the High Middle Ages – or indeed earlier – slavery 'was neither industrial nor agricultural: with the exception of armies, it was not collective but individual . . . a personal service in the widest sense of the word'. The acquisition of a slave, in these circumstances, was 'a great affair' in which a man was congratulated almost as if a son had been born to him. And no wonder: for a slave fulfilled tasks similar to those performed by a son, 'and belonged, more or less, to the world of commerce and finance'.*

The standard cost of a slave in tenth-century Cairo, during the

*S. D. Goitein, *A Mediterranean Society*, vol. 1, *Economic Foundations* (Univ. of California Press, 1967), p. 130. This important contribution is, essentially, a study of the Jewish trading archives, happily conserved, of Fatimid Cairo, and will remain a major source for an understanding of long-distance trade in the ninth to twelfth centuries A.D.

high period of Fatimid prosperity, was evidently around twenty dinars. Since the dinar was a gold coin and the measure of monetary value, the purchase of a slave represented a solid outlay of capital. Elsewhere the cost could be higher still. In the Cordoba Caliphate of Andalusian Spain, during the eleventh century, the standard cost of a black slave – that is, a slave brought from south of the Sahara – stood at 160 mitcals (more or less equivalent to the same sum in gold dinars). And at about the same time the Cordoban historian, al-Bakri, is telling us that a 'slave cook' purchased at Awdaghost, on the southern 'shore' of the Sahara where one of the great caravan trails started for the north, was likely to cost a hundred dinars. Perhaps these cooks were especially expensive because especially skilled: it remains the case that they cost little less at the 'point of source', allowing for subsequent costs of transport and the rest, than at the 'point of delivery'.

None of this is compatible with any picture of millions being taken north over the Sahara every hundred years or so. The flow was constant, but it was much more like a stream than a flood, even if, exceptionally, black slaves were used in agricultural labour on an extensive scale, as in southern Morocco during the fifteenth century.

There is similarly no good evidence for thinking that the East Coast slave trade across the Indian Ocean was on any large scale before the nineteenth century, when very large numbers were involved. Much has been made of black slaves who became 'military usurpers' in the kingdoms of western India. But they could do this, being employed as military specialists, without being numerous; and the evidence suggests, in fact, that they were relatively few. There is one limited though important exception. This was the development in southern Iraq, during the ninth century, of a system of cultivation on large estates that made use of forced labour, including forced African labour. African captives were brought in to help in the toil of draining water-logged land. Finding themselves ill-treated, they organized revolts between 869 and 883. But this plantation-type economy appears to have been 'the one big attempt on these lines'.*

* H. Brunschvig, in *Encyclopaedia of Islam*, vol. 1, A–B, ed. H. Gibbs et al. (Humanities Press, New York, 1960), s.v. '*Abd*. The whole question is

Still, we may add to the totals for the Atlantic trade another series of totals, for the Arab-Asian trades, which must add up to several millions. Yet it was the Atlantic trade after about 1650 which continued to have the lion's share of human export.

The social and cultural impact of these losses will be considered in the concluding sections of this book. The mere totals of losses, in so far as they are ascertainable, give only a crude measure of that impact. Lost to Africa, in this period, were countless young men and countless, if fewer, young women; and, with them, the children they could have given to their native lands.

2. The System Installed

THEY were carried away from Africa under all manner of conditions, but the general run of the Atlantic trade can be said to fall into three phases, of which the third was much the most important. These were slaving by piracy, by warlike alliance, and by more or less peaceful partnership.

In the first of these phases Africa faced mere raiding by small parties of Europeans; and this differed from 'inter-tribal warfare' in little more than the new fact that the raiders came and went by sea. Thus the Portuguese raider João Fernandes saw some 'Moors' coming towards his landing party and resolved to fight. But 'all five were women, and these they took with right good will, as something that increased their capital without toil; and then they conducted them with others to their ships'.

Raid soon gave way to alliance, for the Europeans could offer goods that African chieftains greatly desired: horses to begin with and then, increasingly, firearms and alcohol. Then came motives of what one may call mutual convenience. Nearly a century after 'Mamadu, the lord of Mali' had sent to the Portuguese captain at Elmina for help against his enemies, the English got themselves involved in wars by one chief against another.

In 1567 Hawkins set forth upon his third slaving voyage to the

---

authoritatively discussed by Claud Cahen in *Der Islam*: *Vom Ursprung bis zu den Anfängen des Osmanenreiches* (Fischer, Frankfurt 1968), pp. 137 ff. Cahen points to the same conclusions as those summarized here.

lands of Guinea and, as before, passed down the Coast by what was now a familiar route: from Cape Verde to the Rio Grande (in the modern republic of Guinea-Bissau); thence to the Islands of the Idols (Ihlas dos Idolos, corrupted to Isles de Los off the modern city of Conakry, capital of ex-French Guinea); and so onward, raiding for slaves all the way, to the coastland of Sierra Leone. By the time he had come as far as this he had collected 150 captives and was ready, having suffered some losses, to sail with them to the West Indies and sell them there to Spanish planters. But events took a new turn.

'And being ready to depart from the Sea coast', runs the account of this voyage, 'there was a Negro sent as an Ambassador to our Generall, from a King of the Negroes, which was oppressed with other Kings, his bordering neighbours, desiring our Generall to graunt him succour and ayde against those his enemies, which our Generall graunted him thereto.' With reason: for the ambassador added a promise 'that as many Negroes as by these warres might be obtained, as well of his part as of ours, should be at our pleasure'. The local chief, in other words, cared nothing or knew nothing about any difference between the condition of African captives and that of captives who were sold to the Europeans. He considered selling prisoners to an ally who came by sea in the same light as selling them to an ally on land. Anyone who was not of his own people – a 'believer' – was fair game. The precedent would mark a fateful step.

Hawkins thereupon took two hundred Englishmen ashore and joined the 'king of Sierra Leone' and the 'king of Castros' against the hostile kings 'Zacina and Zetecama'. The object was to storm and ruin a town which was said to have some eight to ten thousand inhabitants; and they marched on it forthwith, a curious army of mercenaries mingled with feudal vassals.

'This towne was built after the use of the countrye, very warlike, and was walled round with mighty trees bound together with great wythes and had in it soldiers that had come thither 150 leagues. The kings within it had in it of principall soldiers Negroes 6,000, besides thereof innumerable sight of other menne, women and children.' Eager for his booty, Hawkins pressed this feudal assault. But the taking of the town proved no easy matter, the besieged having 'made many engins, as false ditches covered with light sticks, leaves and such trumpery, to overthrow our men in and with their envenomed arrows and darts so defended the walls, having made loopes in every place to shoot out at for their safety . . .' In the end the English fired the town. There was great slaughter, and Hawkins eventually weighed for the Spanish Main with 470 captives.

Such rough and ready systems of alliance occurred elsewhere. The Portuguese often made them. Not many years later, to quote one case, they signed a treaty of 'mutual aid' with the paramount ruler of the inland empire of the Monomotapa in the lands that were to become Southern Rhodesia. They exchanged their fire-armed discipline and skill against a promise of mining and land concessions. This proved fatal to the Monomotapa and his independence, and was not the only case of its kind. But wherever the social structure proved strong enough to resist infiltration of this kind, warlike alliance gave way in turn to a regular pattern of peaceful trading. With the growth of triangular trade in the seventeenth century, when slaving was the dominant factor in the African-European connection, collection of slaves on the coasts of Guinea and the Congo became increasingly a business with an accepted though often highly complicated scheme of rules and prohibitions. This business was always that of powerful men on either side, operating directly or indirectly through appointed agents, merchants and captains; but it was increasingly, on the African side, an affair of chiefs and rulers who understood the value of monopoly and how to defend it.

At the point of sale and purchase it was peaceful more often than not; but it was also perilous. What Mary Kingsley at the end of the nineteenth century would call 'the steady kill, kill, kill of the West African region' was already at work; and death is never long absent from the slaving record. The ships would sail in from Europe and approach the tropical shore, search for their land-marks on charts that showed a promontory, a cluster of palms or a 'tall tree' here and there, send out a boat to make soundings ahead of the blunted prow, usually with the master or his chief officer in charge, and land at last with their arms at the ready. But they dared not stay there for long.

Speed was vital for the slavers, since the longer they stayed on the coast the more deaths they suffered from fevers that were irresistible. Often enough, as the years passed, coastal chieftains with slaves for sale learned to operate signalling systems; they would light fires to call in ships, or else leave their coast in darkness so that the slavers should go elsewhere.

'Sence our coming into this river [of Gambia]', runs a characteristic early comment, that of Captain John Blake of the English Guinea Company in 1651, 'it hath pleased the Lord aflikt us with much Sicknes that wee have buried three and twenty men. My Chefe and my Second maite and botswaine are three of them; both my Guneres maites and botswaines mait, three more, Mr Dobes one of your factores, the rest of them being the lustiest men wee had in our Shipe.'

Except for those who drove the trade and throve on it – whether investors in Europe, planters in America, or chiefs in Africa – the game was hard and merciless on all it touched. Whether from London or Liverpool, Nantes or Amsterdam, the man before the mast was in some respects even more of a victim than the man battened below decks: the choice he faced, as often as not, lay between starvation at home or death on the Coast.

Little by little, as slaving settled into a regular system, the Coast was divided by Europeans into regions considered good or bad according to their speedy or slow delivery of slaves. This had its profound effect on the course of much African experience. And something else happened at the same time, something that was even more binding and pervasive in its consequences. Men became mere trade goods. Not only that: with the expansion of the 'Great Circuit' enterprise in the seventeenth century, men often became the *only* trade goods that really mattered. African chiefs found that the sale of their fellow men was indispensable to any contact or commerce with Europe: unless they were willing – and not only willing, but active in delivery – the ships went elsewhere. That is how the system was installed.

Trapped in this unforeseen and fatal circumstance, pushed by their desire for European goods (and firearms often became essential to chiefly survival), or blackmailed by the fear that what one or two might refuse their rivals would consent to give, the rulers of coastal Africa surrendered to the slave trade. They struggled against its worst excesses from time to time; but the trade was always too strong for them in the end.

It would be foolish to moralize. As it was in Europe, so it was in Africa: 'the trade in slaves', wrote John Barbot of the Guinea Coast at the end of the seventeenth century, 'is the business of kings, rich men, and prime merchants.' This is the necessary key to understanding the nature of the system, its success and its consequences, throughout coastal and near-coastal Africa.

Within its institutional context, the slave trade became inseparable from the workings of chiefly rule. Wherever the trade found strong chiefs and kings it prospered almost from the first: wherever it failed to find them it caused them to come into being. Whether in the accumulation of wealth by customs-dues, gifts or trading profits; or in the political authority which slaving lent to those who organized it; or in the military superiority which derived from the buying of firearms, slaving built chiefly power where it did not exist before, or else transformed that power, where it was already present, from a broadly representative character into an autocratic one.

All this might have gone differently if only the demand had slackened. But the demand incessantly grew; and, along with this, an ever-renewed insistence on speed of delivery. Hitherto the slavers had often been obliged to cruise along the coast, picking up a dozen captives here and a dozen there, enduring long weeks and months in pestilential misery and paying the price with an appalling death rate in their own ranks. But now the productive regions shortened the period of collection by laying in a store of slaves ahead of delivery. A handful of European castles on the Gold Coast had already become centres of collection: the more powerful chiefs followed suit and the barracoon appeared – the coastal warehouse where slaves could be kept until ships should call.

Here and there the Europeans themselves established floating barracoons, hulks permanently anchored in creek or estuary for the storage of slaves. Often these storage ships were heavily armed so as to be able to defend themselves from slave revolt, attack from the land or assault from rivals at sea. Off Dahomey in 1739, for example, the French slaver *Affriquain* found 'an English ship of forty guns . . . serving here as fortress and trading station for an English company'.

Africans had long watched how Europeans fought each other

for monopoly of the maritime side of the trade – for exclusive enjoyment, that is, of the African alliances and thus of rapid access to many captives. For their part the coastal chiefs were not slow in understanding where their own commercial interest lay. They in turn endeavoured to win a monopoly of the landward side of the trade, not so much against each other as against any European attempt to penetrate into the near-interior lands whence most of the captives must come. On the whole they succeeded. The story of much of the Coast during this long period is the record of how coastal societies obstructed contact between Europeans and the peoples of the interior, and built for themselves a powerful middleman position.

They also fought each other as the Europeans did, sought alliance with this or that European nation, stormed their rivals, enslaved them, sold them off; or were themselves seized and sold. In this grim sequence of cause and effect the slave trade foundered gradually into a ruthless manhunt. Ruthless, but not therefore chaotic. For the rules of the connection were well established, and they grew in number. In this the manners of Africa were no different from those of Europe.

3. Rules and Customs

'THIS day aboutt nine in the morninge', says the journal of the *Arthur* of London for a slave-and-sugar voyage in 1677, 'Came on Board the King of New Calabarr with some others of his gen'tes, and after a Long Discourse Came to Agreem'tt for Current for negro man 36 Copper Barrs: for negro woman 30...'

Many have pictured the slave trade at its zenith as a desperate affair of raid and war: much more often than not, at least at the point of sale and purchase, it was nothing of the kind. That morning's scene of long and earnest haggling aboard between partners who knew one another well, and had long since learned to tolerate each other's peculiarities and methods of bargaining, was much closer to the general run of the trade. Highly organized on the European side, it was scarcely less so among Africans.

By this time custom regulated the trade in almost all its contingencies and not least in price and payment. Here the slave-ship supercargoes and the coastal chiefs needed all their skill if they were to 'see their profit'; and it was clearly understood on both sides that a good half of the success of a slaving exchange would lie in this battle of wits. The inexperienced or the ill-informed went quickly to the wall. Chiefs and supercargoes were required to know not only the state of the trade at any given moment – including the likely supply of slaves on one hand and the likely supply of ships on the other – but also the varying values of many different standards of payment.

Coins were seldom or never used on the Coast. Mostly the chiefs and supercargoes dealt in rolls of tobacco, pipes of rum and firearms, or more generally in lengths of iron or copper or in 'pots and basins' of brass. The slavers' log books are eloquent of all this.

'On the twenty fifth in the morning', runs the log of the *Albion-Frigate* in 1699, trading at New Calabar, 'we went ashore also to compliment the king and make him overtures of trade, but he gave us to understand he expected one bar of iron for each slave more than Edwards had paid for his; and also objected much against our basons, tankards, yellow beads, and some other merchandise, as of little or no demand there at the time.' Such was the customary opening: the great thing was not to lose heart.

'On the twenty sixth, we had a conference with the king and principal natives of the country, about trade, which lasted from three o'clock till night, without any result, they insisting to have thirteen bars of iron for a male, and ten for a female slave . . .' This was too dear for the Europeans: they took supper with the king and went back to their ship.

'The thirtieth, being ashore, had a new conference, which pro-produced nothing . . .' The king's representative held forth once again on his 'difficulties'. 'He was sorry we would not accept of his proposals; that it was not his fault, he having a great esteem and regard for the Whites, who had much enriched him by trade. That [the reason why] he so earnestly insisted on thirteen bars for male, and ten for female slaves, came from the country people holding up the price of slaves at their inland markets . . . but to moderate matters . . . he would be contented with thirteen bars for males, and nine bars and two brass rings for females, etc. . . .' And at last, on the following day, they fell into agreement.

Such haggling was accompanied, especially at prosperous harbours like New Calabar in the Niger delta, by a vast deal of entertaining, bestowal of gifts, arguments, teasing on both sides and alcoholic refreshment. On this particular occasion there was a luxuriant reception on board the *Albion-Frigate*, everyone being filled 'with drams of brandy and bowls of punch till night'; and the king was presented with a hat, a firelock, and nine bunches of beads. His various counsellors and sub-chiefs, garnished in the slavers' records with a fine sequence of names and titles, benefited likewise. Thus: 'To Captain Forty, the king's general, captain Pepprell, captain Boileau, alderman Bougsby, lord Willby, duke of Monmouth, drunken Henry, and some others, two firelocks, eight hats, nine narrow Guinea stuffs . . .'

As the trade expanded and was regularly installed, Africans grew more skilful in extracting profit. They evolved a whole system of 'tax and tribute'. This varied greatly from place to place but generally the slaving captains and supercargoes were pushed from one small concession to another. The forceful kings of Dahomey became adept at this game. At Great Ardra, Barbot notes, ''tis usual for Europeans to give the king the value of fifty slaves in goods, for his permission to trade, and customs, for each ship; and to the king's son the value of two slaves, for the privilege of watering; and of four slaves for wooding'.

In the same way the hire of canoes and crews for the transport of goods and slaves back and forth through the coastal surf was also subject to accustomed payment in goods-per-slave, and gifts were expected on top of that. 'The factor or supercargo, having finished his sale, is to present the king again with two muskets, twenty-five lbs of powder, and the value of nine slaves in other goods', as well as making presents to lesser luminaries.

What profits could be realized on either side depended, of course, on the factors of cost and the eventual prices paid or received. All this was obscurely complex because the factors were many, various, and often hard or impossible to define. The African king or merchant had to pay for a whole series of services by his own agents before they could deliver captives to European dealers. And most European investors, by the eighteenth century, had scarcely any interest in the actual bargaining on the coast: what they wanted to be sure of was a profit on the 'round voyage', taking into account the overall cost of the goods they exported and the prices they could realize for the American produce with which their ships eventually returned.

All this was made the more hazardous by the absence of agreed standards of monetary exchange. These had to be forged by rule of thumb, or little more, from initial practices of straightforward barter. Yet the trade had to go on, and procedures were invented. Generally, in one form or another, these took the form of inventing 'units of account', on the European side, whose validity became acceptable to the African side. The most famous of these 'units of account', at any rate in the English trade, was the so-called 'trade ounce'.

Formally, in the eighteenth century, the 'trade ounce' was an assortment of goods exported from England whose cost, in England, represented half the cost of an ounce of gold on the West African coast: in other words, the 'mark up' that you aimed at was 100 per cent. But of course the African side, while accepting that the risks of the European trade justified a mark-up, was naturally concerned with reducing its size and was often able to do that. Besides this, the price of gold fluctuated as did the fortunes of trade; and the 'trade ounce' could never be used as more than an approximate guide to the relative values (for their respective partners) of whatever was being exchanged. Even so, the 'trade ounce' was long used in one form or another for calculating deals.*

Often the manner of payment was bafflingly complex. In one characteristic transaction a 'young woman' was bartered against one roll of tobacco, two patches, twenty-four linen handkerchiefs, one gun, one jug, four pint mugs, and three 'garsets' or textile measures. 'A man and a fine girl' were exchanged, in another typical bargain, against:

One roll tobacco, one string pipe coral
One gun, three cutlasses, one brass blunderbuss
Twenty-four linen handkerchiefs, 5 patches, 3 jugs rum

* For an introduction to this extraordinary subject, see Marion Johnson, 'The Ounce in Eighteenth Century West African Trade', *Journal of African History*, VII 2 (1966), pp. 197 ff.

Twelve Brittanicas, 12 pint mugs
One laced hat, one linen handkerchief.

In 1676 – to quote another representative case – the *Sarah Bonaventura*, a ship of the British Royal African Company, bought exactly one hundred men, women, and children – all duly branded with the Company's mark, DY (Duke of York) – for various lengths of cotton cloth, 'nittones', 'Tapsells' and so on, whether made in England or in India, and five muskets, twenty-one iron bars, seventy-two knives, half a barrel of powder and various odds and ends.

Much of the trade was carried on in cowrie shells, a standard of value long accepted on some parts of the Coast as well as in the interior. 'The best commodity the Europeans can carry thither', reports Barbot of the Gold Coast at the end of the seventeenth century, 'is Boejies, or Cowries, so much valued by the natives: being the current coin there, as well as at Popo [Ivory Coast], Fida [Dahomey], Benin [estuary of the Niger] and other countries farther east [Congo and Angola]; without which, it is scarce possible to traffick there.'

Slaves at Ardra on the Slave Coast, Barbot goes on, 'are usually purchased, one half with Boejies [cowries] and the other half with European goods; and when they [cowries] are scarce and dear in Europe, as it happens sometimes, we endeavour to satisfy the Ardrasians with one-third or fourth part of them, and the other parts in merchandise; of which, generally, flat iron bars are next to Boejies the most acceptable.'

Sometimes the currencies were elaborated into multiple units. Dahomey is a case in point. In 1793 Archibald Dalzell gave the current values there in the following curious list:

40 cowries	= 1 tocky	=	$1\frac{1}{5}$*d.*
5 tockys	= 1 gallina	=	6*d.*
5 gallina	= 1 ackey	=	2*s.* 6*d.*
4 ackey	= 1 cabess	=	10*s.* 0*d.*
4 cabess	= 1 ounce 'trade'	=	40*s.* 0*d.*

(16,000 cowries weighing 42 lb)

All these complicated reckonings had to be learned by the traders on either side. In addition, prices had to be fixed for the right of watering and timbering ships on the Coast, as well as for the yams that the slaves would eat on their ocean passage. Over and above this, extensive systems of credit soon came into operation. 'If there happens to be no stock of slaves at Fida', notes Barbot, 'the factor must trust the Blacks with his goods, to the value of 150 or 200 slaves; which goods they carry up into the inland to buy slaves at all the markets.'

Even after all this bickering and bargaining was done with, there remained the quality of captives to be considered; and, for those who were accepted, the branding of them. Here, too, custom ruled. 'As the slaves come down to Fida from the inland country, they are put into a booth or prison, built for that purpose, near the beach, all of them together; and when the Europeans are to receive them, they are brought out into a large plain, where the [ships'] surgeons examine every part of every one of them, to the smallest member, men and women being all stark naked. Such as are allowed good and sound, are set on one side, and the others by themselves; which slaves so rejected are called Mackrons, being above 35 years of age, or defective in their lips, eyes, or teeth, or grown grey; or that have the venereal disease, or any other imperfection.' Only the best were good enough; and this is no doubt one reason for the often amazing resistance, physical and moral, of the slaves who reached the Caribbean and the Americas.

'These being so set aside, each of the others, which have passed as good, is marked on the breast with a red-hot iron, imprinting the mark of the French, English or Dutch companies, that so each nation may distinguish their own, and to prevent their being chang'd by the natives for worse, as they are apt enough to do. In this particular, care is taken that the women, as tenderest, be not burnt too hard.

'The branded slaves, after this, are returned to their former booths', where they await shipment, 'sometimes ten or fifteen days.' When that happens they are stripped naked before being put into the canoes 'without distinction of men or women'; but, adds Barbot, 'to supply which [deficiency of clothing], in orderly ships each of them as they come aboard is allow'd a piece of canvas to wrap around their waist, which is very acceptable to the poor wretches'.

With this systematic degradation, one brutal innovation leading to another, one cruelty opening the way to the next, it was inevitable that indifference to human suffering should grow. It did grow mightily, and on both sides. On the African side there is much evidence, as we shall see, that this process helped towards a breakdown of social structures and a collapse of security and self-respect. On the European side there was increasing thought for raising the rate of profit at the expense of the slave commodity. Often enough this was carried to a point where it utterly defeated its own end, for the commodity was rendered so wretched and reduced as to deprive him, or her, of any market value or even of life itself. On all this, too, the records speak clearly and without shame.

'Concerning Captain Woodfin's Negroes whereof 160 died and no complaint made of their goodness,' report the factors of the British Royal African Company at Cape Coast in 1681, 'wee are apt to believe that had he taken in only 400 there had few miscarried ...'

A year later Captain Japhet Bird is writing to his Bristol owner from Monserrat in the West Indies. 'I arriv'd [here] ... with 239 slaves which Now all sold better than Expectation; so that I am in hopes to make a Tolerable good voyage Notwithstanding I've had the misfortune of beuring [burying] seventy odd slaves, as good as any Now sold. I am somew't Dissatisfied that it should happen to a young beginnar, but thank god it Can't be said that its owing to Neglect for I can assure you that it have been the Constant care and Indeavour of me for the Interest of those Gentlemen that have Imploy'd me.' Seventy slaves might die, but the interest of the gentlemen of Bristol came first; and in thinking so the youthful Captain Bird did no more than honestly interpret the spirit of the times.

Those captains who lost a large number during their voyage to the West Indies – and they were a minority of captains – were understandably defensive in their reports. 'This with my Humble Servis to you and Rest of the Gentlemen Owners', Captain Edward Hollden of the *Grayhound* galley is writing to Bristol in 1723, 'and is to certifie you of my Arivall hear haveing seven weeks Passage from Bony [Niger delta] but very Dismall and Mortall for outt of 339 Slaves I brought herr butt 214 ... the Like Mortality I think Never was known for Jolly Likely Men

Slaves to Eatt their Diett over Night and the Nex Morning Dead 2 and 3 in a Night for severall Days . . . as for Management I think it Could Not be Better I allways had their Victuals in good order . . .'

In somewhat later times there were spasmodic efforts and 'inventions' to avert such calamitous blows at the profit of investors. Towards the end of the eighteenth century it was a common practice to bring the slaves on deck and exercise them by making them jump in their irons. 'This was so necessary for their health', it was explained in evidence before the House of Commons, 'that they were whipped if they refused to do it.'

Systematic inhumanity more often than sadism marked the trade. Yet the inhumanity knew no limits. Slaves who fell sick were simply pitched overboard. In the nineteenth century there were many cases of slavers who threw their whole living cargoes into the sea when pursued by British anti-slaving patrols, since capture with slaves aboard meant the impounding of their ships.

Fear on both sides added to the brutality of everyday custom. Slave revolts at sea were put down with grim ferocity. John Atkins has left an account of how the master of the *Robert* of Bristol, one Captain Harding, dealt with an insurrection early in the eighteenth century:

'Why, Captain Harding weighing the Stoutness and Worth [of the ringleaders] did, as in other countries they do by Rogues of Dignity, whip and scarify them only; while three other Abettors, but not Actors, nor of Strength for it, he sentenced to cruel deaths; making them first eat the Heart and Liver of one of them killed. The Woman [who had helped in the revolt] he hoisted up by the Thumbs, whipp'd, and slashed her with Knives, before the other Slaves, till she died.'

Bloody clashes were the order of the day: between Europeans and Africans, but also among Europeans and among Africans. 'That day came into the Road', William Smith wrote of his voyage in 1726, 'the *Friendship* Brig, of Bristol, one Barry Commander, who likewise din'd aboard the *Queen Elisabeth*, and towards night, having drank pretty freely, insulted the two Captains, who not being able to bear it, return'd him proper marks of their resentment; which so enrag'd him, that he immediately went aboard his own ship, and in a piratical manner fir'd a shot at the *Queen Elisabeth*, which had like to have carried away her forestay . . .'

African manners along the slaving coast developed the same reckless attitude. There is the example of one Thomas Osiat who became the grand caboceroe, or principal trader, of Cape Coast, in what is now south-western Ghana. Osiat had been enslaved as a boy and carried to Ireland. There his master had died and 'left him in Care with a widow, whose name was Pennington, who kept the Crown or Falcon tavern near the 'Change in Cork'. Having in the course of time come home again, Osiat 'now lives in very great grandeur, and is of the utmost service to the English, both for carrying on this trade in the inland country, and preserving peace with all their neighbouring powers . . .'

But Osiat's way of 'preserving peace' was peculiar to the times. He fought in many of the skirmishes between Cape Coast and neighbouring Elmina, then held by the Dutch. In one of these flurries he 'took a great many prisoners, among whom were nine of the petty caboceroes of Elmina, whose heads Tom Osiat (tho' a Christian) caus'd to be cut off, and sent them next day in a bag' to his opponents.

With a commerce of this sort, little else could be expected. Once again the habits of the seamen prove the point. 'Men on their first voyages', noted Clarkson, 'usually dislike the traffic; and, if they were happy enough then to abandon it, they usually escaped the disease with a hardened heart. But if they went a second or a third time, their disposition became gradually to be accustomed to carry away men and women by force, to keep them in chains . . . to behold the dead and dying . . .' Clarkson, it is true, was an abolitionist eager to prove that slaving meant sadism. Yet by the time he wrote those words he had traipsed round the docks and quays of London and Bristol and Liverpool, sat and listened endlessly in seamen's taverns, interested himself in many cases of injury, and collected the names of twenty thousand seamen engaged in the trade.

His judgement may stand. The trade was always vicious. But it became worse with the passage of time.

4. Attitudes and Opinions

MISUNDERSTANDINGS grew apace. Fear and ignorance quickened – on either side – into beliefs that were strange but also strangely alike. There came into being a 'community of legend'. Nothing shows this better than the currency of thought about man-eating.

Cannibalism certainly existed in Africa. Some African peoples had long practised the ritual eating of the flesh of their especially honoured enemies. Now and then, besides, famine drove men to eat each other. None of this was exclusive to humanity in Africa; although at one or two points, and for reasons that were evidently not disconnected with the slave trade, cannibal habits appear to have gained a destructive hold.

Yet most Europeans who thought of Africa were convinced from early times that it was the general custom in that continent for men to eat their fellows from taste and preference. A good illustration of this fantasy may be found in Cavazzi's celebrated description of the three African kingdoms of Congo, Matamba and Angola. The artist in that fine quarto volume, published at Bologna in 1687, gave free rein to popular belief. He offered a splendidly graphic line-engraving of a cannibal scene: several Angolans butchering human limbs and cooking them on a grid-iron.

Now the odd thing is that this cannibal myth worked both ways. The drawing in Cavazzi's book occurs on page thirty-two. But a little beyond, on page one hundred and sixty-four, Cavazzi is describing how the slaves of Angola have a particular horror of being shipped away. Why? Because, he writes, they are convinced that Europeans want them not for labour, but for turning into oil and charcoal. Or simply for eating. Europeans learned with great surprise that Africans generally believed them to be great and irredeemable cannibals.

Many of the old descriptions of the Coast record this belief, but none better than that of Olaudah Equiano, an Igbo (east Nigerian) slave who afterwards lived in London as a free man and whose book deserves respect. Captured as a young boy in about 1756, he retained a vivid memory of his fear that the stewpot was his fate. 'When I looked round the ship', he recalled of the moment when he was delivered to the European slavers, 'I saw a large furnace or copper boiling, and a multitude of black people of every description chained together, every one of their countenances expressing dejection and sorrow.' He 'no longer doubted of his fate'. He turned to his companions, newly enslaved as he was, and 'asked them if we were not to be eaten by those white men with horrible looks, red faces, and long hair?'

The belief was encouraged in Igbo country, as we shall see, by the famous *Aro* oracle. Yet it has had a long life in several parts of Africa. Even in the early twentieth century a Scottish missionary's wife in Nyasaland could describe it clearly. 'It was commonly asserted that our chief . . . had eaten his child by a slave wife. Some of our boys believed us capable of this abominable practice ourselves. When a very stout man, a land surveyor, called by the natives, "Che Cimimba" (Big Stomach) visited our station and stayed in the Doctor's house, the table-boy there fled in terror lest he should be eaten by the fat man. And another time when the Msungu [European in charge] was smoking a piece of wild boar in a barrel, a boy believed firmly that the "nyama" [meat] was one of his comrades.'

By the eighteenth century this slaving mythology was in full bloom on either side. Yet it remains an interesting fact that this period of the largest extension of slaving was also the period of a revised European estimate of African society. Moreover, at about this time the 'noble savage' came on stage. This is noticeable as early as 1744 when William Smith, together with his own memoirs of the Coast, published the account of Charles Wheeler, an agent of the Royal African Company's who had seen ten years' service, evidently at Cape Coast. Wheeler's description of African life is strong on lascivious detail and was possibly written with an indulgent eye to the eighteenth-century public; but there is no doubting the idyllic note. He dwells with fond amusement on his concubine with 'jetty breasts' but argues strongly for the 'sexual liberty' which, he says, Africans accept. They are never, he claims, tempted to rape as European men, through constant frustration, are tempted. 'All the time I liv'd there, I never once heard of those detestable and unnatural Crimes of Sodomy and Bestiality, so much practis'd among Christians.'

'A Guinean,' says Wheeler, 'by treading in the paths prescrib'd by his ancestors, paths natural, pleasant, and diverting, is in the plain road to be a good and happy man; but the European has sought so many inventions, and has endeavour'd to put so many restrictions upon nature, that it would be next to a miracle if he were either happy or good.' Not entirely a balanced view, perhaps: but certainly a new one in the literature of the Coast. 'And I doubt not upon an impartial examination of the premises, it would be found that we Christians have as many idle ridiculous notions and customs as the natives of Guinea have, if not more . . .'

This note was struck repeatedly in Britain and France as the anti-slavery campaigns grew stronger. Long accepted beliefs were challenged by the most unlikely observers. In 1796, for example, a pensioned officer of a brigade of Scottish mercenaries in the Dutch colonial service published his memoirs of an expedition against rebel slaves in Surinam (on the north coast of South America) during 1772–7. The frontispiece shows the young man, whose name was Stedman, leaning on his gun while a rebel Negro lies dead at his feet. But there is a ravaged expression on Stedman's face, and the rubric underneath has these surprising words:

> 'From different Parents, different Climes we came,
> At different Periods': Fate still rules the same.
> Unhappy Youth, while bleeding on the ground,
> 'Twas *Yours* to fall – but *Mine* to feel the wound.

Some of the most useful memoirs during the eighteenth century were those of ships' doctors and surgeons, men who were trained to look facts in the face. One such writer, Thomas Winterbottom, observed of the coastal Africans of the region of Sierra Leone in 1796, that they 'are in general shrewd and artful, sometimes malevolent and perfidious. Their long connection with European slave traders has tutored them in the arts of deceit, so that false weights and measures, damaged goods, and all the various cheats which the ingenuity of the more enlightened European has strained itself to invent, are now detected almost as soon as they are attempted to be put into practice. It is in great measure owing to this cause that traders who visited the coast of Africa in hopes of becoming suddenly rich, disappointed in finding the natives better acquainted with the value of their country's produce than they at first supposed, and too well instructed by dear bought experience to be so grossly imposed upon as formerly, have drawn of them so foul a picture as they could invent ...'

This new tone of cool inquiry, cutting through the mist of legend, was partly cause and partly effect of the anti-slaving agitations of the last quarter of the eighteenth century. It is of great importance in European literature about Africa. Henceforward Europeans would be increasingly divided into two opposed views: one, the traditional, tending to hold that Africa had never possessed cultures that were worthy of respect or even of serious investigation; the other, the scientific, tending to argue the reverse.

One may reasonably think that the ending of the slave trade must have reinforced this spirit of inquiry. This happened to some extent. But the trade was followed without much interval by colonial conquest and the 'scramble for Africa'; and a new spirit of obscurantist reaction soon carried all before it. Otherwise intelligent men were writing about Africa, by the beginning of the twentieth century, with much the same condescension and contempt as their predecessors of earlier times. 'People more animal-like than reasonable', Cavazzi had declared of the Angolans in 1687: 'Dancing among these barbarians, having no motive in the virtuous talent of displaying the movement of the body, or the agility of the feet, aims only at the vicious satisfaction of a libidinous appetite.' Such words read oddly in our day; yet the records of the 'scramble' period of the nineteenth century are full of remarks no less absurd.

By 1900 the average European opinion about Africa – though there were some memorable exceptions – showed scarcely a trace of the stubborn curiosity which men like Winterbottom had deployed a century earlier. Sir Harry Johnston is a case in point. He knew several regions of Africa fairly well; yet none of his experiences stopped him from accepting the doctrines of the day. Indeed, he swallowed some of them whole. For him, as for others, all signs of civilization in Africa were to be attributed to outside influence. 'Undoubtedly', he wrote in 1910, 'the influence of the Portuguese . . . wrought some surprising movements all along the coast regions of West Africa and in the southern basin of the Congo, by which organized kingdoms arose which created and stimulated commerce, and which in their general effects on the people were perhaps less drearily horrible than the anarchy of cannibal savages.' Yet the truth – as any diligent inquirer could have known even in 1910 – was precisely the reverse. For the kingdoms of the Congo had preceded the Portuguese; and the Portuguese, far from creating them, had in truth helped to destroy them.

The tide of reaction flowed far and wide; and some of its racist inundations are mournfully with us to this day. Johnston was a man of liberal reputation in the England of his time, yet he could airily dismiss the consequences of the slave trade for Africa as small or non-existent. No doubt unconsciously, he repeated the opinions of the Liverpool slavers of the eighteenth century who had claimed that the trade could even bring 'an access of happiness' to Africa. 'So far as the sum of human misery in Africa was concerned,' he wrote, 'it is probable that the trade in slaves between that continent and America scarcely added to it. It even to some extent mitigated the suffering of the negro in his own home; for once this trade was set on foot and it was profitable to sell a human being, many a man, woman or child who might otherwise have been killed for mere caprice, or for the love of seeing blood flow, or as a toothsome ingredient of a banquet, was sold to a slave-trader . . .'

Such language passed for serious comment in high colonial times. Only at the end of the imperial epoch, still many years ahead when Johnston wrote his books, would Europeans and Americans begin to look at Africa systematically, and as a subject in its own right rather than a mere object of pity, amazement or contempt.

5. Where Did They Come From?

THE modern reader will not think it likely that the brutal extraction of millions of men and women from Africa could have brought any 'access of happiness' to anyone save those who profited from their removal. The totals, true enough, may not seem very large – if mere size is any measure of misery – when divided into an 'annual average' over the three main centuries of the trade. There are several reasons, however, why it would be misleading to regard it in this light. One reason is that the most intensive years of slaving were concentrated between about 1700 and 1850. Another is that the areas from which slaves were consistently taken in great numbers were relatively few, and often relatively small.

Trans-Atlantic records are helpful here. There is the convincing case of Mexico. African labour in Mexico early took the place of 'Indian': no wonder, for the 'Indian' population was cut down by more than half in little over a century. As early as 1570 there were said to be as many as twenty thousand African slaves in Mexico. In 1584 the king of Spain passed to his vice-regal council in Mexico an order that 'the Indians, a weak people, be left to their own business, and that the labour of the mines, construction, fields and mills be undertaken by mulattoes, negroes and mestizos'. And so it was.

Most of the Africans who came to Mexico in those early days were probably of the Mande-speaking groups who lived then, as they still do, in the lands behind the western bulge of the Guinea Coast. These captives were generally known as Mandingos, (Mandinkas) and this word Mandingo appears to have survived in Mexico as the popular name for a devil. But the careful records of the Inquisition in Mexico, records that were kept as part of the process of 'safeguarding Christianity' by ensuring baptism, show that the land was fertilized by many African peoples.

Some of these were brought into the country not under their own names but under those their captors knew them by. Thus Nupe captives from central Nigeria who were taken and traded by the Yoruba people of western Nigeria were generally called Tapas, and as such they were delivered by the traders to the markets of the New World. In their turn the Yoruba, enslaved by the Fon people of Dahomey to the west of them, were known as Nagos and entered America under that name. The Susu people of the coast of the modern Guinea Republic do not appear in the Mexican records: they were registered as Xoxo. Bambara captives from the Middle Niger were known to the Inquisition as Bambura; the Tuculor of Senegal as Tucuxui; the numerous Foulah or Fulani under various labels and derivations. Among tribal names that suffered no distortion one may note the Kissi and the Senufu, who came from the lands of the Forest Belt behind the coast of present-day Liberia and the Republic of Guinea.

Often enough the captives were given two names, the first being that of the market where they were purchased on the African shoreline, and the other the name or nick-name of their tribe. Thus the records speak of Mina-Popos going to Cuba – Ivory Coast captives bought at the castle of Elmina; of Mina-Nagos going to Brazil – Yoruba people acquired at the same market. Igbo slave captives from eastern Nigeria generally arrived in Mexico as Calabares, having been purchased at the markets of Calabar in the Niger delta.

Most of the slaves were undoubtedly from western Africa. They were taken from about a score of principal markets or market-zones, and from many smaller ones, on a three-thousand-mile coastline between Senegal in the north and Angola in the south. A few were taken from East Africa even in the sixteenth century. The Mexican Inquisition archives mention at least two of the East African city-states: Melin, presumably Malindi, and Mozambique (by which was meant the island capital of that name, and not the later Portuguese colony). Those carried from the Mozambique coast were called Kaffrarians, after the Arabic word *kaffir* or pagan. Sometimes they were more clearly labelled. Thus 'Zoza' slaves in Mexico were probably Xhosa from the far south-eastern part of South Africa. And other victims came from places still farther afield: the Mexican records tell of slaves from Burma, Malaya, Java and even China.

Once in the New World, African peoples were often strong and numerous enough to revive and recreate the customs and beliefs of their homeland. Some of the West Indian islands and Brazil show this very clearly; nearly all the slave-populated lands of the Americas show it to some extent. Transported to Brazil in large numbers, Yoruba captives evolved a compound of their own beliefs and Christianity. Children of a strong and venerable culture, they printed a deep African accent into the everyday culture of the cities of the coast. Thus the *orishas* of the Yoruba – the national gods – were reborn in Brazilian Bahia as Christian saints. At Rio de Janeiro the god of war, Ogun, became St George, the sainted knight of the Catholics. And in their cult houses, their *macumbas*, the Africans of Rio, says Ramos, sing: 'Ogun! Ogun! My Father! Oh Jorge, sarava (save) Ogun!' Yemanja and Oshun, goddesses of the Yoruba, have in their turn become fused with Our Lady of the Conception, and other female *orishas* have here and there undergone the same transformation. Even African languages have sometimes survived, though in truncated form.

So a study of the ex-slave communities of the New World can still throw much light on their African origins. Modern research seems to indicate two conclusions. The first is that few African peoples were spared their tribute of slaves. But this is considerably qualified by a second conclusion: that most of the slaves came from lands that were near the coast.

Some writers have depicted the slave trails reaching right across the continent, plunging their merciless thrust into the most remote corners of the far interior. This certainly happened during the brief and bloody Arab slave trade from Zanzibar in the nineteenth century. Even in earlier times it was now and then the case, captives from the inland countries being handed from one set of traders to the next until they were finally delivered to Europeans at the coast. 'They sold us for money', recalls the narrative of a West African ex-slave who wrote his memoirs in 1831, 'and I myself was sold six times over, sometimes for money, sometimes for a gun, sometimes for cloth . . . It was about half a year from the time I was taken before I saw white people.'

Another memoir tells how a French slaving captain purchased at Cabinda, near the mouth of the Congo river, 'an African woman who seemed to him pretty familiar with Whites, or at least showed no surprise or fear at sight of them. Struck by this unusual confidence, the slaver asked her the cause of it. She replied that she had already seen White men in another land where the sun rose out of the water instead of hiding itself in the sea, as it does in the Congo. Pointing to the east, she added the words *monizi monambu* – I have seen the edge of the sea. She had been *ganda cacota* – many moons – on the way.' This story, adds the writer, appears to confirm what the seventeenth-century Dutch geographer, Olfert Dapper, had said about slaves of Mozambique being sold in the Congo.

There is nothing improbable about Africans having repeatedly and even regularly traversed the continent from one ocean to the other. From experience at the end of the seventeenth century, the trader James Barbot had already observed that peoples in Angola extended their trade as far eastward as the frontiers of the kingdoms of Mombasa, Kilwa and Sofala, all of which are on the east African coast. Slaves were brought to the Angolan coast, he noted, from '150 or 200 leagues up the country'.

'All that vast number of slaves which the Calabar Blacks sell to all European nations', James's uncle, John Barbot, was writing a little earlier of the Niger delta trade, 'are not their prisoners of war, the greatest part being bought by those people of their inland neighbours, and they also buy them of other nations yet more remote from them.'

Both the European and American records generally agree, though with exceptions, that the coastal peoples seldom supplied slaves from their own ranks. They purchased or otherwise got hold of them, as one would expect, from the peoples in their rear; and these in turn, while delivering some captives from their own region, looked for their main supply to other peoples still further into the interior. How far did this shunting process go? The answer seems to be that it went much less far than the slaving totals would at first sight suggest. From one century to the next, the bulk of the slaves were evidently drawn from a belt of territory that reached inland from the coast (but seldom included the coast itself) for several hundred miles but seldom further.

Thus the Fon slaving kingdom of Dahomey never seems to have taken prisoners, at least in any significant number, from regions more remote than a couple of hundred miles into the interior. Another large source of slaves was the Gold Coast. Here the slaving middlemen were the Fanti people who purchased captives from the Ashanti to the north of them and sold them to the Europeans at the coastal forts. 'Yet all evidence from recognisable survivals such as the many Ashanti-Fanti place names, names of deities, and day names in the New World', Herskovits has reported, has argued 'that the sources of the slaves exported by the Fanti were in greatest proportion within the present boundaries of the Gold Coast colony [modern Ghana].'

Summing up for West Africa, one may say that the strong peoples of the coast and its immediate hinterland raided or purchased northward, but not very far. They drew their regular supplies from the relatively abundant peoples of the Forest Belt and to a lesser extent from the sparser peoples of the grasslands beyond the forest. Somewhere in these grasslands a 'slaving watershed' seems to have existed: to the south of it captives were drained off the coast, while to the north of it they were channelled to the Niger and thence taken either to Senegal or to the Island of Gorée for the trans-Atlantic trade, or sold for transport across the Sahara to the markets of North Africa. But the main impact of the trade was felt on the southern side of this 'watershed', and it is there, near the coast and along the coast, that one must look for its principal effects.

6. Three Regions

GLANCING through the records of this long-enduring trade, you may get at first the impression of a hopeless muddle. Sudden quarrels are smoothed into unexpected peace. Bloody insurrections shatter long-established custom. Chaotic and haphazard strokes of fortune are interspersed by days of the most detailed and calculated haggling. On top of all this there is a flood of strange names and tortuous jargon. Yet the confusion is less baffling than it seems. It can be straightened out with patience into a fairly clear sequence of cause and effect.

To begin with, it soon becomes obvious that the African-European connection had powerful influence on the growth and manner of trade. Currencies expanded. Methods of calculation grew. There came a new sophistication in methods of dealing: along with this, a new fraudulence. Africans learned from European tricks; and the tricks were many and various.

In much of this the African-European connection was no different in its general effects from the African-Arab or the African-Indian connection. Indeed, one should think of the main continent of Africa in these centuries as of a vast island surrounded by three oceans, the Atlantic and Indian Oceans of water and the Saharan ocean of sand. Within this great continental 'island' there was barter and exchange by standard weight or value. Cities dealt with cities, rulers with rulers, one trading community with another; and often enough their dealings reached over very great distances. Along all three 'seaboards' there grew up new trading towns and merchants who specialized in oversea or overland commerce: Walata, Djenne, Timbuktu, Gao, Kano and others on the southern 'shore' of the Sahara; Kilwa, Malindi and their like on the coast of East Africa; and new settlements and city-states along the West African seaboard of the Atlantic.

Trade had long become important to these communities before the first ships from Europe came over the skylines of the ocean. All of them engaged in local trade and possessed effective marketing systems, often of great antiquity. Some of them were deeply involved in 'external' trade over long distances. Yet all these trading systems, often important though they were, had been grafted into economies in which the element of community subsistence continued to be a large one. It is probably safe to say that trade for a large proportion of rural people – and most Africans were rural people then – was of secondary importance in the general run of everyday life. But this ceased to be the case wherever large and long-distance systems of trade had come into existence. Towns and cities might be small when compared with those of Africa today, but they still provided a valuable market for imported luxuries and other goods not otherwise obtainable at home. These urban or long-distance trades became a highly sophisticated form of business, but not for the majority of people.

When Leo Africanus reported in the sixteenth century that Timbuktu made 'a big demand for books in manuscript, imported from Barbary', and that 'more profit is made from the book trade than from any other line of business', he was not necessarily guilty of any exaggeration. But he certainly did not mean that people all over the Western Sudan were buying books. He meant only that Timbuktu itself was an important centre of Muslim learning and well able to afford private libraries. Much the same may be said of East Africa's large imports of porcelain from China; those fine pots and vases were destined for the homes and tables of the rich and powerful, and not for the huts of lesser men.

The lesser men, for their part, had no zeal for accumulation. It was to be one of the great complaints of European settlers in Africa that the 'savages' were immune to the offer of monetary reward: that their objection to earning money lay not only in their unfamiliarity with money or with what money might be made to do, but also and above all in their unwillingness to work beyond the mere point of providing for themselves and their families. Schooled in a sterner tradition, these settlers saw in such 'stubborn idleness' a sore proof of damnation. For them, more often than not, there was only one road to Heaven – whether the Heaven of immortality or the more immediate Heaven of respectability – and that was to accumulate.

Both Protestants and Catholics saw matters in this way; but the Puritans said it most clearly. 'The standing pool is prone to putrefaction,' said Richard Steele in *The Tradesman's Calling*, published in 1684, 'and it were better to beat down the body and keep it in subjection by a laborious calling, than through luxury to become a castaway.' Such ideas would serve later on as a moral veneer for methods of coercion. Speaking on his Glen Grey Act of 1894 – a measure which imposed an annual money tax on Africans in South Africa so as to force them to leave their villages and go to work for European-paid wages – Cecil Rhodes uttered a comment which may stand as typical. 'You will', he told the Legislative Assembly of the Cape Province, 'remove [the Africans] from that life of sloth and laziness: you will teach them the dignity of labour and make them contribute to the prosperity of the State: and make them give some return for our wise and good government.' Across a crazy paving of such ideas as these the clumsy steam-roller of subjection and 'trusteeship' has gone testily through the years; and only of late have men begun to question its right of way.

Most Africans found such notions, whenever they came across them or were forced to take account of them, useless or unacceptable. The majority of peasants and stock-breeders lived in communities where the idea of private property had scarcely appeared, let alone the much more objectionable notion of private enterprise. 'All the land occupied by the tribe', writes Schapera of the Bantu-speaking peoples of southern Africa, but the definition will apply more widely, 'is vested in the Chief, and administered by him as head of the tribe . . . the land is not his personal possession . . . The natural resources of the land – earth, water, wood, grass, clay, edible plants, and fruits – are all common property, never reserved for the use of any particular persons . . . It is only in regard to land for residence and cultivation that private rights are universally recognised . . .'

Such systems varied in detail. That is understandable. But they were common to much of Africa, the product of trial and error over many centuries. They carried with them and required a general sense of collective responsibility; codes of law that were none the less effective for being unwritten; well-understood sanctions and rewards. There seems little doubt that the economy and ideology of this lineage mode of production was raised among a majority of African peoples to a point where it had solved, if far from perfectly, all the root problems of survival at a pre-industrial and pre-capitalist level.

Trade was therefore useful but not essential. It grew with the development of states and centralized rule. It became the prop and stay of merchants and craftsmen. It supplied the luxury and prestige of courts and rulers. Here and there, too, the growth of trade developed towards the growth of capitalism. Islamic scholars exercised their wit in finding ways to evade religion's ban on usury in much the same way (and with much the same success) as Christian scholars in Europe. But generally the lineage mode held firm.

Even where trade was promoted by the mighty, there was still no accent on accumulation in the capitalist meaning of the term. The proof and power of wealth came from display, not from investment. Sometimes there was glittering display. When the Mali emperor Musa passed through Cairo on his way to Mecca in the fourteenth century he presided over a spending spree of prodigious dimensions, and practically wrecked the value of the Cairo currency by paying lavishly in gold that he had brought with him. Earnest bankers in European cities, catching the distant echo of that event and others like it, came mistakenly to think that the whole country beyond the desert must be replete with wealth. But in fact the prodigality of rulers like Mansa Musa, in Suret-Canale's words, pointed 'less to the wealth of the mines of Bouré than to the enormous accumulation that the social condition of the country made possible – and to the exercise of the old tribal principle that wealth is an instrument of power because it can buy the loyalty of others, rather than the labour of others'.

So long as trade conformed to this pattern, its profits merely enhanced the pride and reputation of local rulers. It added another element to everyday life, but one that was easily absorbed by systems which possessed great inner stability. Yet once the European connection developed into a massive exchange of slaves for firearms, this old stability began to be undermined. Trade came to have special and disrupting consequences. These were generally not present, or present in a lesser degree, with the trans-Saharan and East Coast trades. This was partly because of the smaller volume of these non-European trades. But it was above all because, in the non-European trades, the economies 'at either end' were far closer to each other in type and structure than with the Atlantic trade. They could continue to trade with each other without the external economy becoming dominant over the corresponding African economy. This had been the case at the beginning with the Atlantic trade. The 'technological gap' between the Portuguese and other venturers of the fifteenth and sixteenth centuries on one hand, and their new African partners on the other, was effectively small. Much damage could be done, as will be seen. But the 'European connection' led to another consequence. Feeding the technological progress of western Europe, the Atlantic trade gradually created, for the Africans involved, a partner whose strength was going to prove too much for them.

To unravel the course of this European connection, often devious but never dull, I have selected three regions where its impact was decisive but of widely varying effect.

These are the region of the old states of the Congo, reached by the Portuguese in 1482; the region of the East African coastal city-states and trading empires; and, thirdly, some parts of the Guinea Coast.

All three regions have a large place in the records, but there is another and perhaps stronger reason for choosing them. This is that they throw up contrasts and parallels which are often strikingly instructive. Through these, I suggest, one can measure with a greater accuracy than in any other way just what the consequences of European enterprise in Africa really were.

PART FOUR

MANI-CONGO

I fetch my life and bearing
From men of royal siege . . .

Othello

With an assortment of sundry goods amounting to about fourteen hundred pounds sterling, it may be reasonably expected to get about three hundred slaves or more, which brings them to near the rate of five pounds a head.

JAMES BARBOT in 1700

1. Discovery

SOMETIME in the second half of the year 1482 an expeditionary fleet of three Portuguese caravels anchored off the Gold Coast castle of Elmina, then less than a year old, and sent in boats through the surf for food and water. They were bound on a long journey. Replenished by their fellow-countrymen in the new-built castle on shore, they at once set sail for the eastward, pressing on to fresh discovery.

For the first few hundred sea-miles after leaving Elmina they were on a route that was already roughly known. Several Portuguese ships had come this way since Ruy de Siqueira, ten years earlier, had first entered the Bight of Benin. But near this Bight their commander changed course for the southward. He and his crews passed Cape Saint Catherine – Cape Lopez in the Gabon of today – and entered seas that no European mariner, and probably no mariner of any continent, had ever sailed before.*

In the annals of European discovery the commander of this expedition, whose name was Diogo Cão, undoubtedly deserves a high place. He was the true forerunner of Bartolomeo Dias and Vasco da Gama who would soon afterwards round the Cape of Good Hope into the Indian Ocean. It was Cão's central task to bring back the answer to one great question of consuming interest: how far to the south did this continental coastline reach before yielding passage to the eastern seas? For it was to complete their turning of the Muslim flank along the Mediterranean coast of Africa that the princes of Portugal mainly promoted the discovering voyages which gave them fame. Once their ships could sail right round and behind the Muslim barrier, they could send expeditions to the lands and peoples of the East. They were convinced that this was possible, since earlier maps had

*Herodotus recorded a Phoenician circumnavigation of Africa; but the fact seems more than a little doubtful.

shown a southern termination of the continent; and for some time they believed that this eastward channel must lie not far beyond the Gulf of Guinea. But Diogo Cão proved them wrong.

He failed to sight the southern cape. His farthest point on this first voyage was Cape Lobo, about a hundred and fifty miles beyond modern Lobito. There he erected a stone column – 'in the year of the world's creation 1681, and that of Our Saviour's birth 1482' – to the honour of his king and himself. But on the way to Cape Lobo he had already discovered something else, the estuary of a vast river flowing from the interior of Africa; and it was this discovery that made his name and fortune. So great was this river, he reported, that its silt-laden waters discoloured the ocean for many miles from the shore.

Lisbon sent him back to this river, the Zaire or Congo. An estuary as wide as this must surely offer an overland route to the first of the great eastern lands on the Portuguese list for discovery, the 'empire of Prester John'. On his second voyage Cão sailed up the estuary, landed near the Matadi of today, and there met with some of the people of the country. The encounter was peaceful. Failing a common language, neither side could learn much of the other, but the Portuguese understood they were in the territory of a powerful ruler whose capital was distant from the coast. Cão left four Franciscan monks with orders to visit this monarch if they could, and renewed his voyage to the south.

Returning northward some months later, he again sailed up to the head of the estuary but found his monks were missing. He accordingly seized hostages from the people on the shore and carried them back with him to Portugal. The records say that these Congolese discoverers of Europe were well treated on their involuntary journey, and had already learned to speak some Portuguese before being delivered to the king in Lisbon. They were certainly well received by the king, clothed, converted to Christianity, and encouraged to act as future interpreters. In 1487 they were sent back to the Congo with Cão's third expedition. And now Diogo Cão himself, together with a retinue of fellow-countrymen and these Congolese interpreters, was invited to visit the ruler of this land, the Mani-Congo (or *Mweni*-Congo, lord of Congo), at his capital of Mbanza in the hills behind the coast.*

* More accurately, *Mweni*-Kongo, or lord of the baKongo (Kongo people).

Frontiers of kingdoms after D'Anville (1749) and Fage (1958)

There the Europeans found this African ruler seated on a royal stool of ivory, surrounded by his counsellors and men-at-arms; and the meeting was a great success. Each side recovered its lost ones, the king his subjects who had spent nearly two years in Portugal, and Cão his four Franciscan monks. The long history of Portugal in south-west Africa had begun.

It began in friendship and alliance. Within a few years of this visit to Mbanza, the 'royal brothers' of Portugal and Congo were writing letters to each other that were couched in terms of complete equality of status. Emissaries went back and forth between them. Relations were established between Mbanza and the Vatican. A son of the Mani-Congo was appointed in Rome itself as bishop of his country.

Not for another two hundred years would the Portuguese succeed in destroying the Mani-Congo's independence. Not until 1883 – four centuries after Diogo Cão had first gazed in wonder at the wide brown flood of the Congo where it surges into the Atlantic – would this African state be formally annexed by Portugal to the neighbouring colony of Angola. The whole early history of this intercourse makes a clear and often startling illustration of the organizational similarity of these two states; and, at the same time, of the inner contrast in their forms of rule and growth that would lead, little by little, to Portuguese dominion. Here, if briefly and fitfully, there was the promise of a genuine partnership between Europe and Africa, as well as a demonstration of why the promise failed.

2. Royal Brothers

NOTHING more clearly shows the curious perversity of the European-African connection, as it developed through the years, than this history of the Congo (that is, in modern usage, of the kingdom of the Kongo and its neighbours). The connection undoubtedly began with something of a golden age of peace and friendship. It just as surely degenerated into violence, hatred and distrust. So complete was this decay that when the nineteenth century finally brought colonial conquest, the conquerors seemed to have utterly forgotten the experience and accumulated knowledge of earlier Europeans. They proclaimed their 'mission to the heart of darkness' as though nothing was previously known of any of these states or peoples. They and their backers in Europe saw this land as a twilight zone of mystery and mumbo-jumbo where the Ancient African had somehow managed to survive in primitive squalor and simplicity, a little better than the animals but not much: and not enough, in any case, to justify regarding him as a man who deserved the same respect as other men.

No one expressed this approach and attitude more clearly than Joseph Conrad although he, of course, did it only to expose the bitterness of the case. His Marlow would remember of a journey in about the year 1900 how the wide reaches of the Congo river opened before his river vessel and closed behind

> as if the forest had stepped leisurely across the water to bar the way for our return. We penetrated deeper and deeper into the heart of darkness. It was very quiet there. At night sometimes the roll of drums behind the curtain of trees would run up the river and remain sustained faintly, as if hovering in the air high above our heads...

No good thing, surely, could ever have come out of such a place.

The impressions of the early Portuguese had been altogether different. They found much that was strange and puzzling but nothing that seemed to allow of an easy contempt or special sense of mystery. They ran into many surprising beliefs and superstitions, but few or none that seemed more disconcerting than others they could find at home. Victorious Congolese armies tended to see signs and ghostly symbols in the sky, yet there was nothing out of the way in that. The Portuguese themselves regularly saw angels, and so of course did other Europeans. More often than not they found it easy to accept the peoples of the Congo as natural equals and allies.

Of this the most striking evidence is to be found in the correspondence exchanged between King Manuel of Portugal and his remarkable Congolese contemporary, the Mani-Congo Nzinga Mbemba who was baptized as Dom Affonso. This outstanding African ruler seems to have become a Christian soon after the first large Portuguese missionary expedition reached the Congo in 1490; after defeating his rivals, probably with Portuguese armed assistance, he became Mani-Congo in 1506 or 1507 (the date remains uncertain) and entered at once into a close alliance with his 'royal brother' of Portugal. He reigned for some forty years and was long remembered with honour and respect. Even as late as the nineteenth century a Portuguese missionary could say that 'a native of the Congo knows the name of three kings: that of the present one, that of his predecessor, and that of Affonso'.

Some twenty-two of King Affonso's letters, preserved in the royal archives of Portugal, are known for the years 1512 to 1540. Written by various secretaries – the most important of whom, baptized as João Texeira, was evidently Congolese* – they show a good command of the Portuguese language and bear on a wide variety of topics. They also illuminate the relations of equality that marked this early contact.

'Most powerful and excellent king of Manycongo,' King Manuel wrote from Lisbon in 1512, 'We send to you Simão da Silva, nobleman of our house, a person whom we most trust ... We beg you to listen to him with faith and belief in everything he says from our part ...' And King Affonso, who was still Nzinga Mbemba to his subjects, generally began his own letters with the words: 'Most high and powerful prince and king my brother ...'

What medieval Lisbon thought of this remote land and its people may best be seen from the famous *regimento* of 1512. This 'set of instructions' was composed by the Portuguese court for the better ordering of Manuel's relations with the Mani-Congo. It consisted of thirty-four points 'in none of which', as James Duffy has lately pointed out, 'is there a suggestion of authoritarian constraint on the people of Congo'. The *regimento* remains one of the most interesting documents in the tortuous saga of Europe in Africa. It reveals a strikingly keen appreciation of the difficulties of conducting a commercial alliance with a distant people of whom little was known, and foreshadows many of the bitter problems which were soon to beset the enterprise of European discovery.

The 'instructions' from Lisbon were in four parts. All of them portray the central misunderstanding that dogged these early

*I am following here the opinion argued by Cuvelier.

efforts in the Congo. Affonso asked for friendly help and was willing to pay for it in whatever goods the Portuguese might care to buy. But the Portuguese, having won over an African ruler to Christianity, thought that the best way they could respond (while duly furthering their own interests) was to transfer Portuguese institutions bodily to the Congo. Simão da Silva, bearer of the *regimento*, was recommended as a resident adviser to Manuel's royal 'friend and brother'. Not foreseeing the consequences, Affonso eagerly accepted this: later on, when the consequences became clearer, it was too late to reverse the course of events. Yet it is fairly certain that the Portuguese themselves had as yet no thought of outright invasion of the Congo: their *regimento* was intended as a gesture of friendship to a newcomer by one of the leaders of the Christian world. In sending it, Manuel seems to have had in mind that he was dealing with a pagan but strongly organized people – now, fortunately, with a Christian king at their head – who were fully masters of their own land, non-literate but not therefore savage or especially barbarous, and capable of taking the graft of Portuguese culture without any long period (this idea would develop much later) of 'trusteeship' or direct Portuguese government.

In the first two parts of the *regimento* it was provided that the Portuguese should help the king of Congo towards a better organization of his realm, introduce Portuguese notions of law and warfare, build churches, teach Portuguese court etiquette, and, writes Duffy, move in all matters 'with tact and discretion, to offend no one, but to create where possible an African parallel to Portuguese society'. It was also suggested that the conflicts and quarrels of Europeans and Africans should be settled amicably, but local Portuguese were to have 'extra-territorial rights' and be dealt with in a case of need by Portuguese law. Offenders were to be sent home for punishment in Lisbon.

Such was the 'civilizing mission'. Manuel was also mindful of the material profits. The last two parts of the *regimento* insisted that the Mani-Congo should supply cargoes for the ships of Portugal. 'This expedition', noted Manuel, 'has cost us much: it would be unreasonable to send it home with empty hands. Although our principal wish is to serve God and the pleasure of the King [of Congo], none the less you [Simão da Silva] will make him understand – as though speaking in our own name – what he should do to fill the ships, whether with slaves, or copper, or ivory.' Lastly, da Silva was told to collect information of every kind, whether political, military, or commercial.

By the better organization of the Congo kingdom, Manuel intended a tighter and more reliable feudal hierarchy. He knew that Affonso had won his throne in the Congo only against violent opposition from other claimants, and he seems to have been convinced that if Affonso were going to survive the ambition of his turbulent feudatories, he must take an altogether firmer grip on his fiefs. Manuel himself, after all, had the best of reasons for distrusting feudal chieftains, his predecessor having put to death a number of rebellious noblemen. He accordingly abounded in good advice tending towards autocratic rule, and thoughtfully added an appendix to the *regimento* that set forth the titles and armorial bearings which the king of Congo should adopt and bestow on his nobles. Here in this curious list there figured 'principes, ifamtes, duques, marquezes, comdes, bixcomdes, barões'.* The six greatest feudatories of the Mani-Congo – chiefs of the regions of Mbata, Nsundi, Mbamba, Wembo, Wandu and Mbala – were to be dukes; lesser notables were to be marquises, counts and barons; while the children of the king were to be princes and princesses. Manuel also sent a specimen signature 'which it seems to the King our lord that the King of Manycongo should make and sign from now on'.

It is hard to know what the Congolese really made of all this. Affonso accepted it, at least outwardly, in its entirety. On receiving the *regimento* – presented by a 'husbandman' called Alvaro Lopes, da Silva having died on the way – the Congo ruler at once sent down four hundred and twenty slaves for choice by the Portuguese at their anchorage near the mouth of the Congo, and of these the Portuguese selected three hundred and twenty and duly carried them off. There is also extant a long manifesto or circular letter which Affonso addressed to the 'chief lords' of his kingdom; but once again it is difficult to guess how far Affonso could have intended this to be taken seriously.

The King of Portugal 'sent us the arms painted in this letter', Affonso told his chiefs and counsellors according to this mani-

*'Princes, royal heirs, dukes, marquises, counts, viscounts, barons.'

festo, 'for us to use them as ensigns on our shields, as the Christian kings or princes of those lands generally carry so to show to whom they belong and whence they come . . . Those arms which he so sent to us represent the Cross seen in the skies, and also the Apostle St Tiago with all the other Saints with whom he fought for us . . . together with that part of his own arms which he added to the mentioned ones which the Almighty God our Lord gave through his Angel to the first King of Portugal while he was fighting in a battle against many Moorish Kings, enemies of his holy faith . . .' This was no doubt a letter written for consumption in Lisbon.

Sincere or not, Affonso increasingly adopted the Christian ideas and arguments of his 'royal brother' in pressing frequently for aid, and in complaining when aid as frequently failed to arrive. There must in any case have seemed no other way of winning access to European knowledge and technique; and Affonso's letters leave no doubt that he was fully sincere in wanting both of these new things. Whenever he had the chance he sent cargoes of young men to be educated in Portugal, persisting in this even when he had learned by experience that many would be lost to Portuguese enslavement on the way.

He also strove to by-pass the Portuguese maritime monopoly and enter into direct relations with the other 'important European' of whom the Portuguese had given news, the Pope in Rome. Manuel at first was not averse to this: the appearance of a Congolese embassy in Rome would necessarily reflect great prestige on the Portuguese discoverers. He suggested that his brother of Congo should send a mission to Rome, helpfully explaining that twelve noblemen with six servants would be the right number. One of Affonso's sons, baptized as Dom Henrique and then being educated in a Portuguese seminary, should lead this mission and, as ambassador, should formally address the Pope in Latin. King Manuel would request the Pope to make Prince Henry a bishop.

All this, however unlikely it may now appear, came to pass with little delay. Accompanied by gifts of ivory, rare skins and the fine-woven raffia textiles of the Congo – and, as far as Lisbon, by the three hundred and twenty captives whom the Portuguese captains had chosen – the mission arrived in Portugal and was sent overland to Italy, crossing the Alps and making its way slowly down to Rome, where it safely arrived in 1513. With it went Prince Henry, who was then eighteen years old.

Five years later, on May 5, 1518, Henry of Congo was elevated to the rank of bishop on the formal proposal of four cardinals, Pope Leo X having two days earlier published a bull to that effect: *Vidimus quae super Henrici* ... Three years later Henry returned to his native land. He appears to have died in 1535, having achieved little or nothing. Like the rest of his people – and like his memorable father – Henry was the victim of an impossible contradiction. The 'civilizing mission' and the 'commerce' of the *regimento* had been supposed to march gently hand-in-hand, the one aiding the other. In fact they were sharply and even violently opposed from the very first; but it was the commerce that won.

Yet 'relations of equality' persisted as long as Dom Affonso remained alive. So did the Christian texture of his correspondence. 'Most high and most powerful prince and king my brother,' he was writing in 1517, 'it is due to the need I have of several things for the church that I am importuning you. And this I would not probably do if I had a ship, since having it I would send for them at my own cost ...' He had repeatedly asked Manuel to give him a ship or the means of building one; but Manuel, being determined to keep the maritime monopoly strictly in his own hands, had as regularly refused to oblige. 'The things needed for the church are the following ... a silver cross, a monstrance for the Corpus Christi, curtains for the altar, half a dozen surplices . . .' and other items of the kind.

In 1526 Affonso had news by a Portuguese vessel of the death of the queen of Portugal. He at once hastened to send Manuel assurances of 'the great sorrow and mourning' he felt because 'the Queen Dona Leonor our Sister had passed away from the present life, and only Our Lord knows how sorry and regretful we were for that ...'

In the same year he wrote again, with fresh requests for 'technical aid', asking this time for medical staffs:

> Your highness has been kind enough to write to us saying that we should ask in our letters for anything we need, and that we shall be provided with everything, and as the peace and health of our kingdom

depend on us, and as there are among us old folk and people who have lived for many days, it happens that we have many and different diseases which put us very often in such a weakness that we reach almost the last extreme; and the same happens to our children, relatives and others owing to the lack in this country of physicians and surgeons who might know how to cure properly such diseases . . . We have neither dispensaries nor drugs which might help us in this forlornness . . . We beg of you to be kind and agreeable enough to send two physicians and two apothecaries and one surgeon . . .

Like other of Affonso's efforts to introduce European techniques, this appeal for doctors seems to have been fruitless. Yet even as late as 1540, when the early partnership had run hopelessly into the sands of commercial greed, and Affonso had seen all his plans and ambitions reduced to nothing, the Congo monarch was still writing to Lisbon – now to John III who had meanwhile succeeded Manuel – in the same language of Christian persuasion. He argued that the King of Portugal's assumption of the title of 'Lord of Guinea' should be a reason for showing special consideration for the needs of the Congo, 'since we have helped you to sustain this title with unfailing support'. He gently complained of the repeated disappointments that he had suffered at Portuguese hands. He renewed his appeal for help.

It will not seem wrong that . . . as adequate income should be awarded us for our legitimate necessities . . . since we have to spend a lot of money [in furthering the interests of Christianity] and have nobody to help us, unless we turn to Your Highness and ask for assistance for the sake and honour of Our Lord Jesus Christ's passion: We beg of you to lend us five thousand cruzados to provide for the expenses of our brother and ambassador Dom Manuel, who on our behalf goes to see the Holy Father, accepting in exchange one hundred and fifty *cofos* of coins of our Kingdom [three million cowries] with which slaves can be bought [and the King of Portugal thus repaid].*

But to John III and his counsellors the request did seem wrong; and it fell, like the others, on deaf ears. By this time the Portuguese court had taken the measure of their own interests in the Congo, and these were not the same, by a long chalk, as the interests of the people of Dom Affonso. To see why this was so, one needs to look at the old Congo as it really was.

*The actual words read: 'units can be ransomed', *units* being a Portuguese euphemism for slaves, and *ransomed* being another for bought.

3. Congo: Ngola: Matamba

MUCH can be learned of the old states of the western Congo basin and the neighbouring coastal regions, for the Portuguese were curious travellers and, from time to time, acute historians. Many early missionary writings have survived. Lately, too, sociological investigators such as Vansina, Balandier and Miller have added much useful knowledge to the record, filling out the picture of the way these peoples lived before conquest by the Portuguese, and suggesting how they were related to their neighbours in the north and east.

The last of the 'Lords of Congo' died some seventy years ago, unhonoured and unsung, an obscure nonentity whose authority had vanished and whose prestige lay hidden in the half-remembered traditions of a captive people. His baptismal name was Dom Martin, and he counted in the world of Africa for nothing but a memory. Yet it was a great memory. Dom Martin came of a long line of rulers. He himself was the fifty-fifth Mani-Congo. His 'founding ancestor', whose name was written by the early Portuguese as Nimi a Lukeni, appears to have begun his rule near the end of the fourteenth century; and was perhaps contemporary, to make a European comparison, with the early years of Joan of Arc.

Two sons of the sister of Nimi a Lukeni came after him, succession being matrilineal then just as it is today among some of the peoples who occupy this country; and then another Mani-Congo whose name is lost, at least to the Portuguese records. Fifth in the line was Nzinga a Nkuwa, who was Mani-Congo when the caravels of Diogo Cão turned eastward into the estuary of the great river in 1482, and whom Cão's missionary fellow-venturers christened as João after their own sovereign lord. Nzinga a Nkuwa was followed by Nzinga Mbemba who, as Dom Affonso, became King Manuel's 'royal brother'.

The lands of the Mani-Congo's dominion varied in extent. As in Europe a little earlier, this was a time of constant if limited warfare between powerful rulers whose authority was buttressed by the spiritual powers they were believed to possess. At their greatest extension, probably not long before the arrival of the Portuguese, the Mani-Congo was the liege lord of territories of fealty and tribute whose boundaries may have measured about three hundred miles from north to south and perhaps two or three hundred from west to east, or a country rather more than half the size of England. To the north of the Congo estuary these lands included Loango, roughly coterminous with modern Cabinda, and the states of Congo, Ngola and Matamba to the south of the river, all these three lying in northern and western Angola as we know it now.

The 'home kingdom' of Congo was the extreme northern part of modern Angola. Its frontiers, at their greatest extent, may have reached inland from the Congo estuary for about two hundred and fifty miles. There is no means of knowing the exact size of the population of all these countries: perhaps six or seven millions today, it was certainly a good deal less five hundred years ago. It will have been considerably larger, in any case, than the population of Portugal.

Self-confidence and a vigorous sense of independence were the characteristics that repeatedly struck the Portuguese about these rulers and their counsellors. They thought themselves, wrote a seventeenth-century Italian, 'the foremost men in the world', and nothing would persuade them to the contrary. 'Never having been outside of Africa, they imagine that their country is not only the largest in the world, but also the happiest, most agreeable and most beautiful.' Powerful in war, quick to defend themselves, jealous of their rights and suspicious of foreign intervention, they were seldom or never defeated in outright battle by the Portuguese. Pushed back by European fire-power, they retreated to their mountain strongholds, nursed their wounds, recouped their losses and returned time after time to the attack. Many of their leaders became famous in the memories of the people of Angola.

Where had the Mani-Congo and his people come from? Their own traditions suggested that they – or at least their ruling families – were relative newcomers to the country when they first encountered the Portuguese. Picking up two hundred years later what Lisbon had learned of these traditions, Oliveira Cadornega has an interesting passage in his *Description of the Kingdom of*

Congo, published in 1680. 'About the origins of this kingdom ... this nation has always been considered as foreign ... [and as being people] who had come from the interior to dominate this kingdom: as it happened, we may say, with the Romans, Sueves, Vandals, Goths and Semi-Goths who occupied our Lusitania, Spain and other kingdoms and domains ...'

This comparison was strikingly perceptive. For the African period that was contemporary with the over-running of Roman Europe by 'barbarians' from the east and north was also, as modern research confirms, a time of great movement of peoples. These were the centuries that saw many new developments in the great migratory spread of Bantu-speaking and other African peoples who populated much of central and southern Africa with the nations that are known today. They spread across lands that were relatively empty of people in directions that were mainly from north to south but were also, as migratory spread became more complex, in lateral and northerly directions too.

In this way there came into the western Congo, in their turn, the ancestors of the Mani-Congo. Probably they were no more than a small group of closely organized and well-armed intruders, tempered and toughened by their travels and adventures. They would have conquered their lands in Congo in much the same sense as Duke William and his four thousand knights had seized control of Saxon England some three or four hundred years earlier, subjugating the peoples whom they found, settling among them, intermarrying with them and gradually building a new state and social system. Little by little they spread their influence among their neighbours, contracted 'royal marriages', and established the right of tax and tribute. Sometimes these neighbours revolted against such impositions, as fief-holders regularly did in Europe, and the Mani-Congo was obliged to call out his levies and go to war for his 'rights'. It was precisely this endemic rivalry between 'king and barons' that made the early Portuguese alliance attractive to Nzinga a Nkuwa and his successor, Dom Affonso, and gave the Portuguese their early chance of military intervention here.

Recent archaeological research indicates that these south-western states (Congo, Ngola, Matamba and their like) were off-shoots of the main stream of Iron Age development in central-southern Africa during the first centuries of the present millenium: a development that culminated, so far as southern Africa was concerned, in the plateau states which built Zimbabwe and other notable stone structures. There is evidence of similarity between the organization and culture of the Congo states and those of Zimbabwe and Mozambique.

Among this evidence there is that of the 'royal palaces'. The paramount rulers of the Zimbabwean states were generally established in large dwellings, often of stone, and sometimes, as a Great Zimbabwe or Khami, of elaborate construction with one large wall encircling another – a labyrinth of mystery built less for safety than for means of celebrating the spiritual power and prestige of this or that ruler. Commenting on the large stone ruin of Khami, near Bulawayo, Robinson has defined its evident function as being 'to provide a suitable residence for the chief and his followers. The site for such a residence had to possess certain qualifications. First, it must be centrally placed in relation to the other important dwellings. Second, it must occupy a prominent and dominating position, and provide outstanding sites for important huts. Third, it must be sufficiently fortified to defy attack by jealous rivals. Fourth, it must be near permanent water. Fifth, it must be so constructed that in spite of its prominence it provided sanctuary for the tribal relics, and privacy of movement for the chief and his advisers.'

Obviously the need for security would vary with time and circumstance. At Great Zimbabwe the palace of the ruler was guarded by a strong fortress established on the hill above. At Khami there seems to have been little or no fear of attack. Elsewhere, and notably at Mapungubwe in the northern Transvaal, the central dwelling was placed on a steep-sided 'table mountain' up on to the top of which its dwellers had carried many thousand tons of soil. This was a technique widely followed. Mosheshwe, the great nineteenth-century leader of the Basuto, followed the same tradition when he built his royal village on the flat summit of a steep-sided hill.

What is known of chiefly dwellings in Angola, west of Zimbabwe, shows the same pattern of need and intention. Here and there the parallels are remarkably close. 'The king of Angola or Dongo', James Barbot noted in 1700, 'resides a little above the city Massingan, on a stony mountain seven leagues in compass, in which are many rich pastures, fields and meadows, yielding a plentiful provision for all his retinue: in which there is but one single passage, and this according to their method well fortified; so that he needs fear no enemies . . .'

That the states of the Congo were an integral part of the Central African Iron Age is confirmed by evidence from other groups of stone ruins and graves which have lately come to light two hundred miles south of Massingan, near Amboim on the Angolan coast, and southward again near the port of Benguela. Some of the larger graves are thought to be those of chiefs, although close archaeological investigation, as everywhere in the Portuguese colonies, has still to be undertaken. 'The importance of the chief', Clark has written of them, 'is shown by the amount of ornament on the stone-work. The same geometric patterns are repeated here as in the Rhodesian Zimbabwean ruins. Monoliths are also found on these graves and are said to be symbolic of the power of the chief, a suggestion that throws an interesting reflection on the purpose of the Zimbabwe bird monoliths . . .'

Thus the states of the Congo must be seen as members of the great community of Africa's Iron Age: loosely articulated constellations of state-power and social organization that spread across the central and southern continent through the middle centuries of the present millenium. Beyond them to the eastward, across the heartlands of the Upper Congo, there were the long-established and powerful states and empires of the Lunda and Luba peoples. Eastward again, over the frontier mountains of the Congo, there were the feudal states of the Banyoro and their like, while to the south lay the lands of the Monomotapa,* first thought by the Portuguese to be Prester John himself, and the states of the southern and south-western Bantu. North and west of the Congo there were others no less famous, Oyo and Benin, Kanem and Songhay and Akwamu. This was a world that was specifically African in its outlook, beliefs, culture and organization: a network of organized peoples who had tamed a subcontinent.

* Mono is clearly *Mweni* (lord). Various meanings have been ascribed to Motapa. The area was central Zimbabwe: the people were members of the Shona group.

4. Law and Order

It is easy for us to see, even today, why the sixteenth-century Portuguese should have interpreted the organization of the states they found as being essentially like their own: as being what we now call feudal. Though keen observers, as their many narrratives and memoirs show, they lacked the means of getting beneath the surface of what they saw. It was not their fault, but it led them into many problems. In later years the Portuguese discovered their mistake and were suitably mortified. 'The Government of Bailundo', exclaimed a nineteenth-century report on one of the peoples of inland Angola, 'is democratic. These heathen mix with the infamous humiliations of the orientals, the unbridled coarseness of the English people at election time in England. The kings defer to and flatter their counsellors: these are they who elevate a king to the throne and also cast him down.'

Yet to the medieval eye the general picture of government in the Congo was remarkably close to that of government in Europe. Lesser chiefs were found to pay tribute to greater chiefs, and greater chiefs to owe fealty to the Mani-Congo himself. Chiefly marriages were contracted with the aim of sealing loyalties or alliances. The whole land of the Mani-Congo's dominion was divided into 'provinces', each with its governor or paramount ruler: in the late seventeenth century there were eighteen such provinces, but the number seems to have been much the same at the time of European arrival about a hundred years earlier. There is plenty to indicate that these arrangements, though orally defined and casual in their integration, were part of a solidly-grounded state system. They represented far more than a loose confederation of tribes, as later Europeans, victims of the myth that 'Africa has no past', would generally but mistakenly assert.

This organization was described in some detail by the Portuguese and Italians who lived and worked in Angola during the seventeenth century, usually as missionaries. Provincial governors – and all men who had 'fiefs of the king' – had to go to court once every three years and renew their vows of loyalty to the

Mani-Congo. Every time a new Mani-Congo was enthroned he had to redistribute fiefs and powers. 'For the conferment of offices and dignities', an Italian missionary, Cavazzi, explained in 1687, 'they have another rite which shows the majesty of the king and the great submission that is given by those whom he honours. Early in the morning they announce the ceremony with a triple discharge of muskets and other military noises: at the third discharge the king comes out and seats himself on his throne. Everyone prostrates himself in an act of adoration rather than of courtesy,' and after due ceremonial the chosen subject is invested with 'a bonnet, a scimitar, a standard, and a carpet with permission to use it'.

Perhaps the ceremonies had grown in pomp with Portuguese example, and the muskets, of course, were of European provenance; yet the meaning of the investiture could not have greatly changed since pre-European times. The lord of Congo, in common with other rulers of the time, was conceived as having divine powers. He was believed to embody in himself the immortal substance of God, for the Congolese, again in company with other African peoples, believed in a High God, though flanked by lesser deities. Mani-Congo Nzinga a Nkuwa, like his forebears, was customarily forbidden to eat in public, as were other such rulers; and it became a sore point of religious strife when his successor, Dom Affonso, decided to abandon the rule and eat as a Christian in the sight of his court.

According to Father Carli, who wrote a little earlier than his fellow-Capuchin Cavazzi, the most important fiefs were those of San Salvador (Mbanza Congo, the capital province) 'where the king resides'; Bamba 'where the great duke Don Theodosio rules'; Sondi 'where there is another duke'; Pemba 'where a marquis lives'; and Songo 'in which there is a count who has not given fealty to the king of Congo for some years'. North of the river, the state of Loango likewise had its sacred king who was forbidden to eat in public; and here, too, there prevailed a clear hierarchy of duties, rights and responsibilities.

Methods of government reflected this political organization. Writing in the second half of the eighteenth century, the Abbé Proyart mentions a number of 'ministers' of the king of Loango: the Mangovo, who was in charge of 'external relations', the

Mafuka, who was responsible for trade with the Europeans, the Makaka who was 'minister of war', and the Makimba who was 'minister of rivers and forests'. To the south of the river, the Mani-Congo had much the same kind of government at his disposal: Pigafetta, drawing on Portuguese sources for a book that was published in 1591, also described the Mani-Congo's postal system, 'runners who stand ready to go from one place to another with the King's messages and to carry the post'.

Military levies were raised in a manner which early European travellers found perfectly familiar. 'The sovereigns of these countries', Proyart would note a good deal later, yet validly for the earlier period too, 'maintain no regular troops. When a king has determined on war, his Makaka, minister of war and generalissimo of his armies, transmits orders to the princes and governors of provinces, to levy troops; the latter never fail to lead to the rendezvous the quota that is demanded of them.' Portuguese reports in the seventeenth century credited the Mani-Congo with power to raise some eighty thousand men, though this was probably a large exaggeration.

European opinions varied on the degree of bloodiness of these wars. Father Girolamo de Montesarchio thought that generally there were few men killed, and spoke of a pitched battle between the lords of Sevo and a rebel army numbering many thousands when only forty fatal casualties had occurred. Cavazzi, on the other hand, believed that the wars were very destructive of life. A hundred years later Proyart noted of Congo warfare that it was 'very rare that the armies advance ... to encounter each other with the intention of coming to blows. The great art of making war is to avoid the enemy and to pounce on the villages known to be abandoned, in order to pillage them, reduce them to ashes, and take prisoners there.' But there is little doubt that by Proyart's time the old feudal and ceremonial manners of Congo warfare had degenerated into the ravage and rapine of wholesale slaving for export. Bloodshed for the sole purpose of taking captives had by then become an everyday affair.

Solidity of state organization was reflected in other aspects of daily life. It would be said in later times that anarchy and chaos had reigned supreme: the colonial system, it would be argued, had brought the blessings of law and order to peoples incapable of fashioning their own. The truth was otherwise. In evidence of this a former Apostolic Delegate of Matadi on the lower Congo, Monsignor Cuvelier, has lately suggested a comparison of the laws of Congo with those of Portugal. True enough, the laws of Congo were somewhat modified (at least in theory) by the *regimento* of 1512; but these Portuguese innovations were never applied to Loango, north of the river, and a comparison of the legal position in Loango with that of Congo shows that the *regimento* made little or no impact on such matters as the scale of punishment.

Another reason for misunderstanding was that Congo law was never written law: moreover, it reflected the easygoing judgements of a much less rigidly organized society. Affonso certainly found the Portuguese legal codes bafflingly severe. 'What,' he is said to have asked a Portuguese adviser on one occasion, 'is the penalty in Portugal for anyone who puts his feet on the ground?'

Writing to his brother of Congo in 1511, the king of Portugal had opined that the Congolese might find Portuguese law unduly severe in comparison with their own law; and it is easy to see why. Like other Europeans the Portuguese punished some forms of theft by death; for other forms, the thief must hand over nine times the value of the property he had stolen. Elsewhere in Europe the developing notion of private property caused theft to be punished with an ever-increasing brutality: in the England of 1740 a child could be hanged for stealing even so little as a rag of cotton.

In the Congo, by contrast, where communal ideas of life were still very much alive and notions of private property vague in the extreme, comparatively little importance was attached to theft. Small thefts were punished by fines or 'public shame', or else by reduction to domestic servitude or payment of a slave. Larger thefts were generally punished by enslavement or by a fine equal to the value of a slave. Such slaves were not chattel slaves, of course, but domestic slaves who could generally expect to win their freedom.

On murder the sanctions were evidently much the same in Portugal and Congo: death except in the case of reasonable self-defence. High treason and rape were also punished in the same way in both countries. And it is an interesting comment on the vigour of native Congo law that much of Manuel's *regimento* was in fact preoccupied with the problems of engrafting Portuguese law on to native law, while at the same time providing that Portuguese subjects in the Congo should be judged in Portuguese and not in Congo courts.

Another common belief in later times was that colonial rule had enabled Christianity to destroy the savage and superstitious fear of the supernatural in which, it was held, Africans were hopelessly plunged. Until the coming of Europe, it would be said, the heathen in his blindness had bowed down to wood and stone and suffered appalling mental tribulations in the process. Whatever the truth about African animism – and anthropology has stripped off much of its European-woven clothing of legendary horror – this view of the matter did less than justice to the extravagant nature of contemporary Christianity.

Here, for example, is Father Merolla's description in 1683 of his method of dealing with 'hellish delusions' in the Congo. The delusions concerned female purification rites and habits. Perfectly harmless and possibly hygienic, as we should think now, they were coupled by Father Merolla, who was an otherwise intelligent Capuchin priest, with the whole body of 'foul superstition' in which Africans were believed to flounder and perish.

He began his task of enlightenment with a powerful sermon. He admonished his flock to turn away from heathen practices and concluded, so as to improve the lesson, with a little demonstration of a practical sort. 'The better to move the people,' he relates, 'I had placed on the altar the image of this blessed saint [the Virgin], covered and with a dagger through her breast from which the blood flowed. This done, I began to discourse against those women that observed the hellish delusions before mentioned [such as . . . not to speak to any man, to wash so many times a day . . .], proving that thereby they not only offended the Saviour but likewise did great injury to his immaculate mother. At the same time I drew aside the curtain and revealed the image . . .'

One may wonder what a seventeenth-century African could have thought of that blood-stained Virgin. Many years later, when a British expedition penetrated to the city of Benin (far from the Congo, yet visited by the same Christian missionary zeal in the sixteenth and seventeenth centuries), a local theocracy was found to have practised crucifixion as a means of propitiating God. It would be interesting to know how far the image of a god demanding such a sacrifice was supported by the muddle and misunderstanding of early missionary teaching like that of the good Father Merolla.

Long-distance trade was undoubtedly practised by the early Congo states. Later on, with the arrival of European goods along the coast and a demand for ivory, captives and other items for export to European shippers, this long-distance trade became extensive throughout the southern 'half' of the Congo river basin, and in due course it had its influence on the rise and fall of political powers, especially in states of the Luba-Lunda complex. Before the establishment of the 'coastal connection' this long-distance trade was much smaller and less influential. But it was not insignificant. Early records show in any case that the Mani-Congo was far from being the impoverished beggar his successors would become. His revenues were large. They were paid in kind and also in currency – the goods in kind being domestic slaves, ivory, textiles woven in raffia and skins, while the currency of the realm was the cowrie shell, as it was also that of some of its neighbours. There were officials whose duty was to gather the royal dues: the *mfutila*, charged with collecting tribute, the *mani-mpanza*, the *mani-samba*.

In the matter of cash the Mani-Congo was unusually fortunate. He appears to have possessed a 'mint' of his own. 'The island of Loanda', noted Pigafetta, 'is the mine from which the king of Congo draws what I should call his metallic riches – more valued than gold or silver by him and by neighbouring peoples. Women are used to go into the sea and fill their baskets with sand from which they extract small shells: these are washed, weighed, and carried to the treasury of the king.'

In Loango, north of the river, the currency seems also to have consisted in local textiles (of palm fibre, not of cotton); but cowries were used extensively by all the peoples of the estuary. These *nzimbu* were put through a sieve at the royal treasury. The smallest were rejected, but large ones might still be worth ten times as much as small ones that were considered big enough for use. To avoid the labour of repeated counting there were fixed measures in the form of containers which could hold forty, a hundred, two hundred and fifty, four hundred or five hundred shells. The measure that consisted of containers amounting to a thousand shells was called a *funda*; that amounting to ten thousand a *lufuku*; while a *cofo* was a measure holding twenty thousand.

From early times the Portuguese established a regular rate of exchange between cowries and their own currency. Thus Father Garcia Simões, writing in 1575, reported that ten cowries at Loanda were worth one Portuguese *real*. These exchange conventions were remarkable durable. In 1619 it was said at San Salvador, the Congo capital, that 25 *cofos* (half a million shells) were worth 187½ cruzados. Since the cruzado at that time was reckoned at about four shillings of English money,* a *cofo* would have fetched about thirty shillings, no mean sum in the early seventeenth century. Two years later, no doubt defending his currency, the Mani Congo was claiming that the *cofo* was in fact worth twenty-five cruzados, or five pounds sterling.

Here lay one of many reasons for dissension between the Mani-Congo and his Portuguese visitors. Oversea traders were quick to see their advantage in devaluing the Congo currency. They began to bring in cowries from abroad. The effect was such that the Mani-Congo tried to prohibit the practice since, in Felner's words, 'the money of the country had fallen so much in value that the king was losing two-thirds of his revenue'. The prohibition seems to have had some effect. By 1622, according to the Mani-Congo Pedro Affonso, a *cofo* could be exchanged for only five cruzados; and a report of 1649 returns the same value. In this latter year Cadornega gave four cruzados for one *cofo*, and the rate appears to have stayed at about this level, falling only slightly, for many years thereafter. Exchange in cowries continued late into the nineteenth century. The Congolese had not defended their currency in vain.

What this stable and comparatively prosperous society clearly needed was neither the autocracy of Portugal, religious paternalism, nor military intervention, but trade and knowledge that could stimulate internal changes in a social structure which owed

*Boxer gives this exchange value for 1635; according to Dames, the cruzado of 1510 had been worth nearly ten shillings.

almost nothing to the outside world. The Portuguese were in any case poorly placed to offer such help, for they themselves laboured under forms of government and commerce that were beginning to be outmoded and grossly inefficient even for the sixteenth century. All they were able to achieve, in the event, was a doubtful sovereignty for themselves and ruin for their former partners in alliance.

5. From Alliance to Invasion

For the Mani-Congo and those whom he ruled and claimed to rule, the crisis came with cruel speed. It was down on them even before the ink could dry on Manuel's *regimento* of 1512. Formally, the early partnership of Diogo Cão's time might continue: in any real sense of the word, it was dying fast. As the early years of Affonso's rule brought experience of what Portugal really intended, it became clear that his allies were pursuing dangerously different aims from himself. What he wanted for the Congo was aid in the form of priests, schoolteachers, carpenters, boatbuilders and the like: the skills and education that could really give him and his people an opening to the new world of Europe. But what these newcomers wanted for themselves, increasingly and soon exclusively, was slaves. They saw no profit in sending 'technical aid'. Little or none was ever sent.

How much could Affonso have understood of Portuguese motives and intentions? It is impossible to know, although his letters suggest that he eventually grasped a great deal of the essential truth. Certainly he persevered. Eager to learn, bold to innovate, tolerant of what he failed to understand, Affonso was also under political compulsions that he could never afford to ignore. His vassals were often on the verge of revolt: it would only need Portuguese encouragement to push them to the deed itself. So the Portuguese had to be mollified and kept friendly. Affonso could not afford to throw them off.

Yet he allowed himself a tone of increasing reproach as the years went by, and he continued playing the Christian card to the top of his bent. No kind of revolutionary, he must have thought this card the only one he had to play. He was bitter, but he was also dignified. 'It is unworthy to remind you', he wrote to John III towards the end of his life, 'that you should not forget us, since the reasons why you ought to remember us are perfectly obvious; but I shall take the trouble of bringing some of these to memory in case you have forgotten them.'

The immediate cause of Affonso's troubles lay somewhat to the north of his liege of Loango and two hundred miles out to sea: the island of São Tomé. First settled by the Portuguese in 1490, this island had become a valued staging post for vessels on the journey to and from the East. That would not have mattered to Affonso. But São Tomé was also something else: a settlement of rogues and vagabonds, many of them deported from Portugal, who were governed by a Portuguese vassal empowered to make his fortune if he could. This the vassal of São Tomé could achieve in two ways: first, by exercising a monopoly on trade with the adjacent African coast – that of the Congo states – and secondly by importing African slaves for plantation labour on the island itself. Both activities were in full swing by the time of Manuel's *regimento*. They bore heavily and in the end decisively on the relations between Portugal and Congo.

Like Nzinga a Nkuwa before him, Affonso found himself faced in practice not with the 'partnership' of the king of Portugal but with that of the vassal of São Tomé and his thieving traders, concerned now to procure slaves for their own sugar plantations which were then coming into production, as well as to prevent any other Europeans from gaining access to the Congo coast. The interest of these settlers on São Tomé was to interpose themselves between the Congo states and the outside world and this they did with great attention to detail, and an unrelenting eye for profit.

Affonso tried to circumvent this fatal obstacle to intercourse with Europe. He attempted it on many occasions and in several different ways; but he never secured any lasting success. First of all, he appealed to Lisbon against the great cupidity and greed, as he freely said, of Lisbon's vassal of São Tomé, one Fernam de Mello: such complaints echo repeatedly and vainly down the years. Next he tried to persuade Manuel to let him have a ship of his own so that he could communicate directly with Lisbon.

'Most powerful and most high prince and king my brother,' pleads one of his letters of 1517, 'I have already written to you a few times about how much I need a ship, and telling you how grateful I would be if you would let me buy one . . .' But the sugar island had stronger friends at court, and no ship was ever allowed to fall into Affonso's hands, much less a crew to man it.

Failing in that, Affonso asked that São Tomé should be simply handed over to him as a fief, a proposal which only served to inform Lisbon how little he understood of realities in the outside world. By this time it had become a confirmed practice that all slaves from the Congo states – and already the number was considerable – must pass through São Tomé; and the vassal of São Tomé had secured the right to seize a quarter of such slaves for himself, and then a twentieth part of the remaining three-quarters. Often he took more, so that the Mani-Congo would as often find that half his 'slaving currency' had disappeared in transit to Lisbon. But the notion that Lisbon would ever willingly forgo its claim to São Tomé must have raised a laugh from any Lisbon courtier who heard of it.

As the years went by, and slaving grew in volume, the situation in the Congo states began gradually to shift towards a chaos not known before. In 1526 Affonso tried an heroic measure. He attempted to control, reduce, and even stop the slave trade. It had begun some thirty years earlier – easily, almost imperceptibly, at that time the mere customary act of one monarch turning over to another, his ally, a quantity of captives. The custom was common enough in Iron Age Africa. It was far from rare in medieval Europe. African rulers could have had no more anxiety about the giving of slaves than their European partners about the receiving of them; and this, of course, was still at a time when European merchants and sea-captains were selling European slaves to the markets of North Africa. Yet oversea slave purchase in the Congo had now gone far beyond any question of royal custom. It had become, even in these early years, a social plague and a daily source of fear and dispute. Affonso tried to cut it down again. His motives were both political and social.

These varying motives were clearly expressed in a strong letter to John III. In the first place, Affonso deplored 'the excessive freedom given by your factors and officials to the men and merchants who are allowed to come to this Kingdom to set up shops with goods and many things which have been prohibited by us and which they spread throughout our Kingdoms and Domains in such an abundance that many of our vassals, whom we had in obedience, do not comply because they have the things in greater abundance than we ourselves ...' The incoming traders, in short, had undermined the Mani-Congo's trading monopoly, on which rested much of his power and prestige, and thereby weakened his control of the country.

But there was more, and worse. 'We cannot reckon how great the damage is, since the above-mentioned merchants daily seize our subjects, sons of the land and sons of our noblemen and vassals and our relatives ... Thieves and men of evil conscience take them because they wish to possess the things and wares of this Kingdom ... They grab them and cause them to be sold: and so great, Sir, is their corruption and licentiousness that our country is being utterly depopulated.' The king of Portugal should not countenance such practices. 'And to avoid [them], we need from [your] Kingdoms no other than priests and people to teach in schools, and no other goods but wine and flour for the holy sacrament: that is why we beg of Your Highness to help and assist us in this matter, commanding your factors that they should send here neither merchants nor wares, because it is *our will that in these kingdoms* [*of Congo*] *there should not be any trade in slaves nor market for slaves.*'*

Probably Affonso wanted only to reduce slaving to its former small proportions; but in any case the hope was vain. Once begun, the trade could be neither stopped nor contained. It was worth too much to the coastal chiefs under Affonso's often purely nominal control. It was far too valuable to the men from São Tomé. Every Christian intention of the Portuguese went forfeit to that inexhaustible commercial appetite, and, on the African side, every reasonable hope of direct and fruitful contact with the world of the far north.

Yet Affonso, for his part, clung to his hopes of aid. Often his letters give dramatic evidence of the plight that overwhelmed him. In a long one of 1539 he is found explaining to John III, still his 'royal brother', that the ship which carried the letter also

*Emphasis in the original as printed by Paiva Manso in 1877.

brings to Portugal five of his nephews and one of his grandsons, two of whom are to be taught to read and write, two to be forwarded to Rome, and two to be prepared in Lisbon for minor holy orders. Then comes a passage that abruptly sweeps away the centuries and brings one face to face with this extraordinary man:

> We beg of Your Highness to give them shelter and boarding and to treat them in accordance with their rank, as relatives of ours with the same blood . . . and if we are reminding you of this and begging of your attention it is because, during the life of the King your father, whom pray God to have in His glory, we sent from this Kingdom to yours, according to his orders with a certain Antonio Vieira . . . more than twenty youngsters, our grandsons, nephews and relations who were the most gifted to learn the service of God . . . The above-mentioned Antonio Vieira left some of these youngsters in the land of Panzamlumbo, our enemy, and it gave us great trouble later to recover them; and only ten of these youngsters were taken to your Kingdom. But about them we do not know so far whether they are alive or dead, nor what happened to them, so that we have nothing to say to their fathers and mothers . . .

A sad 'partnership' indeed: for these twenty young Congolese students had gone to Europe in 1516, twenty-three years before that letter was written, and ten of them, as the records show, had been seized by the vassal of São Tomé. Yet so little did the court in Lisbon care for religious vows and promises, grandiose and sweeping though they were, that no official word had reached the Congo of the fate of these travellers. The case was typical enough.

One reason for this callousness – and Affonso can hardly have grasped its full importance – lay in Portuguese discoveries elsewhere. Throughout Affonso's reign, Portugal was sending almost yearly fleets to the Indian Ocean and others across the Atlantic to Brazil. The Congo had to take third place; and the position was a poor one that was rendered all the worse by the Congo's evident deficiency in precious metals. There was consequently an ever-recurring shortage of transport to and from the Congo. One can see this from the complaints that were voiced by hard-pressed agents on the spot. Slaves might be available in apparently inexhaustible supply; the ships that were needed to take these slaves away remained few and far between. 'During these five years that I have been here,' a Portuguese royal agent was writing from the Congo in 1526, 'the [available] cargo has never been less than four or five thousand units [slaves], besides many others who die for lack of ships.' In later years the same complaint of a lack of shipping would be heard time and again.

Yet after their fashion, and in spite of other interests, the Portuguese also persevered. They were disappointed in their hopes of penetrating the interior by way of the great river, for the states of the Congo resolutely barred the way. They were also wrong in their belief that gold and silver could be found in these lands. But there remained the slave trade, and the need for slaves became hungrier year by year. Affonso's tentative protests had availed for nothing. All his chiefly vassals of the coastal territories, whether great or small, were in the trade by now, and not one of them seems to have cared a whit for the social consequences of slaving or to have tried to follow Affonso's example. The slave trade grew by leaps and bounds until it had engulfed the whole connection with Europe. To European observers it came to seem that the sheer abundance of this African humanity could never be reduced. 'And the fabulous amount of people inhabiting these kingdoms', Cadornega was writing in 1680, 'can be estimated if we say that the conquest of these kingdoms began about one hundred years ago, and since then there have been despatched from this port in most years [*um anno por outro*] about eight to ten thousand slaves, which sum up almost to a million of souls.'

One million slaves from Angola in the first century of European contact, together with a further half a million, as other reports suggest, from the neighbouring land of Congo: such was the gloomy balance sheet. Already the fabric of Congolese society had begun to crack beneath the strain. Now came a new factor. Impatient for more direct control of this wide seaboard and the lands behind it, the Portuguese turned to thoughts of military invasion.

They began by strengthening their links with the ruler of Dondo to the south of the Mani-Congo's domains. This ruler's title was the Ngola, a word from which the territorial name Angola soon derived. Advised by priests and traders from São Tomé, the Ngola threw off his allegiance to the Mani-Congo in

1556. The Mani-Congo sent an army to punish and subdue him, but the warriors of the Ngola were victorious: Portuguese settlers, driven by their trading interest, actually fought on both sides in that curious battle. Having won a foothold on the mainland by dint of this military intervention, the Portuguese proceeded to enlarge it. Within a few years the king in Lisbon had appointed Paulo Dias as 'Governor and Captain General' of this part of the coast, granting him hereditary rights over thirty-five leagues of seaboard and as much of the interior as he could seize and hold. There now opened a hundred years of bitterly destructive warfare as the Portuguese thrust repeatedly inland extending their hunt for captives, and leaving havoc in their wake.

And from now on the pattern would repeat itself. Little by little the Portuguese undermined the social order of the Congo states and inserted their own vacillating but destructive power. The story of their intervention and penetration is too long and complicated for rehearsal here. It was slow, erratic and seldom successful except in ruining the social fabric they had found. Many of its wars and adventures, and many of the personalities associated with them on either side, have remained warm in African memory; none more so, perhaps, than that famous Queen Zhinga of Matamba who held the invaders at bay for year after year. Fighting from her rock-bound strongholds in Matamba, Zhinga held out even when the Portuguese had defeated, at least for the time being, the neighbouring armies of the Mani-Congo and the Ngola.

Pretext for the first invasion of Congo in 1665 was the king's refusal to allow free prospecting for mines of gold and copper, although his predecessor had in fact ceded this right to the Portuguese. The Mani-Congo's call to arms has survived in the Portuguese archives. It reads valiantly now:

> Listen to the mandate given by the King sitting on the throne at Supreme Council of war: and it is that any man of any rank, noble or base, poor or rich, provided he is capable of handling weapons, from all villages, towns and places belonging to my Kingdoms, Provinces and Domains, should go, during the first ten days following the issue of this Royal proclamation and public notice, to enlist with their Captains, Governors, Dukes, Counts, Marquises, etc., and with other justices

and officials who preside over them ... to defend our lands, wares, children, women and our own lives and freedoms, which the Portuguese nation wants to conquer and dominate ...

The language, no doubt, was that of Portuguese feudalism, but its application to the Congo was clear enough. An army was raised to fight the Portuguese. It was smashed in battle and the Mani-Congo killed. His successors were never to recover from this disaster.

The next two hundred years became a repetition of much the same sequence of intervention and destruction. Although they retained the formal sovereignty of their lands, African rulers found themselves linked ever more firmly to the fortunes of Portugal and Brazil. Here and there the Portuguese built coastal forts – at Luanda in 1576 and Benguela in 1617 – and held them through the slow centuries but for a brief interlude of Dutch control. Yet their direct control of the country, magniloquent proclamations notwithstanding (and there was never any lack of those), seldom extended more than a few miles from the coast.

Why, then, did these African states prove incapable of recovery and progress? How was it that chiefs who were forceful and intelligent and well aware of the nature of their adversaries – and Queen Zhinga was only one of a number of such rulers of this period – failed repeatedly to learn the lesson of their losses and defeats? Where was the root of the evil?

6. Root of the Evil

THE answer to these questions lay largely in the character of the trade: a demand for slaves on one side, and, on the other, a monopolist interest among African chiefs in obtaining European consumer goods, especially firearms.

There were, true enough, occasional scruples. In the year 1700, for example, Protestant slaving captains were finding it difficult to buy 'units' because African dealers in the Congo harbours 'were possessed with an opinion that we were not Christians, and that we used to carry the slaves to the Turks, and other infidels and hereticks, where they were never baptis'd'. There was also, at least in theory, a right of appeal against sale abroad. 'Every slave in the kingdom', a French observer in Loango was noting in 1776, 'is under the protection of the Mfuka [one of the king's chief brokers] and may appeal against his master, should he be inclined to sell him to the Europeans, unless he has given him that right through his own misconduct.'

But generally it was true that the slave trade had carried all before it. As elsewhere in the world, those who dealt in slaves could make their fortunes: what was more, they could not make their fortunes in any other way. If 'everyone in Liverpool' was investing in the trades that derived from slave labour in the Americas, so was 'everyone in the Congo'. There grew up along the coast a tightly organized and self-defending system of monopoly. It was interested in importing European firearms, strong drink, textiles and metal goods; and in buying from the peoples of the interior as many slaves as were required in payment.

The monopoly was closely guarded. 'Those who have made captives', says the same French report of 1776, 'sell them to the merchants of the country or bring them to the coasts, but they are not allowed themselves to sell them to the Europeans: they are obliged to address themselves to brokers nominated by the [King's] ministers of commerce, who treat with the captains of the ships . . . The function of these brokers is not limited to facilitating the slave trade: they are also charged with superintending the execution of regulations established by the king or the Mfuka. the most important of which is, that there shall not be sold any slaves to the Europeans except those which have been taken in war, or purchased from abroad.'

This pattern of trade and contact carried the coastal peoples inextricably into a system of spoliation, and, in so doing, continually deepened their dependence on oversea partners whose own interests were to increase the spoliation, not to lessen it or transform it into productively creative forms. There were gains, it has been lately argued, for the inland peoples who now had access to new imports and a new stimulus to increase their exports. Some of these gains were undoubtedly real, above all in the inland spread of new American food-plants such as cassava (manioc). For the most part, though, the gains were not developmental: gains of a kind, that is, which could advance technologies or systems of production. And wherever these real gains occurred, they were accompanied by the slave trade. Kings and their agents could benefit from that; whole societies could not. The balance was negative, and more often than not it was heavily so.

From their scattered settlements along the coast, the Portuguese followed the same system, and became part of the same pattern. They too despatched small trading expeditions into the interior. These consisted of servants and slaves – mulatto or African *pombeiros*, as they were called – who might be gone for weeks or months or even years. 'These slaves', James Barbot observed in 1700, 'have other slaves under them, sometimes a hundred, or a hundred and fifty, who carry the commodities on their heads up into the country ... Sometimes these *pombeiros* stay out a whole year, and then bring back with them four, five, or six hundred slaves. Some of the faithfullest remain often there, sending what slaves they buy to their masters, who return them other commodities to trade with a-new.'

Through many years this was the only mode of Portuguese penetration into the lands behind the coast except for rare military expeditions that failed more often than they were successful. It was these *pombeiros* who opened the long trails across Africa that European explorers would follow afterwards. Now and then these bondsmen, few of whose names have survived, must have set up new records of travel in linking one part of the southern continent to another. At least one outstanding example is known. In 1806 two *pombeiros* called Pedro João Baptista and Amaro José made the first attested crossing of Central Africa. They walked from inland Angola to the Portuguese settlement of Tete on the Lower Zambesi, and thus anticipated Livingstone by half a century. It was a great feat, but it was not in fact particularly difficult. Baptista left a journal which shows – and Livingstone would afterwards confirm it – that the trails were relatively safe and easy once the goodwill of two or three powerful inland rulers, notably the *Muata* Yamvo and the *Kazembe*, was obtained.

These great chiefs of the interior had understandably little interest in trade and contact with the outside world. They had heard of Portuguese penetration to the east and west of them, and they rightly feared it. Besides, they were the rulers of African societies which had attained a valuable balance of social stability from the socio-political and cultural development of earlier centuries. They had known indirect trade with the Indian Ocean, but it was of limited use to them except for occasional luxuries and perhaps a fillip to their prestige. Otherwise their countries were self-supporting, and the exchange of a few domestic slaves could always make good any temporary shortage.

'The territory of Kazembe [around the head-waters of the Congo],' Baptista noted after long residence there a hundred and fifty years ago, 'is supplied with provisions all the year round and every year; manioc flour, millet, maize, large haricot beans, small beans, round beans . . . fruits, bananas, sugar-canes, yams, gourds, ground nuts, and much fish from the rivers Luapula and Monva, which are near. [The Kazembe] owns three salt districts . . . He possesses victuals, oxen . . . [obtained in tribute from lesser chiefs] or in exchange for slaves . . .' Such was the calm and well-provided 'heart of darkness' before the temptations and disasters of export slaving made their appearance here as well.

If these far countries remained long inviolate, pursuing their quiet journey across the years, the coastal countries were none the less reduced to misery and despair. It was true, of course, that the impact of the slave trade varied greatly in its effect. Most of the common people were threatened by foreign enslavement or entangled in the brutalities of slaving. But the chiefs and their henchmen generally made as good a thing out of the slave trade as their European partners: better, indeed, for they had little risk in the enterprise while slaving captains wagered their own lives on every voyage.

In this failure of the African chiefly system to resist the temptations of the trade, and to see beyond them to their disastrous consequences for the future, one may grasp just where the decisive weakness of Africa in face of Europe really lay. It was not that the chiefs were entirely without scruple even in the high days of the slaving system. They surrendered to it, but not always without a sense of shame and embarrassment. In the year 1700 a French slaver was buying captives in the Congo estuary. He reported that 'as it is the usual custom among Europeans that buy slaves in Africa, to examine each limb, to know whether sound or not; the king of Zaire thus observing . . . burst out a-laughing, as did likewise the great men that were about him. He ask'd the interpreter what was the occasion of their laughter? And was answer'd: It proceeded from his so nicely viewing the poor slaves; but that the king and his attendants were so much asham'd of it, that [the king] requir'd him, for decency's sake, to do it in a private place: which shows these Blacks are very modest.'

Yet the enrichment of the ruling groups could not, in the circumstances, lead to any compensating gain for their peoples as a whole. One can see this from the nature of the goods that were bought in exchange for captives. Almost invariably, these were luxuries or the means of war. Nothing really changed or developed in this commerce except the 'terms of trade': captives became more or less valuable, as items of exchange, according to the fluctuations of supply and demand. Generally, their value grew as the years went by. In 1776 the Abbé Proyart was noting that the 'slave Makriota' – no doubt a *ladino*, a man trained in household work and therefore relatively expensive – had cost him 'thirty pieces'. These 'pieces' were variously reckoned: about half were in textiles such as indienne, guinea and chaffelat; about a quarter were accounted for by 'two guns, two barrels of gunpowder, two bags of leaden musket balls, two swords, and two dozen common sheath knives'; while the rest consisted of 'five pots of Dutch ware, four barrels of brandy, and ten strings of glass beads'. Perhaps the priest had little difficulty in justifying the purchase of a servant for guns and gunpowder and strong drink, for it was characteristic of the times. But it is obvious that the African purchaser had bought nothing that could help to lift his country to a higher level of economic or social life.

On the contrary, even those who worked the slaving system in the Congo were impoverished. And this was so not only because countless thousands of healthy men and women were sent abroad, nor because the goods bought in exchange were largely for warfare or 'conspicuous consumption'. More than that, slaving wrecked the native administration of these lands. Even as late as 1592, a century after the Portuguese had first made contact with the states of the Congo estuary, the kings still enjoyed considerable means of government. A report of that year puts the royal revenue in cowrie shells at a value of sixty million *reis*, but adds that it could go as high as one hundred and sixty millions or four hundred thousand cruzados. With the cruzado worth not less than four shillings sterling, this would give a minimum revenue for the Mani-Congo of about £28,000. From this the local missionaries derived a more than satisfactory living: at about the same time, for example, the curé of the main church of Luanda had a salary from the Mani-Congo of two hundred cruzados or £40 sterling, a lavish stipend for the time and place.

This wealth failed to endure. When fresh missionary enterprises were urged in Portugal at the beginning of the nineteenth century, two hundred years later, it was officially objected that 'the king of Congo is very poor and naked like the rest. A king of this sort can afford nothing for missionaries nor help them in any way.' By the end of the seventeenth century, if not before, a substantial part of priestly revenues in the Congo was in fact paid directly by the slave trade. Thus it had become obligatory on the slavers to pay a 'baptismal tax' of three hundred *reis* for every captive they embarked for Brazil: this was handed to the parish clergy as part of their settled income. Later on, the Bishop of Luanda was also allocated a 'baptismal tax' of one hundred and fifty *reis* for every slave.

One can follow this impoverishment down the years. Its sorry effects struck at local Europeans with much the same force. They were fatally involved in slaving and produced little commercial wealth of any kind. Fathers Angelo and Carli, two Italian Capuchins, were impressed by the city of Luanda in 1666 as being 'large and beautiful enough'. Yet even then, relatively early in the trade, they found that for three thousand Europeans there was 'a prodigious multitude of Blacks' who 'serve as slaves to the whites, some of whom have fifty, some a hundred, two or three hundred, and even to three thousand.'

The inevitable happened. Idle and pampered, the settlers of Luanda decayed with the passing of the years until they were left with little beyond their memories of erstwhile fame and fortune. 'By the beginning of the nineteenth century', writes Duffy, 'the surface splendour of Luanda had begun to tarnish; the fine buildings were falling into disrepair; its streets were unattended; transportation into the interior was in a state of neglect ... The population of Luanda and Benguela was made up predominantly of social castaways.'

Relations between Africans and Europeans suffered the same decay. The old habits of equality and mutual respect had long since vanished. From allies, the Africans had sunk in European eyes to contemptible providers of slaves. What Africans thought of Europeans may be inferred from a forthright judgement of that enterprising Portuguese settler who sent his two *pombeiros,* Baptista and Amaro, across the continent to Mozambique. Writing of 'native opinion' in 1804, this man said that the blacks imagine that the whites 'never do anything except for their own profit, and to their [the blacks'] prejudice; that the whites have no sincerity; and only turn their actions to their own advantage against the blacks'.

By now, the ordered power which Diogo Cão had found in the states of the Congo had equally vanished and for that, too, the root of the evil was easy to find. 'Another great reason for the strife and jealousy existing among the black nations', wrote this same far-sighted settler, 'is that the whites endeavour to profit by their situation of superiority and power' – a power, one should add, that was largely secured by firearms – 'to subject to them other nations inferior in force and position. They are jealous lest the blacks should enjoy the same privileges, and thus be able to remove the yoke in which they are bound. They supply them [the blacks] with some few things they think necessary, adding whatever they think proper to their cost; but preventing the others [the blacks] from obtaining the same articles from whence they [the white traders] obtain them . . .' One may read in these few words the whole tragedy of that 'Christian enterprise' on which the kings of Portugal had once embarked.

Through these years of deepening bitterness and contempt there was laid, little by little, the foundation for future legends of 'savage Africa'. In the eighteenth century there had still been room for tolerance and sympathy. 'The negresses, like the negroes,' a French priest could write then, 'have their arms and bosoms uncovered, especially when at work; but the custom is general. Nobody thinks of it. Nobody is scandalized at it. And it is wrong for authors to have concluded thence that these [people] brave all the laws of modesty. This nudity of a negress, who from morning to night is occupied in cultivating the field under a burning sun, is less insidious and shocking to public decency, in their country, than the half-nakedness of court ladies in our own.' But the judgements of the nineteenth century, the period of outright invasion and occupation, would abound in convictions of a European superiority which was moral as well as material.

Behind all this there lay the driving pressures of the slave trade. No one can be certain how many captives were taken from these lands. The final score was undoubtedly enormous. Up to 1680 and the end of the legal trade in 1836 there were added about another two million from the ports of Luanda and Benguela alone; and more were shipped illegally in the years that followed. Another million must be reckoned for the smuggling trade. This puts the total number of captives taken from the old states of the Congo and Angola at about five millions. Exaggeration? Perhaps, but by how much? What seems likely, in any case, is that the centuries of slaving saw the export to America of populations from these regions that were about as numerous as the population of Angola in 1900.

Every hope of progress, or even of regaining the old independence, went by the board. 'How great was the moral damage of this hunt and traffic for "black ivory"', a German scholar would write in 1928, and his verdict may stand for the social and economic damage as well, 'it is difficult to say. But gradually the last social links were broken, and the whole structure utterly destroyed.'

That this, at least, was no exaggeration is shown by the abundant records of the trade. They are full of shadows. In 1804 the Mani-Congo Garcia V, a mere puppet of the Portuguese by now, sent a son and a nephew to make their Latin studies at Luanda so that they could train for the priesthood. Every year until 1815 these two young men, the 'princes' Pedro and Affonso, received three slaves from their father with whom to pay for their upkeep. But in 1812, finding himself short of cash, Prince Pedro encountered no difficulty in also selling the royal official whom his father had sent to Luanda with the year's quota of slaves. This was too much even for the Mani-Congo's pitiful dignity. He violently protested and the Governor of Angola accordingly wrote to Brazil, asking his colleagues there to find this Congolese nobleman, if they could, and send him home again.

Nevertheless, it was long before the Portuguese could assert control over the lands of the interior or even feel themselves secure along the coast. Their story here, as in Mozambique on the other side of Africa, was one of frantic bursts of bold endeavour followed by long periods of complete stagnation. All through these five centuries there were brave and public-spirited individuals who tried to revive the 'civilizing mission', or else curtail the cruelty to which it had decayed. But they always failed. They were defeated by those other Portuguese, more numerous, whose whole glory consisted in cracking the whip of a futile ambition over the heads of people who were no longer able to defend themselves. Chained to their dreams of medieval grandeur, these invaders seem never to have understood the enormity of their failure or the absurdity of their claims.

True enough, the lands behind the coast were subdued to their command; but the victory was long delayed, and came in the end only by default. The spirit of African independence and self-respect was broken not by Portuguese military prowess, but by the long ensnarement of the slaving years. Portuguese settlers might flow into these lands, but their numbers were few and they were seldom capable of anything beyond the most elementary enterprise. More often than not, these settlers were luckless victims of ignorance and poverty no less than the Africans among whom they had come to live. Sometimes they were political exiles, bitterly regretting their sojourn in the land. Not seldom they were criminals of the common law, *degredados* as they were called, whose achievement was to spread in Africa the sadness and despair, and therefore the cruelty, they had brought with them from Europe.

Prisoners of a poor and antiquated European autocracy, the Africans of these lands were condemned to lose their own civilization – limited though it was – without the chance of gaining a better. Even by the 1950s there was fewer than one in every hundred Africans of Angola who had achieved the rank of *assimilado* and was thus admitted to the 'rights of civilization'.

The record is grey and depressing. Yet in the 1950s, with

Africa beginning to emerge from the colonial period, new voices were heard in Angola. An independence movement was born. Now at last the wheel of history began to swing full circle and in 1975, with the emergence of a new republic, there came also the strivings of a new resurgence.

PART FIVE

EAST COAST FORTUNES

The people were formerly said to be numerous, civilised and wealthy; the city extensive and fortified, its habitations elegant and public buildings numerous ... but whither have they gone?

JAMES PRIOR:
Kilwa in 1812

Madaka ya nyamba ya zisahani
Sasa walaliye wana wa nyuni ...

Where once the porcelain stood in the wall niches
Now wild birds nestle their fledglings ...

SAIYID ABDALLAH,
Utendi wa Inkishafi,
about 1815

1. A Riddle at Kilwa

BEGINNING with such fair promise, European contact with the old states of the Congo had narrowed to the constrictive deadlock of the slave trade. But what might have happened in the Congo if mariners and traders from Europe had followed or been able to follow a different course? What expansion and evolution might these states not have known if their channels to the outside world had linked them with the many-sided development of European civilization, instead of leading into sterile isolation behind the barriers of slaving monopoly?

Such questions are not entirely vain. Some valuable parts of an answer can be inferred, at any rate in broad outline, from the rich experience of the East African seaboard during a somewhat earlier period.

Along these African margins of the Indian Ocean – the coasts of Mozambique, Tanzania, Kenya and Somalia, a seaboard rather longer than the distance from Newfoundland to the tip of Florida – the consequences of direct African involvement with the outside world can be measured against a much wider range of fortune than was ever offered to the lands of the Congo. Here there was intimate contact with the mature civilizations of the East, and especially with India. The results astonished the Portuguese when they first sailed up this coast.

Expecting a wilderness or at best a repetition of Portuguese experience on the coasts of the Atlantic, Vasco da Gama and his crews came on strong stone towns and harbours filled with shipping. They met with men who travelled the eastern seas and knew more of navigation than they themselves. They found city-states and governments that were, it seemed to them, as wealthy and sophisticated as anything they had seen in Europe.

'When we had been two or three days in this place,' recorded the log of da Gama's flagship, the *São Gabriel* (25·6 metres overall and 8·5 in the beam), 'two gentlemen of the country came to see us. They were very haughty and valued nothing that we gave them. A young man of their country – so we understood from their signs – had come from a distant land and had already seen big ships like ours.' The truth was that this eastern traveller must have seen far bigger ships. He would have voyaged in the many-masted ships of India and Ceylon. He might even have known the great ocean junks of China whose sails were like 'great clouds in the sky'.

Much of this East Coast civilization was wrecked. Except on the northern reaches of the coast, little of its material prosperity survived. The city of the 'haughty gentlemen' recorded in the *São Gabriel's* log was probably Quelimane in modern Mozambique. Almost three centuries later a British visitor to Quelimane would find it desolate and in despair, and would remember it as 'the most frightful place on earth'.

Ruins of a better past could be found; but they could not be explained. In 1823, charting this unknown seaboard for the British Admiralty, a ten-gun brig called the *Barracouta* came to anchor in the great harbour of Kilwa. The *Barracouta's* officers thought it one of the finest harbours in the world, and Lieutenant Boteler had himself rowed ashore. As he came landward in his longboat, Boteler saw the crumbled ruins of an old fortress on Kilwa Island, but the rest of the island was screened from view by a thick girdle of mangroves standing in shabby beds of mud. He got to firm ground and pushed his way through the trees. The light of that clear December morning, one hundred and fifty-seven years ago, showed him nothing that remained of the comfort and sophistication of old Kilwa but a heap of stones. He found a 'miserable village, scarcely visited or known', where 'the wretched Arab hovels of the present day are blended among the ruins of the once respectable and opulent city of former years'. And it was the same wherever they went on this coast. 'Even in the most obscure harbours, we could trace the remains of former wealth and civilization, contrasted strongly with present poverty and barbarism.'

Another British naval visitor had formed the same impression a few years earlier. James Prior, surgeon of the *Nisus* frigate under Captain Beaver's command, also found Kilwa a superb

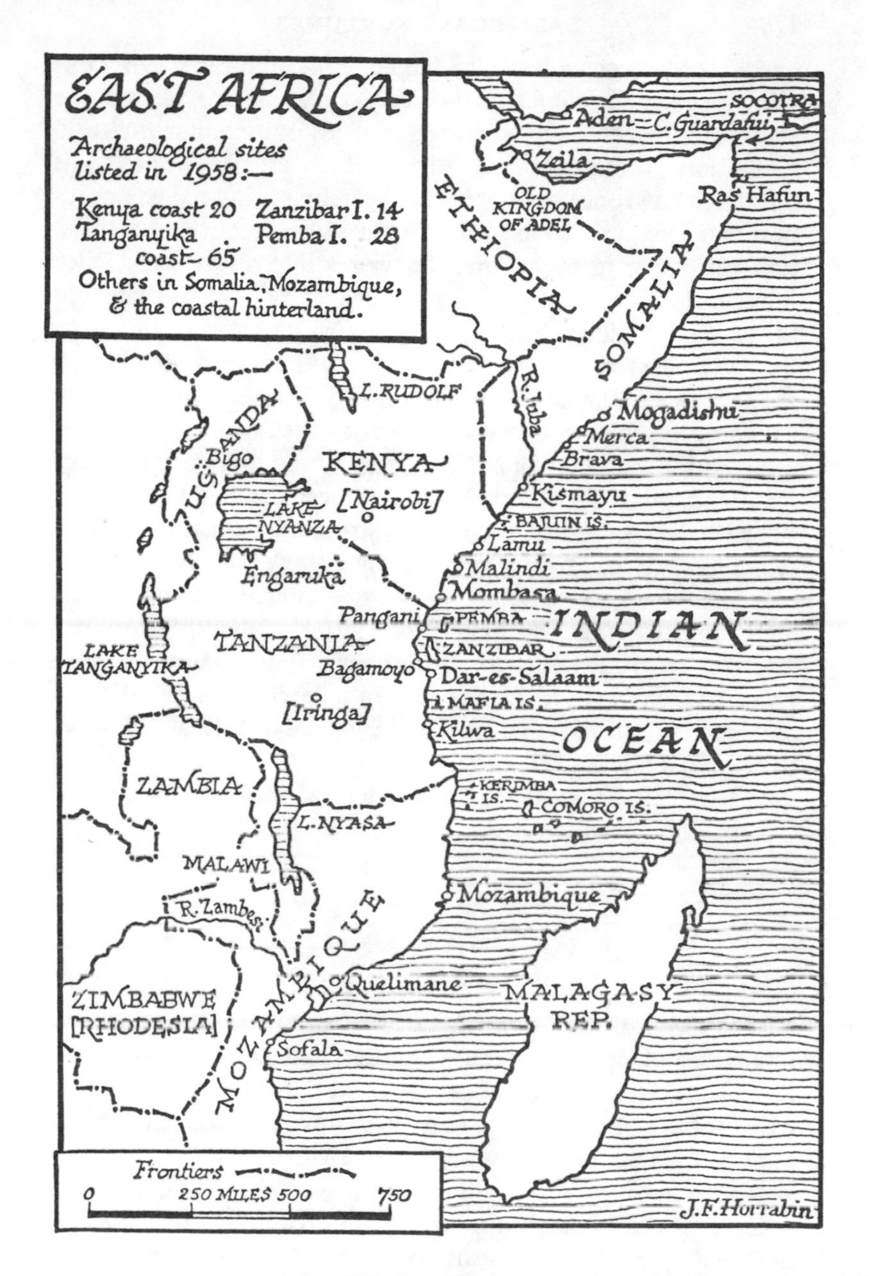

The East Coast

harbour, 'deep enough for the largest ships, and capable of containing nearly the whole navy of England'. Landing there in the year 1812, he noted the 'scattered vestiges of human haunts and habitations, cemeteries and ruins', which all proclaimed 'this district to have once been open and populous'. But the wretchedness and squalor were so complete that earlier reports of civilization seemed hard to believe. Tracing Kilwa's city wall, Prior found himself agreeing with Captain Beaver who 'justly remarked as we walked along, turning the grass to one side in following the line of the foundation, that the older writers gave such flattering accounts of this city in the days of Da Gama, as, from present appearances, to be scarcely worthy of credit'.

Yet Prior found the quantity of ruins, here and on the nearby mainland, puzzlingly large. Rambling over the southern arm of Kilwa harbour, he met with stone structures which included a cemetery forty feet square enclosed by a stone wall, and a 'place of worship' whose tumbled walls were still 'about sixteen feet high, built of stone, cemented by mortar', having 'an arched door in the front and two in the rear'. A few hundred yards away he stumbled on the remains of a large stone building of many rooms, surrounded by the ragged fragments of what had once been a strong wall.

'The ruins,' he wrote, 'are the evidences of a former people. But whither have they gone?'

2. Cities of the Seaboard

THE surgeon of the *Nisus* frigate need not have questioned the reports of older writers. This country had indeed witnessed a notable achievement. Reassessment since the 1950s has left no room for doubt of it. Many strands of influence and culture had gone to the making here of an East African civilization of much specific interest.

Coins from this region offer one surviving field of evidence. So far – and systematic searches have yet to be made – these include five coins of Hellenistic origin (third to first century B.C.), three Parthian coins (first to second century, A.D.), two Sassanian coins (third century A.D.), nine Roman coins and forty-eight from Byzantium, others from Arab and Turkish states, hundreds from China, a few from Ceylon, Annam, and southern India, and thousands from local African mints.

This richness and variety of trading contact with the East is foreshadowed by the earliest first-hand report, which dates from about A.D. 100. This *periplus* or 'shipping gazette', probably the work of an Egyptian Greek, offers in some 7,000 words (of English translation) a brief but factual trader's and mariner's guide to East African harbours and their commerce as far south as a port called Rhapta, which appears to have been near Pangani in Tanzania. Thus East Africa's coastline, some fourteen hundred years before the coming of the Europeans, was already involved in regular and peaceful trade with the cities of the Red Sea, southern Arabia, the Persian Gulf, India, Ceylon and countries beyond. By the tenth century, and probably earlier, Arab writers were well aware of trading ports as far south as Sofala in modern Mozambique.

Archaeology has brought wider understanding of a civilization which became famous and important among the cultures of the Western Indian Ocean, which flourished over many centuries, and which drew the seaboard of East Africa well within the orbit of the evolving East. Much is now known about this east coast civilization. Up to 1959 the number of sites of pre-European towns, harbours and other significant archaeological assemblages was one hundred and forty-one, sixty-five of these being in Tanganyika (that is, the mainland component of Tanzania), twenty in Kenya, fourteen in Somalia, with another twenty-eight on Pemba Island and fourteen on Zanzibar island. Professional investigation of these sites began early in the 1960s, notably by Neville Chittick at Kilwa and on Lamu Island, and by James Kirkman at Gedi, north of Mombasa. Many more ancient sites have been identified. The story revealed by their investigation is long and rich. Culturally and socially, it is a unified story. These towns and harbours with their imposing mosques and graveyards belonged to a civilization common to them all.

The little that remains of this architecture may best be seen on one or two islands not far from the coast, notably on the islet of Songo Mnara near Kilwa Island and on Juani Island in the Mafia group off the Tanzania mainland. Here amid tumbled trees and choking undergrowth, the stone palaces and mosques and merchants' houses of these western terminal ports of the Indian Ocean – product of a trade that stretched in many ramifications to the seas of China and Indonesia – still offer their forlorn and ruined witness to a considerable achievement in civilization.

These various kinds of evidence illuminate the interwoven nature of an African culture that owed some of its origins to constructive stimulus from non-African sources. Already, in times of Graeco-Egyptian navigation two thousand years ago, the trade in these waters was known to be conducted by mariners from southern Arabia who came down the coast for ivory, rhinoceros horn, tortoiseshell and palm oil – but apparently not for slaves – and who bought these goods in exchange for iron tools and weapons, glass beads and 'a little wine'.

Later Arab writers confirmed this nature of the trade, although by A.D. 800 or 900 there seems to have been a steady though never dominant African export of slaves as well. By this time the Indian and Chinese demand for ivory had become of major importance, the African variety being much superior to any other; and it would seem that ivory remained the main export staple for many years. By the eleventh and twelfth centuries the ports of southern China were collecting odd scraps of information about Africa, while Chinese 'cash' and porcelain were arriving in the seaboard cities of Somalia, Kenya and Tanzania. Several Chinese fleets reached the Kenya coast in the early part of the fifteenth century. Books on 'how to treat barbarians' were being published in China, and these 'barbarians' undoubtedly included the coastal peoples of East Africa.

'Treat the barbarian kings like harmless seagulls', advised Chang Hsieh in his *Tung Hsi Yang Khao*, published in 1618 at a time when the great period of Chinese ocean-sailing was at an end, but doubtless drawing on past experience. (The reference was to the well-known story of a sailor who had promised his father to catch a seagull and had failed, because the seagulls, knowing of his promise, would never alight on the water.) 'Then the trough-princes and the crest-sirens will let you pass everywhere riding on the wings [of the wind] . . . Coming into contact with barbarian peoples you have nothing more to fear than touching the left horn of a snail. The only things one should be really anxious about are the means of mastery of the waves of the sea – and, worst of all dangers, the minds of those avid for profit and greedy for gain.' It was wisdom to which the Portuguese in East Africa could have listened with advantage to themselves and still greater gain to those on whom they visited their ravaging fury.

All these influences contributed to the foundation and rise of city-states and coastal 'empires' along this extensive seaboard, starting from about A.D. 750. Looking to Arabia for their 'prestigious ancestors', repeatedly accepting immigrant settlers from Arabia, and taking pride from their membership of the *umma*, the world-wide family of Islam, these states were nonetheless African. Some of them had originated, long before, in Arab settlements; but by at least A.D. 1000 they had ceased to be 'Arab colonies'. European commentators for long refused to believe this. This was a misunderstanding with a long background. It went back to the days of European discovery.

The Portuguese of the sixteenth century had given no credit to African initiative and, identifying religion with race, had invariably referred to the peoples of these city-states of Kilwa, Mombasa, Malindi, Brava and the rest as 'Moors'. Foreign languages were not in their range of study, and there is no known reference to the Swahili language in any of the old Portuguese reports. Writers of the nineteenth century were further confused by the fact of renewed Arab colonization from southern Arabia, and also, one may think, by the prevailing colonialist view that 'Africans have no history of their own'. Hence it became standard belief in the outside world that the ruins of East Africa were those of Arab colonies to which native peoples had brought little or no significant contribution.

This belief has now met with serious revision. It is seen, more and more clearly, that the city-states of the East African seaboard became predominantly African in culture at a relatively early date, though carrying the strong imprint of Arab influence and Islamic religion. One powerful reason for this view rests in the richness and antiquity of Swahili literature and tradition. No one knows how old Swahili may be. But it is certainly not a young language, nor a poor or small one. Its first recorded words appear in Arab reports of the tenth century A.D., and its subsequent literature shows that it early became a flexible and poetic vehicle with a wide vocabulary. Today its spreading influence in eastern Africa, as well as its wealth of slang (resembling, in this, the malleability of English) are modern evidence of old and sound foundations. It abounds in fruity idioms and everyday adaptations. Largely Bantu in construction and vocabulary, it has a rich ingredient of Arabic (and now a notable borrowing from English); and in this, of course, it reflects the essentially syncretic civilization which evolved it and which it helped to evolve.

It would be absurd to deny the formative influence of the Arabs on this old Swahili culture of the coast. Their earliest visitors began to come here more than two thousand years ago. Their little colonies after the eighth century became points of contact with the non-African world. Their religion, architecture and script were only three elements of Islamic culture that helped to bring these peoples of the coast into the circuit of urban civilization.

The essential point is that here – in contrast with the failure of the Portuguese in the Congo – there occurred a genuine and fruitful marriage of cultures. After the thirteenth century, with at least the nominal conversion of much of the coast to Islam, there was also a wide bridge of religion. Ruling men in these cities increasingly felt themselves to be of 'Arab descent' and 'Arabic culture'; but they felt this as men of Africa, not of Arabia, and in rather the same way as medieval Europeans might consider themselves to be of 'Roman descent' and 'Latin culture', but none the less English or French for that. Later on, their rulers would manufacture long genealogies to prove they were sons of the princes of Arabia and Persia; and in this too, they would resemble European families who 'acquired' aristocratic ancestors as the years and gathering wealth allowed.

One can infer this marriage of cultures from many aspects of an often glittering urbanity in Kilwa and some of her sister cities. Mints at Kilwa, Zanzibar and Mogadishu made coins of their own; but the inscriptions were always in Arabic just as those of European coins were infallibly in Latin. These mints served the maritime trade, for coins were probably of no use or value in the commerce with the interior by which the coastal cities acquired their ivory and other goods; and all of them are invariably associated with local rulers who had Arabic names (though sometimes bearing Swahili names as well). The first of them seems to have been founded at Kilwa in the twelfth century, though the earliest coins so far recovered are those of Sultan al-Hasan ibn Talut, who reigned in Kilwa between 1277 and 1294. The sheer abundance of these coins – all so far found being of copper, with a handful of silver – suggests a fair measure of prosperity. Thus more than two thousand coins have turned up from the issues of Sultan Ali ibn al-Hasan (1478–9); nearly three thousand of Sultan al-Hasan ibn Sulaiman (1479–85); and over two thousand eight hundred from the Zanzibar issues of one of its fifteenth-century rulers, Sultan al-Husain ibn Ahmad. But these rulers were no more Arab (and also no less) than King Henry V of England was a Frenchman.

Kilwa itself is said by tradition to have been founded as an Arab trading centre in A.D. 957. Yet the local chieftain who was displaced by Kilwa's traditional founder was called Muriri wa Bari, a name that is manifestly not Arabic and quite possibly Swahili. These pre-Arab rulers of Kilwa must have had close contact with Arab traders and Arab ideas, for Muriri wa Bari possessed a mosque. All that happened here, no doubt, was that incoming Arab settlers took over a going concern in government and commerce; and subsequent rulers of this new Arab line merely traced the 'foundation' of Kilwa to the time of their forefather's advent. They intermarried with the people whom they found; their culture rapidly became both Arabic and Swahili but increasingly, as the years went by, Swahili in language and African in context.

Some time in the twelfth century these energetic traders and warriors of Kilwa seized control of the valuable trade in gold that had long existed between the lands to the south of them and foreign purchasers to the north. Kilwa then became the most important 'city-empire' on the coast. Pemba had earlier held this honour, but now Kilwa's power ran south through trading settlements on the Kerimba archipelago to the gold port of Sofala in Mozambique, and north towards Zanzibar. The Portuguese would find Kilwa sovereign along the southern reaches of the coast, a town with 'many fair houses of stone and mortar, and many windows after our fashion, very well arranged in streets'.

It is a fair inference that through these years of commercial prosperity and expansion the historians and poets of Kilwa and other cities turned to writing in Swahili. But this is not yet proved. Scholars have lately begun collecting works in Swahili and a fair quantity has come to light. Many more are believed to exist, locked away in cupboards and family chests, forgotten or else guarded from the profanity of the public eye. A still greater number may be presumed lost for ever.

Some of this Swahili writing is said to be of high poetic quality. Other documents add to knowledge of the traditions of the coast, sometimes helpfully, sometimes misleadingly. None of those so far found is ancient or medieval, the oldest known document written in Swahili being a version of the Kilwa Chronicle. This is an important repository of local tradition originally set down in Arabic and known in that form to the sixteenth-century Portuguese. But the early Arabic text is long since lost, and the Swahili version is comparatively new. As things stand today, writes Freeman-Grenville, 'no formal Swahili composition, verse or prose', dates from earlier than the eighteenth century. At the same time there is no doubt that Swahili poets were composing lyrical and epic poetry in the vernacular at a date considerably more remote; and it has yet to be shown that they were not writing in the vernacular as well.

This vigorous coastal civilization grew up in no kind of vacuum. Its prosperity, even its *raison d'être*, the explanation of its existence, was in long-distance trade between sea-merchants on one side and land partners on the other. The chief of these inland partners, of course, were the rulers of the plateau states within the Zimbabwe culture, for these were the chief suppliers of gold and ivory whose political power, at least for part of the fifteenth century, reached to the very coast itself. Of that, more in a moment. Meanwhile it will be useful to note that the origins of metal-using cultures, iron being the most influential of their metals, go back to the beginning of the first millennium A.D. in these east African regions, as they similarly do in the central regions of the inland country. In understanding all this the archaeologists have made great strides over the past twenty years, and what was little more than an educated guess when this book was first published is now an established certainty. Pottery and other artifacts show that the spread of cultivating and iron-using cultures, almost certainly by people of the Bantu-language group, reached the confines of the coast by about A.D. 100, and that, following on this, there came the emergence and development of a constellation of Iron Age societies.

Towards the end of the first millennium of our era there seem to have existed a number, conceivably quite a large number, of Iron Age peoples who were organized in more or less coherent groups or units. One can reasonably infer a form of lineage government with clear elements of statehood – a proto-national sense of difference from neighbours, more or less clearly defined boundaries, and a spiritually sanctioned kingship. Popular tradition might be expected to throw light on these early polities of the hinterland, but subsequent invasions and dislocations have erased the old traditions of much of Kenya and Tanzania. Fortunately, this is not the case in Uganda and its immediately neighbouring regions. Here, to history's gain, more traditions have survived; and the picture they offer of the past is rich and valuable. One general conclusion that may be drawn from these 'Ugandan' traditions is that Iron Age society went through important changes about five hundred years ago. Thus the Babito dynasty of the kingdom of Bunyoro counts nineteen generations to its half-legendary founder, while the Ganda dynasty of Buganda has twenty-two. Sometime around A.D. 1450 to 1500, it would seem, society entered a new phase of development.

How and why did this happen? Once again the jostling of peoples had brought social change. The instruments of change in this case are known to tradition as the Bachwezi. Little can be said of them, except that they are remembered as people of new and vital strength and skill. 'They made strange things that had not been made since man first came to this land,' Gray recorded of Bunyoro tradition forty years ago. 'They wandered without let or hindrance to places where no man had ever been before... Hunting was their calling, and they were mighty men therein. They were also traders and wandered about in a miraculous manner.' When the European explorer Stanley reached the kingdom of Ankole in 1887 he and his party were at first mistaken for Bachwezi marvellously returned to earth for a second time. 'We greet you gladly. We see today what our fathers never saw, the real Bachwezi . . .'

These superb newcomers, the Bachwezi, gathered the peoples of western Uganda into a powerful though short-lived empire. Today they are still thought of in western Uganda, writes Oliver, 'as the originators of a pattern of social organization and a religion which were sedulously if uncomprehendingly imitated by the successor dynasties, whose subjects looked back on the Bachwezi much as medieval Europe looked back on the Roman Empire, as the golden age of civilization and pre-barbarian government'.

Here again one sees the unfolding of new forms of hierarchical rule within the enclosure of lineage structure. The Bachwezi vanished, perhaps around A.D. 1500, as mysteriously as they had come. But, continues Oliver, they 'left their regalia, their drums, their copper spears, their beaded crowns surmounted by tall copper cones and underhung with masks made from the skin of the colobus monkey, distributed about the country in the keeping of the district chiefs . . . They left their reed palaces, which were faithfully copied upon the sites of subsequent capitals. They left their slave artisans and even, it is said, their palace women, from whom their Babito successors learned the pastoral duties of royalty. They left, in all probability, a working system of administrative officialdom accustomed to ruling small districts as the local representatives of a centralised monarchy; and a regimental organisation . . . under which young men were conscripted into the military service of the king and were maintained by the peasants occupying areas of land designated for the support of the army.'

Much the same process of social change within early Iron Age society occurred in other east and south-central regions, as also, of course, in western Africa. Comparable evidence is particularly strong for the plateau lands of Zambia and Zimbabwe. Here there is little or no tradition surviving from the medieval past: in place of that, however, there are abundant stone ruins, objects in gold and other metals, pottery from the East Coast, porcelain from China, beads from India. Where the Bachwezi and their immediate successors left great earthworks, the Iron Age innovators of Rhodesia built stone palaces and temples and strong places on high rocks, the most famous of these being the complex of structures at Great Zimbabwe.

Some of these states of the interior had regular and influential contact with the coast from at least the tenth century. Others – but the evidence is notoriously incomplete and may yet be overturned – did not. What can be affirmed with confidence is that the coastal cities had begun to draw these states, or a number of them, into the orbit of Indian Ocean culture and civilization. And the reason for this was that the coastal cities needed ivory and gold, and could obtain them only from the interior.

A steady coastal demand for gold and ivory continued through five centuries or more. It unquestionably caused the states of the southern plateau to open their thousands of gold workings. Among themselves, these inland peoples had little use for gold (although they developed a nice taste in gold ornaments), and Arab commentators were constantly surprised by the ease with which they parted with this precious metal. But they desired trade with the coast. Gold was the way to it. And the opening of a large number of gold workings – many thousands of which were found when European prospectors came this way in later times – must have done much to stimulate the emergence of social divisions, the birth of an embryonic labouring class, and the development of states with hierarchical structures and forms of centralized government.

To the north the influence of the coast may have had much the same effect, though here there was no gold to be tapped and therefore less incentive to penetrate the interior with trading missions. A few archaeological soundings in western Uganda have failed to reveal any contact with the coast; but the available evidence still remains too slender for the drawing of any final conclusions. In Kenya and northern Tanzania the position seems to have been much the same, and much archaeological investigation since about 1965 points to certain conclusions. Some long-distance trade came into existence from early times between inland and coastal states or societies. It may have contributed to several imposing developments, such as the long-term settlement at Engaruka in the Rift Valley. Later on, in the nineteenth century, this long-distance trade – above all in ivory and captives –

became much more influential; and several peoples, such as the Nyamwezi, made it a staple item in their way of life. But the principal effect of long-distance trade, in pre-European times, occurred not here but further south, and was linked to the gold trade from Zimbabwe. This was a case where the long-distance trade proved genuinely developmental. A creative contact, not a system of spoliation, was built between the civilizations of the East, of India and even China, and the rising polities of Iron Age Africa in these regions.

Here the effect of outside contact was not isolation, but communication: not spoliation, but development.

3. The Vital Contrast

IN their impact on Africa there was thus a crucial difference between the Atlantic trade and that of the Indian Ocean in pre-European times. And a clear pointer to the nature of this difference, and the different consequences that flowed from this different nature, is to be found in the driving purpose of these two 'ocean systems' of commerce.

The Indian Ocean trade was never slave-ridden in ancient or medieval times, or indeed any period before the eighteenth century. This is not, admittedly, the standard opinion of European textbooks. There, as Freeman-Grenville has lately pointed out in contesting it, 'the main theme is that the slave trade was the principal occupation of the coast until the British asserted their hegemony' at the end of the nineteenth century. But the evidence will not support this view.

As in most parts of the ancient world, there was a measure of oversea slaving in these regions from the earliest times. Pharaonic Egypt bought captives from the land of Punt; and Punt lay along the northern coast of modern Somalia. Arabia did the same. African slaves were known in Persia and Parthia. Others were taken to the kingdoms of India. And in the ninth century, as we have noted (see *How Many?*), a brief but exceptional venture in plantation-type agriculture assembled a large number of black slaves in southern Iraq. Others were employed even as far as China.

A Chinese document of A.D. 1178, evidently referring to Madagascar, says that 'there is an island in the sea on which there are many savages. Their bodies are black and they have frizzled hair. They are enticed by food and then captured' and sold 'as slaves to the Arab countries, where they fetch a very high price. They are employed as gate-keepers, and it is said that they have no longing for their kinsfolk.' Thus may one see how the legend of 'African inferiority' was no monopoly of the West. In the East the slaves from Africa (for they came from the mainland as well as Madagascar) were said 'to have no longing for home': in the West they would be found 'docile and therefore fit to be enslaved'.

Slaves for the civilizations of the East came of course from all the borders of the Indian Ocean and not merely from East Africa. They were regularly imported into China, for example, over a long period. The same Chinese report of 1178 says that both male and female slaves were bought, 'and the ships carry human beings as cargo'. A Chinese inspector of maritime customs, writing fifty years later, notes that a slave boy was priced at three taels of gold or their equivalent in aromatic wood. He says that slaves were used during voyages for stopping leaks in the hull, even though they had to go out-board and under the waves as well. Many of these luckless victims must have come from Africa.

But there is nothing to show that slaving ever overwhelmed this eastern trade or became, for the most part, more than a minor item of commerce. The available evidence, slight though it is, goes all the other way. 'Slaves of the better sort' could be purchased, according to the *Periplus of the Erythraean Sea* in the second century A.D., at Opone; but Opone was Ras Hafun, almost the far northern extremity of the Horn of Africa. For the ports of East Africa to the south of Ras Hafun there is no mention of slaving in the *Periplus*. Nor is there much mention of it in the medieval Arab writers, and in no single case do these writers place any emphasis on East African slaving. On the contrary, they speak of the importance of East Africa as a provider of ivory and gold and other raw materials.

Sofala, for El Mas'udi who wrote in the tenth century, was the land of gold. He mentions ivory as a principal export from 'the land of the Zanj', the blacks of East Africa. This ivory was taken to India and China by way of Oman in southern Arabia, and 'were this not the case, there would be an abundance of ivory in the Muslim countries'. For Edrisi, two centuries later, iron was the most valued export of the East African coast. The iron of Sofala, he thought, was much superior to that of India, both in quantity and in quality; and the Indians were accustomed to make from it the 'best swords in the world'. There is nowhere here any reference to an East African export trade in slaves. This does not mean, of course, that no slaves were sent abroad. But it certainly suggests that this part of commerce was an insignificant side-line.

Evidence from the Swahili cities of the coast points the same way. The key trades of Kilwa in medieval times were undoubtedly the export of gold and ivory from the states of the interior. Pate Island is said to have dealt in silver as well as ivory. Others are known to have exported, or collected for the export trade of their more important sister-settlements, a varied range of natural products – copal, ambergris, tortoiseshell, copra, coconut oil and mangroves. All this was the body of Swahili trade and the core of its prosperity.

One can reach the same conclusion from the other end. Where in the East were the vast plantations and many mines that required great armies of slave labour? They simply did not exist, with the exception we have noticed, just as they did not exist in the West until the crossing of the Atlantic. Where, again, can one find massive African minorities in the East that are comparable to the African minorities of America? They, too, do not exist. The notion that the old trades of the Indian Ocean dealt in slaves on the same scale as the later Atlantic trade is a pure illusion, product of an uneasy European conscience and the fact of large-scale Arab slaving in the nineteenth century. What really occurred here was slaving on the same persistent but small scale as between many of the states of the medieval world: a useful but subsidiary trade, rarely important in general balance of wealth and enterprise.

The contrast with the Atlantic seaboard is very sharp. A thousand years of Indian Ocean contact, with slaving never of importance, could raise the peoples of the eastern seaboard to full membership in the family of eastern civilization, and send its fructifying influence far into the hinterland. But less than half a thousand years of Atlantic Ocean contact, with slaving of the highest importance in that contact, could make no such claim. On the contrary, the kernel of this western contact became a peculiar if complex and sometimes contradictory system of primitive extraction which, as the times would reveal in due course, led on directly to the far more sophisticated system of extraction of colonial times.

These cities of the eastern coast vanished or dwindled through no fault of their own. They were ravaged by the Portuguese. Loot was the key to the discoverers' ambition. Reflecting on Da Gama's voyage of discovery, the King of Portugal wrote to the ambassador of Venice, then the most powerful city of the Mediterranean, that it would now profit Venetian galleys to come to Lisbon for their cargoes of goods from the East, instead of going to Alexandria. To his cousins of Castile, however, he was a little more forthcoming. Giving them news of Da Gama's exploits, he explained that 'we hope, with the help of God, that the great trade which now enriches the Moors of those parts' – that is, the Swahili Muslims and their oversea partners – 'through whose hands it passes without the intervention of other persons or peoples, shall, in consequence of our dispositions, be diverted to the natives and ships of our own kingdom'.

He took his dispositions without delay. Fleet after fleet was despatched to the East, one almost every year for many years to come. Their orders were to seize the Indian Ocean trade, reduce the coastal cities to vassal status, exact tribute from them in gold and establish Portuguese hegemony. They met with resistance. But the coastal cities, although they too believed that God was on their side, lacked cannon. And the cannon of the Portuguese, together with a ruthlessness and piratical determination not before witnessed in these seas, easily carried the day. Enmity and the threat of violence appeared with the earliest landfalls of Da Gama. After 1501, by which time the Portuguese had taken the measure of their intended victims, there followed ten years of bloody invasion and assault. Kilwa, Mombasa, Zanzibar, Brava and other cities were battered or bullied into submission.

Here and there, as in the Congo, the Portuguese were helped by calls for aid from one African ruler against another. This led to the downfall, for example, of the lord of the Kerimba Islands, a long archipelago lying off the coast of northern Mozambique. In 1522 the Portuguese on Mozambique Island, then their principal base on the East Coast, were approached by envoys from Zanzibar and Pemba, far to the north. These envoys explained that their rulers had formerly paid tribute to the lords of the Kerimba Islands; but now that Pemba and Zanzibar had to pay tribute to the Portuguese they had stopped paying it to the Kerimbas. This had involved them in war with the Kerimbas, and they now asked for Portuguese protection. Another Portuguese version, written somewhat earlier and possibly nearer the truth offers a different explanation but confirms the picture of a closely woven system of political and economic power up and down this long coast. According to this second version, the Kerimba Islands had once been subject to Zanzibar and Pemba but had lately transferred their allegiance to Mombasa.

Whatever the truth of this particular matter, settlers and soldiers on the island of Mozambique saw a golden opportunity in this appeal for aid and alliance. Eighty of them embarked without delay in two *zambucos* – large lateen-rigged coastal vessels – together with 'a skiff and a ship's boat'. After sailing and rowing for five days they landed on the principal island of the Kerimbas, overcame its ruler and his troops (he turned out to be a nephew of the lord of Mombasa), and took a vast spoil reckoned at 200,000 cruzados. Whether exaggerated in the records or not, this booty is fairly conclusive proof of wealthy settlements on the Kerimbas during medieval times. We may learn more of these settlements when archaeology at last finds time and money to conduct detailed surveys there.*

Within fifty or sixty years of frenzied onslaught on the accumulated wealth of centuries, the Portuguese effort had almost spent

* Almost as soon as Mozambique became independent in 1975 the new ruling party, FRELIMO, began to encourage archaeological and historical investigation. This led almost at once to the discovery by a British archaeologist, Peter Garlake, of an important site of the Zimbabwe culture not far from the coast, thereby opening the way to a new and fuller understanding of that culture. Other advances of the same kind seemed likely to follow.

itself. Spreadeagled across the world, imperial Portugal lay dying not from lack of courage or ambition, but from a shortage of men and from an even graver incapacity to move with the times and learn new ways. The Dutch overhauled them. The French and English elbowed them aside. Here and there along the coast they continued to enjoy supreme power; here and there they pushed bravely into the lands behind the coast. But the world soon passed them by. And the cities of the coast, still enduring though often sorely harassed, inescapably shared this decline.

4. In the Wake of the Storm

WITH the ravaging of the Indian Ocean trade, East Africa largely falls from written history for almost two centuries. Much can be reconstructed, but the European materials for the coast remain painfully thin – little more, indeed, than petty correspondence from sleepy Portuguese settlements, chance traveller's tales and the bald facts of Turkish penetration from the Red Sea.

Weakened by their loss of trade, by Portuguese storming and sacking and the payment of heavy tribute, these cities greatly suffered. Yet the story is not all sadness. North of Mombasa, at least, the cities seem to have recovered a good deal of their earlier life and vigour. More than that, they developed their Swahili language into a literate culture of considerable distinction. Here along the northern segment of the coast, Portuguese impact had been sharp but exceedingly short-lived. Once this impact was absorbed, some of the old settlements and city states became focal centres for a new Swahili consciousness. Out of this consciousness there came the written language that has since become a flexible and efficient vehicle of speech for tens of millions of people in Africa.

It would be wide of the mark to see in this revival an early movement of cultural nationalism. The peoples of the coast felt themselves a part of the wide Islamic world, and the ideas of modern nationalism can be ill applied to this time and place. Yet the effect was not so very different. Poets and historians began remembering the past in a new way, dramatically, nostalgically, prefiguring the present and a better future. And although recovery of their writings from private individuals and families is so far disappointing in results, enough is known of their outstanding quality to have moved one careful English critic of Swahili, in a recent letter to the present writer, to declare that 'some of this poetry was the equal, if not to Dante, in certainty to Milton'.

The claim that seventeenth-century Swahili poets in Mombasa and Malindi and neighbouring cities were writing like Milton may seem tall in English ears. Yet there is nothing inherently difficult about it. These writers undoubtedly worked within a rich and various tradition. They and their fellow-citizens had lived and were still living through an heroic age, a time of cultural awakening by assault from outside, a period of repeated danger from the sea and of sudden alarms and disasters and escapes. To many of them it must have seemed that they had wonderfully outfaced these perils and misfortunes. It was the kind of soil from which great poetry can spring.

Not all the Swahili cities were in this condition. Those in the south were overwhelmed, for it was to the south that the Portuguese had their main strength. Kilwa suffered worst of all. Subdued at gun's point by Vasco da Gama on his second voyage in 1502, it was sacked and occupied by Almeida three years later. Its ties with India and the Persian Gulf were cut by the Portuguese. Its trade routes with the interior were severed by the mainland peoples, and its Swahili population dwindled. Some eighty years later its fate was finally sealed by catastrophic invasion from the mainland: the Zimba, marauding migrants from the south, came across the narrows which separate Kilwa Island from the mainland, stormed the town and killed, it is said, some three thousand of its inhabitants.

But here, too, the subsequent history of the coast has its bearing on the course of European-African history. The comment that it makes may be pitched in a minor key, a chronicle of small events and marginal encounters: there is here, none the less, a valuable link between defiance of the Portuguese in the sixteenth century and subjection to imperial Europe in the nineteenth.

The English records pick up the story with James Prior and the cruise of the *Nisus* frigate in 1812. By now the Portuguese settlements were far gone in decay. That was understandable. Given the weakness of Portugal, the wonder is that these settlements should have survived at all. Landing at Mozambique Island, Prior visited a hospital but found 'no specific disease, as far as I can learn . . . except *ennui*. Were I to remain here, I should die of it in three months.'

Rejoicing in the name of Dom Antonio Manuel de Mello Castro e Mendoza, the governor had two residences. The visiting naval party found it hard to find the one he occupied. 'It would be difficult to conjecture its existence without previous information, part of the exterior appearing more like an old storehouse than the mansion of the first personage in the settlement. We were led to it by the clashing of billiard balls, and the confused clamour of contending voices, so that we at first took it to be a tavern or gambling house.'

Slaving was now the main business of the place, partly with Brazil and partly with the French islands of Mauritius and Bourbon, though there still remained a little trade in gold and ivory with the interior. Visiting the governor, Prior and Captain Beaver were poorly impressed by his qualities. He had apparently not visited any part of his government since coming to Mozambique. He affected 'considerable state' but was neither communicative nor inquisitive upon points that his visitors thought interesting. 'He has not once inquired, during the interviews with Captain Beaver, respecting the fate of his own country, the general state of Europe, or whether such places as Portugal and Spain yet existed or were blotted from the list of the independent nations.' Perhaps his pride as a Portuguese nobleman took it for granted, in any case, that they were not. If so, this pride had evidently not prevented him from making a remarkably good thing out of his governorship. 'With a very small official salary, it is said he has realised a fortune of £80,000.' His attitude to gubernatorial responsibilities, in short, was the same as that of his sixteenth-century forerunners. He 'farmed' his colonial 'conquest' as a feudal vassal of his king. In this one may observe, once more, the fatal incapacity of the Portuguese social system to change with a changing world.

On Portuguese evidence, East Coast slaving from Mozambique to Brazil was now running at between ten and fifteen thousand slaves a year. Compared with the West African trade, this was still a modest figure; and although it later rose to 25,000 a year (before finally dwindling to very few after 1850), it emphasizes the relatively small part that was played by European slaving from the East Coast as a whole. What caused the stagnation and decay of this seaboard region was not slaving, though slaving helped, but the reduction of all that vast network of maritime trade which had formerly linked these cities and settlements with the civilizations of the East.

One can see this from a slightly earlier French report on Kilwa. Though the French sailed eastward round the Cape long before the English and the Dutch, they made no impression on the coast itself. At the beginning of the second half of the eighteenth century, however, they began to tap the coast for slaves required by new plantations in their Indian Ocean islands of Bourbon and Mauritius. The pioneer in this commerce was a Frenchman called Morice. Wrecked on Zanzibar with a cargo of 'many piastres' in a ship called the *St Pierre*, Morice escaped to Kilwa where, partly through being a surgeon (like Prior nearly fifty years later), he got on to excellent terms with the sultan, who actually sold him a piece of Kilwa in exchange for four thousand piastres.

Exploiting this success, Morice negotiated a treaty with the sultan that gave him a monopoly privilege on the export of slaves. Signed in 1776, this Kilwa treaty was a distant echo of practice on the Guinea Coast. The sultan promised to deliver one thousand slaves a year at the price of twenty piastres apiece provided that he himself should have two piastres for each slave delivered. No other slaver was to be allowed at Kilwa – '*soit François, Anglois, Hollandois, Portugais*, etc.' – until Morice had obtained his quota and declared himself satisfied.

The trade prospered in a small way. Another French report of the same period, a letter to the French Minister of Marine, Marshal de Castries, contains notes by a slaving captain called Joseph Crasson (or Crassous) de Medeuil, master of the *Créolle*. He was twice at Kilwa on slaving business, evidently in the 1770s. He found the place much as Prior would, a mere shadow of its former self, humbled and yet by no means starving. He says that Kilwa could supply millet, indigo, 'excellent cotton', sugar-cane, gums in abundance, and 'second-class cowries' such as were used to make payments on the West Coast, and notably in Dahomey. Ivory was easily obtained. 'And there are blacks who are excellent when selected with care.'

He selected some of these 'excellent blacks', while the sultan, for his part, recalled the treaty with Morice and asked for French protection against his enemies – who, at this time, were partly his coastal neighbours and partly the Portuguese. Nothing came of this, and the trade remained small. Crasson says that French ships to his knowledge had taken 4,193 slaves from Kilwa in the previous three years, his own share being 387; they cost forty piastres each (double the price that Morice had agreed) and were carried mostly to Mauritius and Bourbon, though some to the French West Indies. Slaves were of course taken to the French islands from other East African ports as well; in 1799 Mauritius and Bourbon were said to have about 100,000 slaves between them.

Slaving and stagnation continued hand in hand. Later British naval visitors – Owen and Boteler in the years 1821–6 – were repeatedly struck by the mournful appearance of these settlements and cities. Warmly hating the slave trade, they were inclined to make it guilty of all the evils they beheld.

'The riches of Quilimane consisted in a trifling degree of gold and silver, but principally of grain,' reported Captain Owen, 'which was produced in such quantities as to supply Mozambique. But the introduction of the slave trade stopped the pursuits of industry, and changed those places where peace and agriculture had formerly reigned into the seat of war and bloodshed . . . The slave trade has been a blight on its prosperity; for at present Quilimane and the Portuguese possessions in the whole colony of the Rivers of Senna [the channels of the lower Zambesi] do not supply themselves with sufficient corn for their own consumption.' He found that between eleven and fourteen slave vessels came annually to Quilimane from Rio de Janeiro 'and return with from four to five hundred slaves each on an average'. Boteler, who sailed with Owen but whose book was posthumously published two years after Owen's, has the same description of Quilimane in slightly different words.

Manifestly the slave trade had played its degrading part here as elsewhere. It had grown much larger since the coming of the

Portuguese. Yet it had remained relatively unimportant. Except from one or two ports at irregular intervals, this trade was too small to explain the failure of these settlements and cities on the southern segment of the Coast to recover from Portuguese devastations in the sixteenth century. Prior had seen the truth more clearly. In addition to the slave trade, he wrote, 'the true cause [of decay] must be sought, perhaps, in the decline of commerce and industry . . . and the only probable reason [for this decline] was the presence and superior power of Europeans in India'. It was now exclusively to Europe that the wealth of the East was channelled. East Africa could have no further part in it.

5. When You Pipe at Zanzibar . . .

BUT European slaving from the East Coast was not the end of the story. Some of the seaboard cities were also in the business. One or two of them were making considerable profits from it; and none more than Zanzibar, now a dependency of the Imam of the southern Arabian state of Muscat. Another British naval visitor, Captain Smee, found in 1811 that the Governor of Zanzibar, an Arab called Yacout, was taking ten dollars a head in 'premium' from every slave delivered to the French for their plantations on Mauritius and Bourbon. As well as selling to the French, Yacout was also supplying Muscat and other eastern markets: perhaps to a total of between six and ten thousand slaves a year, though not necessarily every year. The true totals, as elsewhere, remain obscure.

Such exports, even so, were still on a relatively small scale: in the West, Brazil alone was taking more than five times as many. However evil the plight of the enslaved, East Coast peoples were not yet suffering greatly from slaving, and nor were their neighbours in the interior. But the Arabs of Oman and Muscat were thrusting merchants who now pushed inland from the coast and mightily expanded the slave trade. By 1839, when Zanzibar had the lion's share of slaving, a British observer reckoned that between 40,000 and 45,000 slaves were being sold there every year. About half of these went northward to Arabia, the Persian

Gulf and Egypt. Most of the rest were smuggled southward to the Portuguese in Mozambique, who sent them to Brazil. American slave ships also drew cargoes from this source.

After 1840 the business of extracting slaves from East Africa became a major Arab enterprise. In that year the Sultan of Oman transferred his capital from Muscat to his dependency of Zanzibar. A ruler of great commercial talent, he set about reorganizing the trade of Zanzibar and of much of the Coast on an entirely new basis. He stimulated exports of natural products from the mainland. He established clove plantations on Zanzibar. He sent envoys far and wide across the eastern world to win new markets or reactivate old ones. Arab merchants were again installed, as in early medieval times, at ports as far away as the south China coast. Here was a major effort to rebuild the former prosperity of the Indian Ocean trade between East Africa and its old partners. But now there was a difference: slaving had become a major part of the business, even a dominant part of it.

The years before and after 1840 – but especially after – were those of far-reaching Arab penetration of the East African interior. The Arabs and their Swahili agents went in along the old trade routes – from Bagamoyo, Kilwa, Tanga – and rapidly established trading stations on the Great Lakes and at suitable places in between. Armed with muskets, they overawed the weak and skilfully allied themselves with the strong. They pushed ever further into the interior. 'It will be seen', the British explorer Speke could write in 1864, 'that the Zanzibar Arabs have reached the uttermost limits of their tether; [they are] half-way across the continent, and in a few years they must unite their labours with the people who come from Luanda on the opposite coast.' They had in fact already done so: in 1852 the Angolan archives speak for the first time of direct contact with Arab traders, six of whom had crossed the continent from east to west in that year.

It was this Arab penetration of the interior, having as its main object the provision of slaves for export and slaves for the new plantations of Zanzibar and its immediate mainland holdings, that led to the devastations which Livingstone and other explorers now witnessed. The point here is that the devastations were recent: they were not characteristic of East African history whether in the interior or along the coast. After the coming of the

Sultan of Oman and his traders, Coupland remarks, 'the whole system of inland trade was extended and elaborated far beyond the more or less casual operations in which the Arabs of the coast have been engaged for ages past'. In these years it was said with truth that: 'When you pipe at Zanzibar, they dance at the Lakes.'

But the fact that the inland devastations were recent has often been forgotten. They understandably horrified the European explorers who were now pushing into the interior in the wake of the Arabs. But Livingstone himself was under no misapprehension about the order of events. He knew that he was witnessing the misery of a slave trade that was relatively new. Further to the south, in the Zambesi valley, he even found that the trails he opened were being followed for the first time by slavers in Portuguese employ. Yet in Europe this slaving misery was increasingly believed as being endemic to the East and Central African interior, and as though in some way 'natural' to the peoples of these regions.

From this situation, by routes that were indirect and yet connected, there came colonial enterprise and eventual conquest. This invasion of the African interior was repeatedly justified by the humanitarian aim of suppressing the Arab slave trade. Certainly, the task needed doing; and it was well done, especially by the British and the Belgians. But it was done in exchange for a new subjection; and one, moreover, which was intended to endure and under which Africans were to suffer new forms of servitude. Here, very clearly, one may see how the inability of African institutions to resist slaving became a major cause of their overthrow. Traditional customs of domestic slavery were allowed to slide disastrously into competitive slaving for export; and the damage was all the greater in those regions, notably of East Africa, where other forms of long-distance trading had never flourished.

It is important to understand this process. The ideology of colonial conquest, now growing strong in Europe, was to flourish on the notion that Africans were incapable of promoting and defending their own cultures. This was not true. But slaving made it seem true. Europeans were offered the picture of a continental interior that was unredeemedly savage, a pitiful victim of bloodlust and brutality, powerless to help itself. Every evil tale, and there were many, seemed to strengthen this impression. There could, it was then argued, be only one answer to the problem; and that was outright annexation.

This ideology persisted. One may find it in book after book of the colonial period, whether in the memoirs of those who carried the 'white man's burden' or of those who justified his carrying it. Scholars were as little exempt as colonial propagandists. The outstanding case is that of Coupland, author of standard British textbooks on East African history. A 'new chapter in the history of Africa began with David Livingstone', Coupland was writing in 1928. 'So far, it might be said, Africa proper had had no history . . . The main body of Africans . . . had stayed, for untold centuries, sunk in barbarism. Such, it might almost seem, had been Nature's decree . . . So they remained stagnant, neither going back . . . The heart of Africa was scarcely beating.' In the same large-handed way Coupland wrote off the Swahili cities of the coast. They were, he said, Arab colonies from the earliest times and as such they had remained.

We can see now that Coupland was doubly mistaken. He was wrong about the coastal cities, for he ignored their Swahili nature. He was wrong about the peoples of the interior. They had not 'stayed sunk in barbarism'. They might be 'barbaric' in a narrowly lexicographical sense, since they were non-literate and generally non-urban; but they were certainly not barbaric in the sense that Coupland implied – of possessing no moral codes, laws, governments or civilization of their own. Nor had they 'remained stagnant': on the contrary, they had moved through many phases of social development that were common to other branches of the human race.

What an invading Europe found was not an age-old chaos and insecurity, as many imagined, but the disasters of a sudden social crisis. This was the crisis that opened the way to colonial occupation; and no doubt it is in this that the greatest consequence of nineteenth-century slaving in East Africa should be seen.

Such, in brief but not misleading outline, is the story of East Africa's varying fortunes in connection with the outside world. Yet there were other regions where contact with Europe involved, in pre-colonial times, neither territorial encroachment as in the Congo, nor an outright destruction of existing cultures. And to see the European-African connection in all its astonishing enterprise and vigour, it is to these other regions one must turn. They lay in the west among the peoples of the Gulf of Guinea.

PART SIX

FRONTIER OF OPPORTUNITY

To be a king means to have plenty of slaves, without which you are nothing.

EMIR OF BIDA in 1897

The coastland became the frontier of opportunity.

K. ONWUKA DIKE, 1956

1. Like Nothing Else . . .

THERE is surely no other chapter in human experience like that of the Gulf of Guinea during these years. For sheer complexity of enterprise the records of the West African venture tend to make all other encounters between Europe and Africa seem pale, predictable and sad.

Almost nothing in this story lacks drama or surprise. Little can be foreseen for long. Much death and sorrow there may be, sordid and chaotic; but all the same there persists a steady underlay of humour that goes ringing up and down the scale from the sly ironic to the swaggering absurd. Poker-faced ambition, solemn and socially respectable, is punctured by irreverent laughter. Deliberate brutality walks hand-in-hand with careful restraint. Furious rivalries and frantic *coups de main* are separated by slow periods of peaceful intercourse and dependable alliance. The common man suffers, often appallingly; but humanity, somehow or other, perseveres and doggedly fights back and survives.

It is a strange symphony of expedience that echoes from these years for those who care to listen: a harsh and highly fallible orchestration of forceful men and their wily stratagems, the clash and clatter of cheating and chaffering and agreeing and disputing, the rattle of spears and muskets, the laboured groan of hard-shifting sheets and yards on old ships cluttered with slaves and sick men, slowed to a crawl by the barnacled scum of tropical seas and yet crazily bearing, somehow or other, humanity's past into humanity's future.

It seems to defy all reasonable explanation. Yet it has a pattern. And this pattern on the Guinea Coast, perhaps more clearly than any other aspect of the European-African connection, reveals a gradual transition of African society – the prelude to both subjection and regained independence.

Here, above all, there was great variety. The peoples of the Congo had never known a European connection that was not more or less confined to a single European power, and this a backward and relatively weak one; or to a single interest, the trade in slaves. Their experience of the non-African world was inevitably narrow; their scope for action and reaction necessarily small; their chances of playing off one competitor against another never more than minimal. But along the Guinea Coast there appeared the ships and traders of a dozen nations; and here the trade passed through many hands and phases.

There was also, on the Guinea Coast, a great innate strength of resistance. The peoples of the East African littoral had certainly known a long and varied connection with the outside world, yet they had known it only until the sixteenth century. By then they had built an urban civilization that proved softly vulnerable to the guns and ambition of the Portuguese, and the Portuguese went far to overwhelm it. But the peoples of the Guinea Coast offered no such easy target. They could defend themselves when attacked; and they did defend themselves.

At the beginning there was the same acceptance of equality among Europeans and Africans that occurred in the Congo, and in much the same circumstances. The Portuguese came to Benin as allies and missionaries. They encouraged its ambassadors to visit Lisbon. They helped to build churches. They opened and tried to monopolize an extensive trade in ivory and other goods, and soon in slaves. They established royal agents in the city of Benin. Sometimes their soldiers marched and fought in the armies of the *Oba*. As late as the early seventeenth century the king of neighbouring Warri returned from Portugal with a white wife; his son, who became an important man in 1644, enjoyed the baptismal name of Dom Antonio de Mingo.

There were other such cases along the Coast. But this early equality had a better fate than in the Congo. It continued and evolved. It developed new and unique forms. No matter through what conflicts and miseries the European connection might pass – and it passed through many – the two sides somehow held to each other. They might trust or mightily mistrust each other, enrich or seek to ruin, respect the peace or break it: through thick and thin they were kept together by their common interest in trade. Year

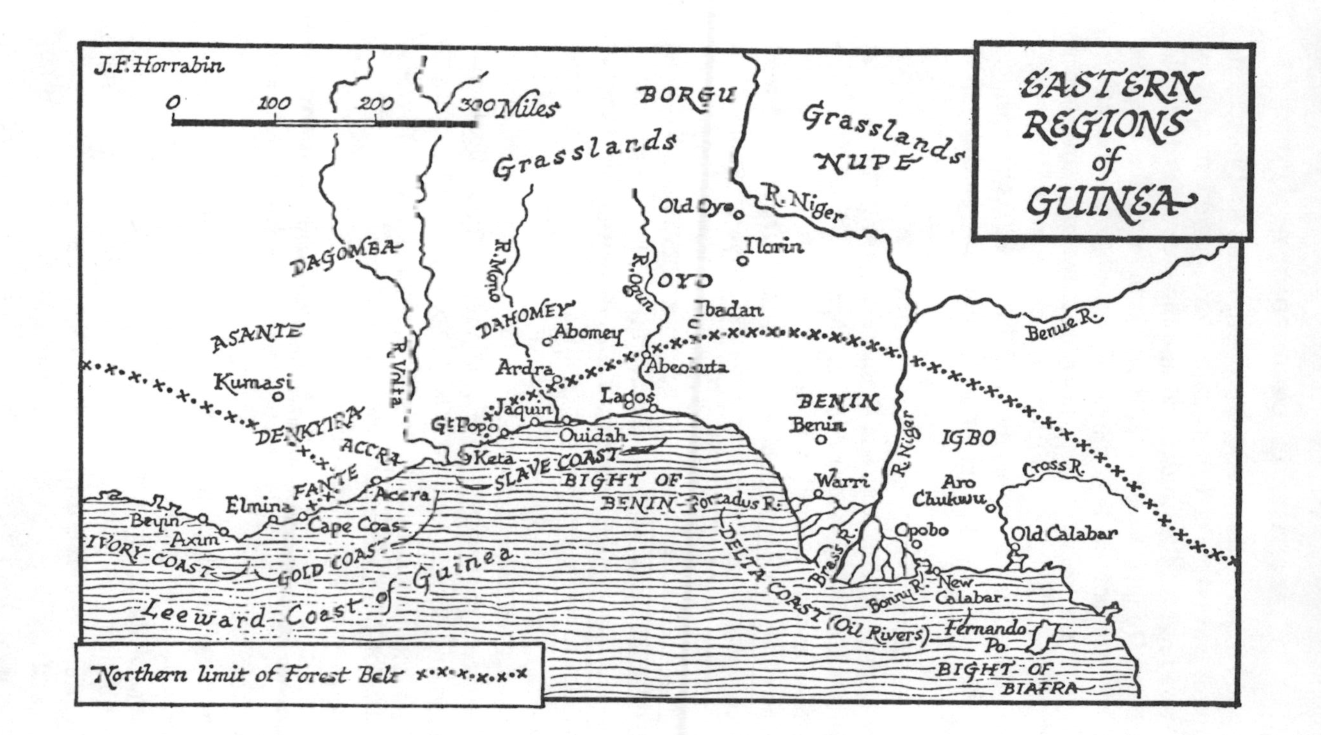

Note: The western limits of the Gold Coast went, in fact, as far as Beyin and a little beyond.

after year, to serve this trade, European crews and merchants underwent mortal risks in navigation and fearful months of sweat and fever on the Coast; and nothing ever availed to hold them back. On their side the African partners in the business deployed patience and commercial cunning, persevered in gauging the manners of these newly discovered peoples from beyond the sea, and little by little took their measure. The history of the Guinea Coast between about 1550 and 1850 is increasingly and continuously the history of an international partnership in risk and profit.

So it is wrong to consider this West African experience as one that was ordered and imposed from outside, with the African part in it a purely negative and involuntary one. This view of the connection mirrors a familiar notion of African incapacity, and it has no place in the historical record. Those Africans who were involved in the trade were seldom the helpless victims of a commerce they did not understand: on the contrary, they understood it as well as their European partners. They responded to its challenge. They exploited its opportunities. Their great misfortune – and this would be Africa's tragedy – was that Europe, more than anything else, wanted captives for enslavement in the Americas.

The states and peoples that became involved in this connection, whether directly or indirectly, were themselves of great diversity of language and social structure. They were states and peoples of the Sudanese grasslands, of the Forest Belt, and of the seaside littoral. Not only were they various; they were also of great antiquity.

By the time of European arrival, late in the fifteenth century, many of these peoples had achieved an Iron Age maturity of social structure. Strong feudal states and empires had emerged and these possessed in their heritage, as modern research now suggests, some reason to regard themselves as occupying the heartland of black Africa.

On this last point, which may have a bearing on their self-confidence and stability, there are two kinds of evidence: archaeological and linguistic. In Central Nigeria, at the confluence of the Niger and Benue over an area of several hundred square miles, archaeologists have lately found the proofs of an Iron Age culture that is earlier than anything else of its kind so far known in Africa south of the Sahara. This Nok culture seems to have had a vigorous life between about 500 B.C. and A.D. 200. It was undoubtedly transitional between stone and iron – a point which is neatly made by a smelting *tuyère* or nozzle that is now on show at Lagos Museum; for inside this *tuyère* there lies, just as it was found, the butt of a stone axe.

This Nok culture, with others of the same nature which are now being gradually identified by the patient work of archaeology, was ancestral to all that long and complex process of societal development which has been called the African Iron Age. And it happens that the outstanding sculptural arts of Nigeria (as of some neighbouring countries) can illustrate this very well. For the terracotta figures and figurines of the Nok people can be seen, beyond any reasonable doubt, to have been ancestral to the rightly world-famous sculpture of Ife in the thirteenth century A.D., and these in turn appear to have been the ancestors of the brass and bronze master-sculptors of Benin, whose work maintained an exceptional standard into modern times.

From those early Iron Age cultures, in other words, there flowed a stream of technological invention and achievement that went hand-in-hand with the 'social engineering' of peoples who built the states and empires of the forest belt: Oyo and Benin, Akwamu, Denkyira, Asante, and their like. And it further seems that this whole 'Nigerian region' has to be seen in a wider sense as a creator of African cultures. For it was here in the Niger–Benue confluence region, or somewhat to the east of it, that modern linguists have identified – and, so far, to their very general agreement – the origins of the 'parents of the Bantu': the remote 'founding fathers', that is, of all that multitude of peoples and societies of the Bantu-language group who form the majority of the populations of central and southern Africa today.

Traditions of Yoruba origin are another kind of evidence. These Yoruba of the powerful state of Oyo, with its spiritual capital at Ile Ife, have generally believed that their remote forerunners came from Arabia. And yet they have also held, by another tradition, that they live in the place where God created man. 'All the various tribes of the Yoruba nation', according to the Rev. Samuel Johnson, a Yoruba clergyman of the Church of England who made an early study of what Yorubas believe, and whose book on the subject was published some sixty years ago, 'trace their origin from Oduduwa [their legendary hero-founder] and the city of Ile Ife. In fact Ile Ife is fabled as the spot where God created man, white and black, and from whence they dispersed all over the earth.'

Now certain forerunners of the Yoruba may probably have reached south-western Nigeria – coming originally, perhaps, from the central Sudan – between A.D. 600 and 1000. But these newcomers were not the only ancestors of Yoruba civilization, any more than William of Normandy's four thousand knights were the only ancestors of English civilization. They were a relatively small group of travellers, but hard-tried and well-armed: they conquered and settled and were then absorbed among the peoples whom they had found. For Yoruba civilization, as Willett has written, appears to be the result of 'a fusion of a small intrusive ruling class, bringing ideas from outside, with a highly artistic indigenous population'. And this fusion is reflected in surviving Yoruba tradition. Thus the Yoruba have remembered their own sagas of travel and settlement, though vaguely and dimly, but they have also remembered another and quite different line of tradition: a much older memory of those who fathered the 'dispersal' from Yorubaland 'all over the earth' – but actually, if the linguists are right, into central and southern Africa.

The principal states of the West African coast and its hinterland were therefore strongly established by the time of European coming. Although non-literate, they had great inner coherence, social self-confidence, moral and customary and artistic vigour. Some of them had been heard of in Europe; most had not. But all of them, by the middle of the sixteenth century, were beginning to feel the tug of the new maritime trade along the coast.

Until now they had looked northward for commerce and contact with the non-African world. The states of the Forest belt had looked to the savannah states to the north of them – to Ghana, Mali, Songhay, Kanem, the Hausa city-states – and these in turn had looked northward again across the Great Desert to the Arab and Berber states of North Africa. Now the position began to be reversed. The empires of the savannah land were losing their potency. And along the coast there appeared the ships and traders of Europe, pushing their way patiently eastward from one anchorage to the next.

And so, for the first time in history, this West African seaboard became a frontier that could be used and crossed. It ceased to be the edge of nowhere, and was henceforward a vital place of meeting with the foremost nations of the world.

The consequences of this great though gradual change of front were felt initially, of course, along the coast itself; and notably among the almost deserted creeks and channels of the sprawling delta of the Niger.

2. The People of the Salt Water

THE swamplands of the Niger delta appear to have been thinly populated before the coming of the sailing ships. Here in this back of beyond, along the profitless edge of an empty ocean, there lived only a few scattered peoples, refugees from the great states of the interior, odd families down on their luck, fragments of minor clans and fishing communities.

Yet within a hundred years there had emerged amid this maze of inland waterways – a Victorian traveller would fancifully call them 'the Venice of West Africa' – a close-knit system of trading states; and within another hundred years these states had built themselves into a well-nigh impregnable position of commercial monopoly. They had become the indispensable middlemen between Europe and the densely-populated lands behind the delta, especially the lands of the numerous Igbo.

The history of these little states, Dike said of them in his penetrating study of 1956, belongs both to the Atlantic and to Africa. They were almost as much the children of the Guinea trade – the slave trade – as were the plantation colonies of the Caribbean and North America. And yet they remained strongly African in accent and ideas. They may be seen as the West African equivalent of the somewhat earlier city-states of East Africa.

From the very beginning of their social growth, these peoples of the delta appear to have shown great ingenuity in getting the better of natural disadvantages – in soil, climate and excess of water – that were as daunting for them as for their European visitors. But they also displayed a persistent political inventiveness. They evolved new ways of unifying peoples of diverse language and origin. They moved far towards complex forms of state organization. Their city-states are among the most interesting of all the products of the African connection with Europe.

Early among the founders of this new society in the delta are thought to have been Ijọ people on the run from Benin's stiff-handed rule. Whether Ijọ or not, these settlers colonized riverbanks and chunks of land amid the water. They lived as fishermen, and they must have lived poorly.

Then came the Portuguese, passing them by at first. 'There is no trade in this country,' Pacheco was writing of the western delta in about 1505, 'nor anything from which one can make a profit.' One should go on up to Guato, port of Benin, and deal with the agents of the monarch of that empire.

Rapidly, this situation changed: partly by initiative of the delta peoples, who found ways of circumventing the royal prerogatives of Benin and tapping the rich trade of the Igbo country behind the eastern river-mouths; and partly by insistence of the European captains and supercargoes, who sought new harbours in which to outwit their rivals and build temporary monopolies of their own. In the event this combination of talent became centred on new settlements that were founded near the mouths of the Brass, Bonny, Opobo and Cross rivers. These became the focal points of maritime trade for the lands that were later to become eastern Nigeria.

New recruits joined these promising settlements. The delta became more than a refuge: it functioned now as a prime connecting point with Europe. Prominent among these migrants were families from Igboland, energetic people whose own customs were those of a democracy that generally tolerated neither chiefs nor kings, human or divine, and for whom the theocratic hierarchy of Benin was perhaps especially foreign. It was these Igbos who gave the delta system its turbulent individualism, famous among West Africans and Europeans alike, and who laid the social foundations on which ambitious men would raise kingdoms and republics in the years ahead.

Yet it would be wrong to consider the society of the delta as an Igbo importation. It became in fact something on its own, a compound of old ideas with new ideas, a mixture that was 'neither Benin nor Efik, Igbo nor Ibibio', but, as Dike says, 'a people apart, the product of the clashing cultures of the tribal hinterland and of the Atlantic community to both of which they belonged. The tribal [inland] Igbos called them *Ndu Mili Nnu* (People of the Salt Water), and so long as the frontier of trade was confined to the Atlantic seaboard, so long did they remain the economic masters of these territories.'

The frontier of trade remained along this seaboard for several hundred years. And with the rise of mass slaving in the seventeenth century the chances of gain became correspondingly large. It was on this that these settlements built their prosperity.

Like their new partners, the Africans who went into this business were people with a long commercial experience, gained partly between themselves and partly by commerce with the northern states and empires of the Sudanese grasslands. What they needed, here in the delta, was not commercial know-how but effective social organization. They had to become strong enough both to obtain slaves from their inland neighbours and, when occasion demanded, to present a common front against the Europeans. It was difficult for them to achieve this strength, because the old and new dwellers in these islands and dry places on the banks of rivers were of many ethnic loyalties.

Faced with such problems, the delta peoples found a solution in their characteristic city-state. These delta states – these multi-ethnic trading corporations – showed themselves both skilful in weaving a common loyalty and flexible in absorbing new immigrants. Each developed its own exclusivist 'citizenship': to the point, indeed, that one may perhaps see in these little states the first thorough-going origins in West Africa of the ideas of modern nationalism. Like the nations of mercantile Europe they competed ruthlessly with one another for trade, profits and even territory. And yet, over and above this rivalry, they felt themselves joined together by common interests and forms of government.

Some of the dozen or so leading states evolved into monarchies, others into republics, their choice depending largely on the influence of neighbouring tradition. But within this broad framework there were new institutions, holding society together, that were peculiar to the delta. The 'house system' was one of these. Dike defines this as 'at once a co-operative trading unit and a local government institution'. Each 'house' was governed by a single powerful trader; and each state, whether monarchy or not, might have many 'houses'. It was through the 'house system' that a new rule of law was found that could be valid for immigrants of many ethnic groups.

The basic idea behind this system was not invented in the delta. It was the characteristically African concept of 'extended family', a group that includes every man, woman and child with acknowledged blood relationship to one another. But the delta system carried this notion much further. Membership of a 'house' came to include not only the ruling families and its relations, but their servants and slaves as well. 'Master and servant, the bond and the free, all became members of one House, a veritable hierarchy, with numerous gradations, each rank with its duties and responsibilities, its privileges and rewards.'

Different origins were forgotten, different languages were discarded, different loyalties were broken; rapidly, all were welded into new customs and traditions. 'The smaller houses numbered anything from three hundred to a thousand members; others, such as the royal Houses, numbered many thousands.' The best slaves were retained to man the armed canoes that went on raid and search for captives needed by the European trade; and, as time went by, these slaves – who were not chattel slaves but men who were bound with special ties of loyalty to this or that master – became important traders in their own right, and sometimes they became kings.

Here and there the house rulers borrowed the old trappings and superstitions of spiritually sanctified monarchy in the interior. Like the ruler of Benin, the little house kings of the delta would expect slaves to be sacrificed whenever one of them should die. Elsewhere the house rulers became a governing oligarchy. They formed exclusive clubs and secret societies which held watch and ward over their states, settled disputes, regulated successions and generally acted as judge, jury and counter-revolutionary police. Later on, when the slaves they kept for their plantations had learned how to organize themselves, these oligarchies would face situations they were no longer able to contain; and slave risings would help to put an end to slave massacres.

Throughout the years of the slave trade, even in times when slaving was past its worst, the delta rulers waxed in wealth and political strength. Dealing as equals with Europeans, jealously guarding their monopoly of contact with the hinterland, proud of their sovereignty, these chiefs and their people transformed this sterile belt of waste and swamp into a prosperous region. A European visitor in 1847 could find that King Eyo of Creek Town 'had in his House many thousand slaves, and four hundred canoes with a captain and crew for every one. Besides his extensive trade ... he employs his people reclaiming waste land, founding towns and planting farms in well-selected positions which give him command of the rivers and channels of trade.'

Here was a case, then, where the development of new forms of long-distance trade – or oversea trade – led to a new demand for labour and new ways of supplying that demand. The boom in palm-oil exports – beginning in the 1830s, growing for decades after that – called for the employment of workers. There being no labour market on capitalist lines, these workers were employed within a system of 'wageless labour'. In other words, they were 'slaves' put to plantation work at home instead of being exported overseas. As such, they were necessarily absorbed within the lineage systems of the Delta. Though maltreatment was no doubt far from rare, they were not chattels.

There was another element making for stability within this new productive system. The latter was socially mobile. 'Wageless workers' – slaves in European parlance – could obtain their freedom of initiative by hard work or individual enterprise on behalf of their masters: that is, of their employers. Dike tells us that 'the wealth produced by a slave eventually set him free, for the master knew his slave intimately and the value of his work, and rewarded him accordingly. It was this incentive, ever present in the House system, that made it in the nineteenth century an institution full of vitality, flexible and in a large measure beneficial to all.'

We may see in the House system one of those transitional 'bridges' which were able, in Europe, to lead from relatively primitive economies into the economy of early capitalism. Why then, could it not do this in Africa: here in the delta of the Niger? The answer is in subsequent history. No sooner had the House system got into its stride than the oversea partner – in this case the British – undertook to destroy it in the sacred name of monopoly. But this is looking ahead. Let us return here to the enterprise of the masters of the Delta before George Goldie with the ambition of British control came on the scene. They accomplished a good deal.

3. 'Children of God'

YET the masters were few, and the oversea demand for slaves was great. Through at least two centuries the demand was so great as to be practically insatiable. Countless thousands of slaves were obtained in the lands behind the delta. Given their numerical weakness, how could the delta states achieve this consistently high rate of delivery? Here again their system revealed a peculiar compound of influence.

On the African side the thing was done by another adaptation of tradition and belief. Like many of their neighbours, the Igbos of the highly populous lands behind the eastern delta possessed a supreme deity. This deity was accustomed to communicate with the Igbos through a famous oracle, Chukwu, which resided in the territory of a large kinship group known as Aro. Other such groups knew the Aro as Umu-Chukwu, the Children of God.

Happy in their gift of fortune, this oracle of great authority, the Aro early fastened themselves into a special position of monopoly inside the general commercial system that linked the hinterland with the coast. 'This they did', Dike says, 'by establishing Aro colonies along the trade routes of the interior.' He compares them with the Greeks, 'the course of whose colonising expeditions was largely directed by the priests of the Delphic Oracle'.

In any case the Aro exploited their oracle with a realism and commercial ardour that would also have done them credit with medieval prince-bishops or tycoons of a later time; and they duly exercised the slave trade as part of their divine (and highly profitable) calling. They became the monopolist operators of the trade between much of Igboland and the busy ports of the eastern delta. In so doing they acquired political influence. This influence continued into colonial times: 'Long Ju Ju', as Europeans called the Aro oracle, was destroyed by the British only in the year 1900.

Slaving was always a grim enough affair, and many captives were certainly taken in war or simply kidnapped. 'Those sold by the Blacks', a French trader observed of Senegal in the 1680s, 'are for the most part prisoners of war, taken either in fight or in pursuit or in the incursions they [the raiders] make into their enemies' territories.' But in the Niger delta the situation was different. 'All that vast number of slaves which the Calabar Blacks sell to all European nations . . . are not their prisoners of war, the greatest part being bought by those people of their inland neighbours.' Many and perhaps most delta slaves were in fact delivered by the Aro system.

It worked through the pressures of orthodox and socially respectable belief among people for whom religion had an everyday compulsion, and for whom death was only the passage from one life to another. Any man who should offend the oracle – and the Aro priests saw to it that nothing was easier – was mulcted of a fine: but it was a fine that must be paid in slaves. Once paid, the 'fine' was supposed to be eaten by the oracle: in truth, of course, the captives were simply handed along the Aro network to the traders of the coast who sold them to the Europeans. Perhaps this was one reason why Igbo thought that Europeans were cannibals.

These priest-slavers had two powerful reasons for confidence in their system. In the first place, they and their oracle provided a valuable and even vital cement for the many factions, tribes, settlements and 'free cities' of this tumultuous delta society. The authority of the Aro oracle was an imperative that many were prepared to recognize and respect: through it, the Aro trader-priests fashioned among these disparate peoples a trading unity, useful though often broken, which they could not otherwise have had. Speaking for a jealous god like others of his kind, 'Long Ju Ju's' word was law.

So harsh a law could scarcely have stood for long, one may

think, without the sanctions of superior force. And sanctions, indeed, were soon found to be necessary. This was where the European connection made its vital contribution to the system. Slaving captains might be powerless beyond the decks of their ships. There was none the less one sovereign means whereby they could push their influence into the hinterland. 'We sell them', a Dutch factor on the Coast was writing home as early in the game as 1700, 'incredible quantities' of muskets and they, the Africans, 'are wonderful dexterous' in using them.

Widespread use of firearms influenced the course of history in the delta as surely as in other parts of Africa. It was their concentration of fire-power that enabled the delta chiefs to outface and overawe the numerically far stronger peoples of the interior. And muskets were almost certainly decisive in enabling the Aro trader-priests to maintain their monopoly – and keep their oracle respected – in face of mounting opposition from those who suffered from the system.

The Aro priests do not appear to have used the guns themselves. They hired others for that purpose. They called up mercenaries from the professional soldier-guilds of Igboland, the famous Abam, Abiriba and their like, armed these with the muskets they had bought, and 'conquered all the people who resisted their influence or killed their agents'. Meanwhile lesser 'Aro systems', presided over by lesser priests in the name of smaller deities and oracles, were engaged in the same business at other points behind the delta ports.

Thus the trade was organized by god and gun on one side as surely as by ship and plantation on the other. Here too, at any rate for the time being, a kind of equality held firm.

4. Partners in Trade

BONNY was the main port of sale for the inland traders. It can never have been a promising or comfortable place. 'Miles of rotting mud water', Mary Kingsley said of the Bonny river ninety years ago, 'fringed with walls of rotting mud mangrove-swamp.' Here were the old hulks of the slave trade, the floating barracoons that were only a memory of the past in Mary Kingsley's day (although a fairly recent past), showing their 'gaunt black ribs like the skeletons of great unclean beasts who have died because Bonny water was too strong even for them'.

This was the 'white man's grave' that Europeans justly feared, the killing seaboard of which the sailors sang:

> Beware and take care
> Of the Bight of Benin:
> For one that comes out
> There are forty go in.

Death by malaria was not so common by the end of the nineteenth century, thanks to quinine, but malaria was not the only killer. Yellow fever slew nine out of eleven Europeans resident at Bonny not long before Mary Kingsley's first visit. A fine show of callous humour was the accepted style among Europeans who were obliged to live in Bonny and its sister-ports: no doubt in self-defence, they felt it a duty to make their visitors' teeth rattle. 'I went ashore to have tea with Captain Boler,' says Miss Kingsley, 'and was told more details about this particular epidemic, to say nothing of other epidemics. In one which the captain experienced, at the fourth funeral, two youngsters (junior clerks of the deceased) from drink brought on by fright, fell into the grave before the coffin, which got lowered on to them, and all three had to be hauled out again. "Barely necessary though, was it?" said another member of the party, "for those two had to have a grave of their own before next sundown."'

Yet at least it could be said of Bonny that its slaves were delivered, decade after decade, with a minimum of violence and disorder. Elsewhere in the delta the organization was less peaceful. There was much armed raiding for captives, especially in the high days of 'King Sugar' when slaves in the Caribbean were always in short supply. At Old Calabar, a little east of Bonny, Efik traders occasionally sold their own 'criminals' – those found guilty of theft, adultery or political awkwardness – but their regular practice was to put small cannon into large canoes and send parties upstream to press-gang any villagers they could find. Now and then they had the practical help of their European partners.

A typical joint enterprise appears in the memoir of an English sailor, Isaac Parker, who was five months in Old Calabar in 1765 and took part in one of these river expeditions.* A trader called Dick Ebro having invited him, they armed several canoes and went upstream into the maze of creeks behind the coast. There they landed and lay 'under the bushes in the day when they came near a village', and took hold 'of every one they could see'. These unfortunates were handcuffed and loaded into the canoes, which then went on to another likely place.

Such terror in the hinterland – yet reaching, perhaps, no more than a few dozen miles from the ocean surf – was generally though not invariably in contrast with the peace and calm of trading operations at the point of delivery. By the eighteenth century, as we have seen earlier in this book, these operations rested on long years of familiar custom. Relations between the two sides were seldom intimate, but they were often marked by trust and a certain rough friendship. There was lavish hospitality on the African side. An eyewitness afterwards recalled of a characteristic banquet in the nineteenth century that the food was brought in by a 'file of stout girls in native undress, each bearing on her head a large covered calabash . . . yams and fish, stewed together with palm oil, vegetables, and pepper . . . laughing and joking', and Eyamba, the house ruler, 'helped them all himself, in succession . . . without asking anyone what he would choose . . .'

There were feasts like this beyond number. After the feasting came the business. Many tales have survived of this tantalizing and often lengthy engagement.† Neither side could ever be quite sure of the other's good intentions because of the violence of the times, but even more because of the exceeding complication in weights and measures and currencies that were used, not to speak of the complexities of the 'trade ounce'. They watched each other warily. Yet most of these stories bear witness to a commercial stability that was strong enough to hold firm through many stiff meetings, hints of dark suspicion of betrayal, sudden out-

* Parker had sailed with the British explorer of the Pacific, Captain Cook, and is said to have had a 'highly respectable' reputation.

† See p. 106 above.

bursts of armed distrust and all the other hazards and hesitations of a trade that had never proved easy.

Something of the complications on the delta coast can be seen from James Barbot's report on prices at New Calabar in 1699. He was buying ship's stores for a voyage to the Caribbean by way of the Congo, and needed fifty thousand yams. These he eventually obtained at the price of one standard-sized bar for sixty 'king's yams' – first quality – and one bar for one hundred and fifty 'slaves' yams'. Butts of water cost two standard-sized iron rings each. 'For the length of wood, seven bars, which is dear; but they were to deliver it ready cut into our boat. For a goat, one bar. A cow, ten or eight bars, according to its bigness. A hog, two bars . . .'

Yet by far the best account of what the trade was really like in these delta city-states has come from an African source. It was discovered some thirty years ago in an Edinburgh library: the diary of an old Calabar House ruler called Antera Duke that tells of the years 1785–8, and vividly projects the African-Atlantic partnership from a delta viewpoint.

At Old Calabar there was neither a sanctified king nor an all-powerful oracle to help both government and trade. Here the 'rich men and prime merchants' of the estuary – at their settlements of Duke Town, Old Town, Henshaw Town, Creek Town – managed their affairs, conducted their administration and maintained their authority not by ancient law or inherited custom but by a new and exclusive society called Egbo, an Efik word meaning leopard. Egbo was something between a wizard's gathering, a municipal executive, and an early African version of a businessman's club; and it possessed powerful religious and legal sanctions. It was not an aristocratic establishment, for anyone who became rich could always buy his way into it. Indeed, its essential function was to defend the interests of the rich and to safeguard their powers of government over lesser men and slaves. Egbo, in brief, was another instance of development towards a 'political society' under the stimulus of new economic conditions and opportunities.

Egbo made the laws and also administered them. 'Under the aegis of the chief and the important elders of the town,' Simmons has written, 'the Leopard Society promulgated and enforced laws, judged important cases, recovered debts, protected the property of members, and constituted the actual executive government.' It punished crime and, whenever this was thought necessary, enforced trade boycotts against Europeans – to the point that some European traders also found it worth their while to buy themselves into membership of Egbo. The system was oligarchical, but not necessarily anti-social in the circumstances of the time. 'For it gave to all men of wealth', in Jones's words, 'an overriding common interest in preserving the stability of the society and the social order of which it formed a part.'

This was the society and social order that is portrayed in Antera Duke's diary. At first sight, even when put into ordinary English from the trading 'pidgin' of the Coast, much of the diary seems incomprehensible. The entry for January 28, 1785, is clear enough:

> About 6 a.m. at Aqua Landing; a fine morning so I worked in my small yard. At 2 o'clock afternoon we two go aboard Captain Small's (ship) with three slaves. So he takes two and we came back.*

The original – to offer an example of Antera Duke's language – reads like this:

> about 6 am in aqua Landing with fine morning so I have work for my small yard after 2 oclock noon wee two go Bord Captin Smal with 3 slave so his tak two and wee come back.

Only two of the slaves were robust enough for Captain Small, so the third had to be brought back again. A small business that day; yet business as usual. Two days later Antera Duke is once again at Aqua Landing at six in the morning –

> a foggy morning, so I was going to work in my little yard, but at the same time we and Tom Aqua and John Aqua joined together to catch men.

A different business, but still as usual.

Next day another note is struck and the obscurities begin. Again the energetic merchant is up at six in the morning and

*'Pidgin', according to Daryll Forde, was 'a jargon which was mainly English in vocabulary although the constructions were often modelled on those of Ibibio'. English renderings here are by Simmons.

walking the quayside. The morning is very foggy and he goes back to work in his yard, not expecting any ship's boats, but

> after that Duke and all of us went to King Egbo to share Egbo money for 40 men.

What is one to make of this? The answer is that the club was sharing out its new members' entrance fees. Whenever a man was admitted to the Leopard Society he had to pay an initiation fee that was divided among all the members. In this case there were forty new members, and their fees were evidently worth a note.

Egbo and its operations are never long absent from the diary. They could not be, for they permeated every aspect of Efik life, an all-embracing system of laws and sanctions grafted skilfully to Efik beliefs in magic and the supernatural. On October 26, 1786, the diarist is not feeling well, so he starts by taking medicine. The day is to prove a busy one:

> Then I heard that Egbo was run and when I heard I walked up to Egbo Young. We saw Egbo come down and the Egbo men said that Sam Ambo and George Cobham had blown on Captain Fairweather. So all our family were damn angry about that blow and we sent to call Captain Fairweather to come ashore and break trade first with our family for about 15 slaves and we fired three guns on shore . . .

Here we have a dispute between a pair of African traders – Sam Ambo and George Cobham – and one of the slaving captains whose ship was anchored in the estuary. They had called out the police – the second grade of Egbo, known as 'Brass Egbo' and responsible for law enforcement – and the police had 'blown on Captain Fairweather'. They had declared, that is, a suspension of trade between the disputing parties until an understanding should be reached. Antera Duke's family were 'damn angry' because Captain Fairweather happened to be a client of theirs as well; so they sent aboard to ask him to come ashore notwithstanding, and fired three guns to clinch their offer. How Antera and his family arranged matters is not explained, but evidently all went off well because –

> at 3 o'clock in the afternoon we saw Eyo and Ebetim come down with Esin Ambo, and they went to Sam and George Cobham to make them settle with Captain Fairweather.

A few days later the Leopard Society is conducting a religious duty peculiar to the establishment of Old Calabar. Duke Ephraim, leading man of Duke Town, has died; and at once there is the customary call for human sacrifice to accompany his funeral.

About 4 a.m. I got up; there was great rain, so I walked to the palaver house and I found all the gentlemen here. So we got ready to cut off heads and at 5 o'clock in the morning we began to cut slaves' heads off, fifty heads off in that one day. I carried 29 cases of bottled brandy, and 15 calabashes of chop for everybody, and there was play in every yard in town.

Human sacrifice at the death of a leading man had long been inseparable from the traditional ritual and religious requirements of a number of Iron Age cultures. It was present in the delta just because it also existed in the cultures of the forest belt – notably at Benin and in other forest states such as Ashanti. There, of course, one should not imagine it as necessarily a matter of terror or dismay. Acceptance of death by royal wives and relatives and servants was a question of moral integrity and of quick passage to an honourable place among the 'other half of humanity' – those who lived as spirits. What seems to have happened in some of the states that were profoundly affected by the coastal trade was that the custom of human sacrifice became increasingly distorted, both into a means of 'conspicuous consumption' by display of wealth in slaves, and as time went on, into an instrument of political repression.

Certainly this distortion grew worse. Its occasional terror reached a climax in the years of acute commercial insecurity that followed on the abolition of the slave trade. Then, with the mainstay of these societies cut suddenly away, superstition sank to gruesome depths: it was into these that Benin would fall. A European missionary has left an eye-witness account of the greatest of the funeral holocausts of the delta states – that which accompanied the death of Eyamba V of Old Calabar in 1847. 'Eyamba', he wrote, 'had many wives, of the best families in the country, as also many slave concubines . . . Of the former, thirty died the first day. How many by the poison ordeal, under imputation of witchcraft against his life, we never knew. Those who were honoured to accompany him into *Obio Ekpu*, or Ghost

Land, were summoned in succession by the message, once an honour, now a terror, "King calls you". The doomed one quickly adorned herself, drank off a mug of rum, and followed the messenger. Immediately she was in the hands of the executioners, who strangled her with a silk handkerchief . . .

'Every night the work of death went on in the river, and screams of the victims were heard both in the ships and the mission-house. Some were sent out bound in canoes, and deliberately drowned. Others returning from distant markets, chanting their paddle songs and glad to get home, but ignorant of what had taken place, were waylaid, knocked on the head and tumbled into the river.'

After Eyamba's funeral and its scenes of blood, Christian missionaries persuaded Egbo to pass a law forbidding human sacrifice. But the law was futile: an accretion from outside, it took no account of what the ruling oligarchy believed. Caught in its own trap of superstition, the law-making and law enforcing Leopard Society of rich men and prime merchants was powerless to control, much less to stop, these periodical though infrequent massacres. By now, moreover, 'sacrifice' had also become a political weapon that was useful to powerful men as a means of destroying rivals. Eyamba had already used it in this way after the death of his predecessor. 'Ordinary folk', Jones has written in his study of Calabar political organization, 'might believe in the genuineness of these witchcraft accusations; the more knowledgeable recognized them as a deliberate method of removing dangerous rivals, weakening powerful houses, and settling old scores.'

But where the law failed to stop human sacrifice, revolt succeeded. There now arose another society – a society, this time, of the slaves of the palm-oil plantations – that was vowed to self-protection. This society was called the Blood Men, but its principal effect (if not its stated object) was to save blood rather than to shed it. In the years after Eyamba's death the Blood Men gathered in the plantations round Old Calabar whenever an important man died, and marched to town in such force as to overawe any dignitary who should try to sacrifice a slave.

Such was the highly specialized society that was called to life by the long years of coastal partnership. Nowhere in the delta –

or, in different circumstances, along the whole of the West African coast – was the product quite the same: and often the contrasts were many and vivid. Yet by and large, along wide reaches of the Gulf of Guinea, there arose a special network of economic and political conditions that would have remained unthinkable but for the oversea trade in general, and the slave trade in particular.

These societies became what they were through African tradition, native ingenuity, local eccentricities of soil and geography and population; but also through the nature of the commerce in which they were engaged. Throughout the whole record one can see this last point repeatedly emphasized. It is clear in the delta. It is clear in the evolution of the small seaboard states of the Gold Coast littoral (the coast of modern Ghana), where no fewer than fourteen statelets were in existence by the seventeenth century. It is clear in the trading stations of the Slave Coast of old Dahomey. The European connection, insisting on slaves, became an inseparable part of a close-woven scheme of cause and effect which brought new societies into being and which kept them alive and energetic, though at bitter cost to others. It is this that makes the underlying theme of Antera Duke's diary.

Week after week the entries recall each other.

'We settled comey' – customs-dues exacted by the towns of Old Calabar from all trading ships – 'on board Potter ...'

'Captain Aspinall's ship goes away with 328 slaves ...'

'Potter and his tender went away with 350 slaves ...'

'At three o'clock after noon Captain Fairweather went away with 377 slaves ...'

'We saw the Combesboch tender go away with 280 slaves ...'

The slavers pulled up their anchors and warped to the broad estuary, broke their sails and took their course for the Americas, the sultry coastal waters heaving in reluctant wake for hour after hour, year after year, century after century. Such speed as they could make was the essence of their business: too long on the Coast would ruin their cargo and probably themselves; and they relied, as they had to rely, on a firm and efficient understanding with their friends ashore. By the end of the seventeenth century the partnership was known and valued and acknowledged. Its spreading influence was in full bloom.

5. Behind the Coast

THE history of the lands behind the Guinea seaboard is in an altogether better position than that of the hinterland of East Africa or the near-coastal regions of the Congo.

Here in the forest belt of Guinea there were powerful states and societies of which much is known and recorded. They had grown in strength and self-confidence from the early years of the present millennium, but their origins lay much further back in the remote beginnings of the West African Iron Age. These forest states had seldom or never lost touch with the trading empires of the Sudanese grasslands and, through them, with the peoples of the Nile and North Africa. Many elements of their broad and varied culture, whether in the symbols of religion, the manners of government or the techniques of art and industry, reveal an ancient and creative interweaving of ideas that were both native to the forest and assumed from northern neighbours.

It was from these forest states that Europe by way of Arab and Berber intermediaries drew the bulk of its supply of gold after medieval times. It was to them that grassland caravans took the copper of Darfur and Saharan Tegidda so that the master artists of Ife might cast their fine sculpture. For many centuries before European arrival on the coast, these countries were profoundly involved with the world to the north of them. But then, with that arrival, their horizon changed. So did the nature of their trade. And their history underwent a corresponding change.

Like all great changes of its kind, this one was slow to take effect and tortuous in its processes. No full review is possible or appropriate here.* All I want to do at this point is to show in outline what were the effects of the Atlantic trade on these large polities through all the period when slaving was its chief component. As will be seen, these effects were not invariably negative; but in the matter of the trade in captives they certainly were.

Developed from lineage systems of community, the major

*See Reading Guide.

states behind the coast were always too powerful for any European military threat before the advent of automatic firearms and modern military organization; and the latter appeared only late in the nineteenth century when the slave trade was virtually over.

Some of these states were of great antiquity and, by the eighteenth century, already had a long history of their own growth in size and development in structure. Others were relatively new centres of political and economic power, arising from structural reorganizations in the eighteenth century. All of them owed much to the long-distance trade with the Central and Western Sudan. They were, in short, *developed* states on any scale of measurement that history can apply. True enough, there were great differences between them and their contemporary states in western Europe. But these differences, in terms of what is nowadays called 'development', consisted chiefly in the technological backwardness of the African states. In all other respects these were not the differences between European 'development' and African 'un-development'; and it never occurred to anyone in those days to apply such categories.

Though mechanical only in a very small degree – they had, for example, no use for wheeled transport in their forests and wooded savannahs, or for literacy, itself the father of mechanical development – these states had advanced through perceptible stages of political, cultural and economic development. They had evolved complex systems of government with in-built checks and balances of a nature that Europeans have usually called constitutional. They had presided over the rise of professional administrations, codes and courts of law, means of law enforcement, professional fighting units and other aspects of what Europeans have usually recognized as civilization. In all ways available to the welfare of communities in the world of that time, they were indeed civilized states. And when the opportunities opened by the Atlantic trade reached them through coastal intermediaries, they invented or adapted ways of dealing with these opportunities as well.

To these notable states 'behind the coast' (though sometimes not far behind it) – Benin, Oyo, Asante, and others – the Atlantic trade proposed several advantages.

It offered a source of interesting and sometimes useful goods from hitherto unknown countries beyond the seas. It opened a view on different concepts of the world, new ideas, curious inventions, somewhat as though our own world of today were visited by an 'unidentified flying object' filled with 'goods from space'. It further promoted a new market for the products of these African countries: for gold, ivory, fast-dyed cloth, malageta (pepper), and, at first as little more than a minor item, for the 'disposable persons' who had lost their civic rights, their 'community membership', by sentence of the courts or by capture in warfare.

We have seen what this last item meant. The selling of a few 'disposable persons' rapidly led to the European demand for more; and after about 1650 this demand for 'disposable persons' carried all else before it.

To this demand these states reacted in diverse ways. The state of Benin, for example, seems never to have become deeply involved in the slave trade. Its prestigious neighbour to the west, Oyo, became involved only in the course of a fairly long stretch of years, but, eventually, was heavily involved. The Fon rulers to the west of Oyo, in Dahomey (modern Republic of Benin), seem to have gone into the trade reluctantly but soon became dependent on it, as did other states, for supplies of guns and gunpowder. It was much the same with Asante (modern Ghana).

All these states were increasingly affected by those aspects of spoliation, of violence and coercion, which the Atlantic trade implied. The hunt for captives, or self-defence against neighbours engaged in the same hunt, called for better weaponry. So the import of guns and gunpowder grew in scale and importance. Not necessarily because these firearms were militarily more effective than well-used swords and spears, since the firearms of those days were short in range and very uncertain in accuracy. But firearms became the badge of military effectiveness, and, in becoming that, they acquired a military value far in excess of their probable killing power. Besides, they got more lethal as the years went by.

All this became interwoven with less easily identified factors leading to instability. Often difficult to isolate and define, these factors arose from the long success of Iron Age development. Small states became larger. Rivalry for markets led to struggles for control over large areas. Kings with professional administrators at their call, as distinct from lineage elders or chiefs who were often king-makers, began to nourish new ambitions of personal power such as the older systems had disallowed. There came, in these indistinct but accumulating influences, a crisis of society. Old structures were challenged. Old hierarchies of control were called in question.

In these upheavals, wars, revolts and the rest, erupting in many regions behind the coast – in the forest regions of the Akan, in the country of the Fon, in the lands of the Yoruba, and increasingly across the savannahs of the Central and Western Sudan – we can perceive the beginnings of a struggle for a new organization of political and economic power. Far from 'standing still', as Europeans liked to think, the history of Africa – in this case of West Africa – was now in rapid movement towards new constellations of power, new governing ideas, a new attempt to master the problems of social growth and change.

It was at this juncture and in this situation that the peculiar nature of the Atlantic trade came in to exercise its influence. There might have been much that the rich experience of Europe, whose own 'movement of history' into structurally and technologically new forms of society had already come to fruition, could have offered to these African polities and peoples. Production by machinery was already underway in the more advanced parts of Europe. Science had recorded startling progress. Literacy remained a privilege, but a rarer one than in earlier times. A whole gamut of appropriate ideas and applications were on the scene.

But the Atlantic trade – and we shall come back to this point – lacked any of that 'development potential' which could have transferred the gains of European progress. It was concerned uniquely with narrow forms of exchange within fiercely guarded systems of monopoly. One can generalize the example of King Affonso's vain demand for shipbuilders; the last thing these Europeans could want, in fact, was the technological promotion of their African partners. If they exported guns to Africa it was only because, in their circumstances of internecine rivalry, they could not refuse them. But they certainly had no interest in prompting the know-how of firearms manufacture; and what went for guns went for everything else of this kind.

The essential factor in this exchange, as we shall see again, lay in an 'equation' between guns and captives. But out of this 'equation', or others that were comparable, nothing could emerge save a growth of the same form of exchange. And this growth could not, and it did not, develop into anything else, at least until the European demand for captives was terminated by Europeans themselves; so that the states behind the coast, involved as they were in any case with their own crisis of structure and authority, found themselves still further undermined and distracted by the very nature of the Atlantic trade.

Only in the wake of the slave trade, or only when the slave trade was in swift decline after about 1830, were the major European partners able to advance their own economy beyond this system of primitive extraction. Then they asked Africans to produce goods which did indeed begin to have a development potential, palm oil for soap and lubricants being perhaps the most notable of these products. By then the technological 'gap' between Europe and Africa had become very wide. By then, too, the capitalism of the major European powers had developed far towards a new imperialism. And in due course this new imperialism strode upon the scene. The European demand now was not for gold or captives, ivory, pepper, or palm oil; it was for territorial possession. The colonial period began, and Africans, far from being able to continue their own adjustment to the modern world, became for many decades the mere objects of the history of other and intrusive peoples.

The sentences I have just written telescope a long and complex process. All this took time, a long time. Yet the records of the pre-colonial decades, in this respect, all point in the same direction.

6. Disaster at Benin

WHEN the early Portuguese voyagers reached Benin they found it the powerful capital of a considerable empire. In 1500 the city was a league long from gate to gate. A large moat, 'very wide and deep', sufficed for defence. Its rule was said to be effective over an area that was about the size of southern England and Wales. All this is confirmed by Bini tradition: Egharevba, the historian of Benin, believes that the city entered its greatest period under *Oba* Ewuare the Great, who ruled in the years immediately preceding Portuguese arrival.

Though continuously in Benin throughout the sixteenth century, the Portuguese do not seem to have written much about it. They were well received as traders or missionaries, and on at least one occasion the king in Lisbon received an ambassador from the *Oba* of Benin: but their records, or at least those so far published, are disappointingly thin. With the coming of the Dutch at the beginning of the seventeenth century the written sources greatly improve, for the Dutch were deeply interested in their trading partners. They wrote letters to their principals in Holland that are full of useful details of Benin.

'The Towne seemeth to be very great, when you enter it,' says one of these Dutch accounts, evidently dating from 1602: 'You goe into a great broad street, not paved, which seemeth to be seven or eight times broader than the Warmoes Street in Amsterdam; which goeth right out, and never crooketh, and where I was lodged with Mattheus Cornelison it was at least a quarter of an houres going from the gate, and yet I could not see to the end of the street . . .

'At the gate where I entered on horsebacke, I saw a very high Bulwarke, very thick of earth, with a very deepe broad ditch, but it was drie, and full of high trees . . . The gate is a reasonable good Gate, made of wood after their manner, which is to be shut, and there always there is watch holden . . .'

But the rulers of Benin, though hospitable, were jealous of their authority and perhaps apprehensive for it, too. They would allow these traders from Europe no more than a limited freedom.

'When you are in the great Street aforesaid, you see many great streets on the sides thereof, which also goes right forth, but you cannot see the end of them, by reason of their great length. A man might write more of the situation of this Towne, if he might see it as you may see the Townes of Holland, which is not permitted there, by one that alwaies goes with you – some men say, that he goeth with you, because you should have no harme done unto you, but yet you goe no further than he will let you.'

Benin was prosperous and comfortable in those early years of the seventeenth century. 'The Houses in this Towne', continues this same Dutch report, 'stand in good order, one close and even with the other, as the Houses in Holland stand.' Steps led up to the entry of the houses of 'men of qualitie', and here there were galleries 'where a man may sit drie; which Gallerie every morning is made cleane by their Slaves, and in it there is a Mat spread for men to sit on . . . but they have other places besides, as Kitchens and other roomes . . .'

The palace of the king, the *Oba*, was almost a 'Forbidden City' within Benin. 'The King's Court is very great, within it having many great four-square Plaines, which round about them have Galleries, wherein there is alwais watch kept; I was so far within the Court, that I passed over four such great Plaines, and wheresoever I looked, still I saw Gates upon Gates, to goe into other places, and in that sort I went as far as any Netherlander was, which was to the Stable where his best Horses stood . . .'

When Olfert Dapper published his great collection of African reports some fifty years later, he was able to include an engraving which showed how Benin appeared to the Dutch travellers of the early seventeenth century. There, in that well-known picture, one may see the *Oba* riding in ceremonial procession with the city massed behind him in its dense urbanity and surmounted by the little turrets of the *Oba*'s wooden Kremlin, each bearing 'a copper bird with its wings spread'.

John Barbot, who was on the Guinea Coast between 1678 and 1682, says that 'the inhabitants of this great city are for the generality very civil and good-natured people, easy to be dealt with, condescending to what Europeans require of them in a civil way, and very ready to return double the presents we make them . . .' And although Barbot was writing at second-hand or even third-hand, borrowing from Dapper who had borrowed from other Dutchmen, he was undoubtedly in a good position to know Benin's reputation among his fellow-traders and travellers.

These were impressed with the efficiency of Benin's government by a system of 'king in council'. Barbot records that 'the king might be considered just and equitable, as desiring continually his officers to administer justice exactly, and to discharge their duties conscientiously . . . He seldom passes one day, without holding a cabinet council with his chief ministers, for dispatching of the many affairs brought before him . . . appeals from inferior courts of judicature in all parts of the kingdom, and audiences to strangers, or concerning the affairs of war and other emergencies . . .' Though based on hearsay, these notes probably offer a fair picture of the main structure of government in Benin at least up to the latter part of the seventeenth century.

There was extensive trade between Benin and vassal states or neighbours that were not vassals. Much of this trade, perhaps most of it, was a royal monopoly; but it was one that was much abused, as the Dutch soon found, by the *Oba*'s chiefs and agents who were entrusted with the duty of bargaining with Europeans. No foreigner, according to Dapper, could bargain or buy except through the *Oba*'s delegates or merchants whom he had empowered for the purpose (to whom, in other words, the *Oba* had 'farmed out' the privilege of dealing with Europeans); and both sides thereafter were at the mercy of these agents and merchants. Sales could take months to complete.

Internal trade was more loosely organized. 'They also have severall places in the Towne, where they keep their Markets; in one place they have their great Market Day, called Dia de Ferro' – a witness to long Portuguese presence here – 'and in another place they hold their little market, called Ferro . . . They bring great store of Ironworke to sell there, and Instruments to fish withall, others to plow and to till the land withall; and many weapons, as Assagaies and Knives . . . This Market and Traffique is there very orderly holden.' Barbot lists the exports of Benin as cotton cloths, jasperstones, skins, ivory, pepper, blue coral beads and female slaves: no men slaves, he says, could be taken from Benin whether they were foreigners or not.

This 'city-empire' had trouble with its neighbours like every other state: sometimes it was successful, thanks to the valour of its kings, while at other times it failed. Like Oyo, Benin imported firearms to bolster the power of its armies and even, in the sixteenth century, made some use of European mercenaries by alliance with the Portuguese.

The Dutch accounts show that these wars were generally to Benin's advantage up to the middle of the seventeenth century. But after that a steep decline set in. Earlier wars of conquest were now giving way to wars for slaves, and the fabric of Benin society seems also to have suffered from this. In 1700 the well-informed Dutch agent at Elmina, William Bosman, was writing home to Holland that Benin no longer deserved the name of city. 'Formerly this village was very thick and close-built,' he told his employers in Amsterdam, 'but now the Houses stand like poor men's corn, widely distant from each other.' By this time, Fage adds in a modern comment, 'the continual warfare was destroying the prosperity and even the structure of the state. Large areas of the country had become depopulated and uncultivated. The armies returned with fewer and fewer slaves and sometimes destroyed each other in conflicts for what little booty there was to be found.'

The decay in Bini state power in any case continued, and fresh ways of manipulating or using that power at the centre evidently failed to reverse the trend. The Atlantic trade could do nothing to help, but it seems that it did less to harm than in some other regions. War-captives were sold to the maritime traders who continued to visit the Benin river, and possibly others were obtained by purchase from neighbours. But 'there is no evidence', Ryder tells us, 'that Benin ever organised a great slave-trading network similar to that which supplied the eastern delta' of the Niger river, or indeed that Benin ever engaged in systematic raiding for captives. Ryder quotes an evidently characteristic case for 1798, when English ships bid for a total of nearly 20,000 captives in the eastern delta as against a mere thousand in the Benin river. 'Benin either could not or would not become a slave-trading state on the grand scale.' If Benin continued to decay, it was from failure to carry through those modernizing adjustments which could have released new energies. Instead, a local priesthood acquired the power of something like a theocratic tyranny, and, with this, progress turned back upon itself.

A little of this may be traced in the decline of Benin's famous sculpture. Inherited from Ife, Benin metalwork was of high technical competence from, at any rate, the fifteenth century. Metal-casters in this city knew how to make heads and figures with great artistic skill and economy of metal, and their art in its best period – the fifteenth and sixteenth centuries – would have been outstanding in any continent. It was, one should note, specifically an art of the *Oba*'s court, drawing on royal *motifs*, celebrating the *Oba*'s power, portraying his soldiers and his allies, and always distinct from the popular work of the Edo peoples of whom the Bini were a part: this popular work, being a branch of the wide-ranging metal craftsmanship of the Lower Niger region, possessed a much more relaxed style and less formal choice of subject.

The courtly art of Benin grew notably coarser during the years of slaving warfare. After the end of the sixteenth century, in William Fagg's judgement, the heads and figures 'became much more stereotyped and lacking in sensitivity, even though gaining a certain impressive quality'. By now the emphatic humanism of Ife heads was completely eclipsed; and one may perhaps even draw an instructive parallel – without meaning to suggest that naturalism is necessarily 'better' than abstraction – between the heavy styles of late Benin work, increasingly crude in conception and dense in weight of metal, and Benin's political decline after the middle of the eighteenth century. Moreover, this process of coarsening can be shown to have continued: the heads became clumsier and more gross in shape and feeling as the slaving years passed by and the old skills were overborne or set aside.

By now, sharpening the anxiety of Benin's rulers, the delta states were in full bloom. They imported firearms of their own and defied the *Oba* as and when they would. Here the consequences were much the same as with Oyo: firearms could bolster the power of a central government, but they could also, in the hands of vassal states, lead to painful disintegration.

In defending their privilege and power, the priests of the *Oba* knew of only one final sanction, and that was ritual sacrifice.

Once again one should be careful of the distinction between customary sacrifice and its distortion. 'No person of rank or wealth', Dapper had recorded of mid-seventeenth-century Benin, 'dies there unaccompanied by bloodshed.' Yet this, one may repeat, had been bloodshed of a special kind. 'They let down the corpse into the pit,' a Frenchman recorded of the 1670s (writing of what Europeans had reported about Benin at that time), 'and then the most beloved domesticks of both sexes earnestly beg to be allow'd the favour of going into it, to wait and attend on their master in the other life; but this honour is granted only to the best qualified among them, and those the deceased king seemed most fond of, which often occasions great murmurings and discussions amongst them.'

Some two centuries later, discussing the same point, Rattray would make the same explanation of sacrificial rites in old Asante. There too the death of famous men was accompanied by bloodshed, but not, once again it seems, for blood-thirsty reasons. 'In the first place, the persons killed on these occasions were supposed to resume after death their various duties under their royal master . . . The ideas and beliefs of the men who acted as executioners on these occasions and of their "victims" with regard to death were the same. Death was merely a transition, like birth, from one kind of life to another.' Secondly, Rattray thought, the attitude towards death in those days was 'one of comparative indifference', since people were not filled 'with any vague, troublesome misgivings' about what would happen to them after death. Thirdly, most of those killed at funerals were 'either prisoners of war, whose lives had only been spared for this purpose, or criminals who had been tried and sentenced to death, but like the former class had been preserved for such an occasion'.

But most important of all, in Rattray's view, there was the positive wish for death among some of the highest in the land – 'high court officials, relatives and wives of the dead monarch, who, no longer having any desire to live once "the great tree had fallen", compelled their relatives to slay them'. And Rattray, who knew the failings of the Asante and yet loved them for their virtues, concluded that: 'The man or woman who, like some of these old Asante, was ready to die for an ideal, however misguided and mistaken it may have been, nevertheless is of the stuff which goes to the making of a virile and courageous nation, and is entitled to our respect and admiration.'

Little of this can be said of the sacrificial habits of Benin government during the last years of decline in the late nineteenth century, any more than similar explanations can be valid for the occasional massacres that the Blood Men stopped. These disasters were the measure of an institutional failure – a failure which should be attributed not to a lack of natural capacity but to a combination of circumstance that pushed steadily towards ruin. It is obviously true, of course, that this ruin was of limited extent. It was particular to Benin institutions, not general to the whole society. It left much of society intact, for these were strong and fertile peoples who have easily survived those bludgeoning years. Yet the old order and dignity of Benin were none the less undermined.

This combination of circumstance may be traced in the Bini system of royal trading monopoly, but even more decisively in the traditional sanctions of Bini religion. As early as the 1780s one may see how matters were tending. Already trade was less than in former times, and already the priesthood seems to have fallen back on its final sanction of human sacrifice in an effort to restore 'the good old days'. Every year, according to one British visitor, three or four people were sacrificed as 'offerings to the sea, to direct vessels to find their course to this horrid climate'.

As the coastal pressures grew stronger and Benin's trade continued to shrink, the priests redoubled their frenzy until Benin, towards the end of the nineteenth century, indeed became 'a city of blood'. The threat of European invasion was almost certainly the last and fatal incentive; and the *Oba*, by now, was powerless to stop the slaughter even when he had wished to do so. 'The king', wrote Captain Gallwey in 1893, 'struck me as being very willing to listen to reason, but he is tied down by fetish customs, and until the power of the fetish priests is done away with', there could be no peace. A couple of years later the British sent in a military force and made peace under a new power. And when the colonial interruption was brought at last to an end, sixty-five years later, the way became clear for institutional adjustment to the needs and opportunities of the modern world.

7. One Gun: One Slave

IT is one thing to note the failure of African kings and governing institutions to parry the disintegrating and destructive pressure of the oversea slave trade. It is quite another to suggest that, given their circumstances and opportunities, they could have succeeded in doing so.

They were in any case never offered the chance of success. At no point were they presented with any choice except that of forgoing European trade altogether – to the almost certain profit of rivals and their own peril – or else of surrendering to the incessant demands of Europe. Cases were not lacking when African rulers struggled against this bitter choice, and tried to limit or even to abolish the export of slaves; but these efforts were always – and, as one may think, necessarily – fruitless.

Affonso of Congo was not the only African ruler who attempted to free his country from the barbs of the slaving hook. A first-hand Swedish report of 1787 tells of an African king of Senegal in the far west of Africa who, 'very much to his honour, enacted a law that no slaves whatever should be marched through his territories'.

This laudable measure could only remain a dead letter. For 'at this time several French vessels lay at anchor in the Senegal [river], waiting for slaves. The route of the black traders in consequence of this edict of the king was stopped, and the slaves carried to other parts. The French, unable on this account to complete their cargoes, remonstrated with the king. He was, however, very unpropitious to their representations, for he returned the presents which had been sent him by the [French] Senegal Company, of which I myself was a witness, declaring at the same time that all the riches of that company should not divert him from his design. In this situation of affairs, the French were obliged to have recourse to their old friends, the Moors. These, who had before shewn themselves so ready on such occasions, were not less ready and active in this. They set off in parties to surprise the unoffending negroes and to carry them all the calamities of war . . .'

Sixty years earlier the rising power of Dahomey on the Slave Coast had prompted another effort of the same kind. In 1727, invading the towns of the Slave Coast, the king of Dahomey captured an Englishman called Captain Bullfinch Lamb and tried, through him, to reduce the local impact of the slave trade – a scourge from which his own people had suffered fearfully in the recent past. After holding him in honourable imprisonment at Abomey, the Dahomeyan capital some sixty miles from the sea, the king allowed Lamb to take ship for England, giving him a present of 320 ounces of gold and 80 slaves, and bidding him inform his masters (the phrasing, of course, is Lamb's) that 'the Natives would sell themselves to us on condition of not being carried away'.

This proposal met with no favour in London, needless to say, since no investor had any interest in buying slaves for use in West Africa; but the trading figures none the less show a remarkable decline after Dahomey had won control of the points of actual export on this Slave Coast.

Hitherto – that is, before 1727 – this fifty-mile segment of palm-fringed seaboard had earned its name in full measure, for its little 'city-states' of Ardra and Ouidah (Whydah or Fida) and Jacquin were tremendous deliverers of slaves. Of Ouidah, a leader among these ports, Barbot could write in the 1680s that 'they are so diligent in the slave trade that they are able to deliver a thousand every month'. And a British naval surgeon some forty years later was still able to note that this was 'the greatest trading place in the coast of Guinea, selling off as many slaves, I believe, as all the rest together: forty or fifty sail (French, English, Portuguese and Dutch) freighting thence every year'. Europeans had made regular establishments here, and in 1677 the Portuguese had even built themselves a little fort at Ouidah so as to manage the trade more efficiently. In course of time this old fort of St John became officially part of the Portuguese 'province of São Tomé and Principe'. A curious fragment of the past, it remained in Portuguese hands until 1961, when the newly independent Republic of Dahomey (now the Republic of Benin) brought the Portuguese presence here to an end.

Up to 1727, when Dahomey broke through successfully to the coast and achieved direct contact with the European traders who were there, annual exports from Ardra and Ouidah were running at about 20,000 captives a year. Thereafter they seem to have fallen sharply and never to have recovered their former scale. The governor of Britain's Slave Coast trading post, Archibald Dalzell, reported in 1789 that 'the greatest number now sent off from this place [Ouidah] and the two great kingdoms of Ardra and Dahomey, together with several smaller ones united to them, is only 5,500'. In a period when total delivery of slaves from Africa was touching levels that were higher than ever before, the Slave Coast no longer deserved its reputation.

For this reason and for several others, Dahomey was a state-organization which remains of high interest in the study of African institutions. Here I want only to draw attention to one or two elements in its extraordinary condition. They show very clearly why the wounds of the slave trade had become really inescapable.

Like the city-states of the delta – and like those of the Slave Coast – Dahomey was a child of the African-European connection. It seems to have emerged at the beginning of the seventeenth century, or about 1625, when the Fon people of the country behind the Slave Coast drew together in self-defence against the slave-raiding of their eastern neighbours, the Yoruba of Oyo. No doubt the Fon were interested in defending themselves from coastal raiders too: whenever the king of Ouidah was short of slaves for sale, declared a British report of 1721, 'he marches an army, and depopulates. He, and the king of Ardra adjoining, commit great depredations inland.'

But the new state of Dahomey could defend itself effectively only if it could lay hold on adequate supplies of firearms and ammunition. And these it could obtain only by trade with Ardra and Ouidah – and, of course, only in exchange for slaves.

Hence Dahomey's power to resist Oyo (itself in turn subjected to the same pressure) depended on delivering slaves to the coast: the drastic but inescapable alternatives were to enslave others – in order to buy firearms – or risk enslavement oneself. This indeed was the inner dynamic of the slaving connection with Europe; and it pushed Dahomey, as it pushed other states, into wholesale participation in slaving. No single state could safely or even possibly withstand this combination of slaves and guns. Almost from the first, and in spite of the reluctance we have noted, Dahomey was caught in the slave trade's ruinous chain of cause and effect.

Even so, their new safety was precarious for the Fon so long as it rested on the will or whim of the coastal towns. Like other colleagues in the delta, these energetic middlemen of the Slave Coast were well aware of the strength of their monopoly, and they defended it and used it as vigorously and ruthlessly as they could. In the end Dahomey found their exactions intolerable. They refused to allow Dahomey to sell its captives to the Europeans except through them, and this was the immediate reason why the fourth king of Dahomey, Agaja, waged successful war on them in 1727 and seized their towns. There on the coast itself, in Biobaku's words, Dahomey made contact with slave dealers of several European nations and Brazil, 'and exchanged slaves captured in forays for rifles and cannon by means of which their forces became irresistible to their inadequately armed neighbours'.

Huge quantities of firearms were poured into West Africa during the major period of the slave trade; and the state of Dahomey, increasingly a militarized autocracy, was among those that had the doubtful benefit. At the height of the eighteenth-century commerce, gunsmiths in Birmingham alone were exporting muskets to Africa at the rate of between 100,000 and 150,000 a year, and it was common talk that one Birmingham gun rated one Negro slave. This last was Birmingham sales talk rather than a statement of fact, since African traders were seldom willing to sell a captive only for a gun and demanded other goods as well; yet the spirit of the saying was true enough. Firearms had become indispensable to the Guinea trade.

European dealers on the coast might regret this flood of weapons, for it strengthened the bargaining power of their African partners: there was nothing they could do about it. Like the Africans, they too were caught in the chain of cause and effect. They had to have slaves, and to get slaves they had to pay with guns.

Even if European traders had wanted to refuse guns, they were far too distrustful of one another to operate any sort of common policy: as William Bosman observed at Elmina on the Gold Coast in 1700, the Europeans could never unite, and each European felt obliged to sell what Africans would otherwise obtain, if he should refuse, from his rivals. And the Africans, on their side, were generally in the same case although here and there, and notably in the delta, they sometimes found enough unity among themselves to apply a boycott on their European partners.

Dahomey became famous – or infamous – in European eyes for the autocratic power of its rulers. It departed from the general pattern of African state organization in being first and foremost a polity that was organized for war and built, almost directly, on superior weapon-power. It was seldom at peace with its neighbours in the east, who regularly invaded the Dahomeyans and whom the Dahomeyans invaded in return; and it fought a long battle for retention of its coastal base, where the maritime towns sometimes secured help from Europeans and sometimes from the Yoruba of Oyo. Its rulers even raised a 'Praetorian Guard' of several thousand fighting women-at-arms, devoted to their persons and reputedly valorous in war. More or less continual warfare confirmed the kings' autocratic power and seems to have encouraged these monarchs, whether for religious reasons or for motives of prestige, or both, into something of the same bloody practices as occurred in Benin.

Late in the eighteenth century an English visitor, Robert Norris, described the royal establishment at Abomey. He took with him 'a very handsome sedan chair and a chamber organ' and with these presents was well received at the palace. 'On each side of it was a human head, recently cut off, lying on a flat stone with the face down, and the bloody end of its neck towards the entrance. In the guard-house were about forty women, armed with a musket and a cutlass each' – these were the 'Amazons' of Dahomey – 'and twenty eunuchs with bright iron rods in their hands.'

Entering an inner court with one of the king's ministers, Norris was received by two other ministers; all three Africans 'knelt down and kissed the ground, pronouncing aloud some of the king's titles as we walked across this court, in which were ranged six human heads'. At last, in a third court, they were greeted by the king himself, 'seated in a handsome chair of crimson velvet, ornamented with gold fringe and placed on a carpet in a spacious cool piazza . . . smoking tobacco and wearing a gold-laced hat with a plume of ostrich feathers'. The king inquired of Norris 'after the health of his brother, King George', and the visit concluded with Norris buying thirty-two slaves.

Such visits to Abomey were rare because the policy of the Dahomeyan kings, no doubt fearing European penetration, was to forbid them. In their day-to-day dealings the traders on the coast were obliged to arrange their affairs with the king's 'viceroy' there, the *Yavougou* (as Dalzell wrote the word) whose by no means empty title signified 'captain of the white men'. These traders understandably disliked Dahomey's power and generally regretted that the coastal towns had lost their independence, but they seem to have had a good deal of respect for the Dahomeyan achievement. And aside from their callous attitude to human life – in which, of course, they were scarcely peculiar in the world of the eighteenth century – the kings of Dahomey may well be thought to have done the best they could with the grim alternatives that were open to them. Their kingdom may have constituted to the outside world, as Biobaku says, 'an odious stronghold of slavery and human sacrifice'; but then the outside world had a useful knack of overlooking its own destructive habits. More slaves were thrown alive into the Atlantic by slave-ship captains, sacrificing to their god of profitability, than were ever beheaded by the kings of Dahomey or the *Obas* of Benin.*

At least to their own peoples these rulers brought a new security. If they bolstered their prestige with a lavish display of human heads, they also boldly faced the implications of musket warfare and sheltered the Fon from the worst ravages of slaving. Out of the deepening chaos of the near-coastal regions they carved a state

*Notorious but not unique was the master of the Liverpool slaver *Zong*, 1783, who caused 133 slaves to be flung overboard alive since they were 'sick or weak, or not likely to live'. He argued that if the slaves should die a natural death on board ship their loss would be borne by the owners, while the underwriters would have to pay if the slaves were thrown living into the sea. So he threw them overboard before they had time to die on his hands. In the event the owners did claim for these slaves, but the underwriters refused to pay the insurance. The owners then brought suit in the Court of King's Bench. They were awarded the verdict.

where law and order, if often summary and at steady cost in the enslavement of others, none the less largely prevailed. It was not glorious; but nor was the world they had to live in.

Just as this militarized kingdom was the product of the African-European connection as moved by the slaving-musket 'equation', so was its ultimate fate inseparable from the further development of European pressure. In the nineteenth century the Europeans shifted their policy. Hitherto they had been content with trading: now they desired conquest. Dahomey found itself faced with a new battle for monopolist control: no longer with Africans or with weakly manned trading posts at Ouidah and Ardra, but with the full might of industrialized Europe. Little by little, the major European powers came to see the Fon state of Dahomey less as a useful trading partner and more as an obstacle to European territorial possession. Given the development of European imperialism – French, in this case – eventual confrontation became unavoidable once the fourth Fon king had seized the coastal towns in 1727 and showed that he could hold them.

Yet the new threat was slow in coming to a head. It was not until 1851 that France obtained a foothold on the coast in the shape of a 'protectorate' over the trading town of Porto Novo; and not until 1888 that Dahomey and France came to blows. Thereafter the process went swiftly: King Behanzin of Dahomey bought arms from the Germans, while the French landed two thousand men at Porto Novo and invaded the country, defeating Behanzin's army in 1892, and declaring Dahomey a French colony two years later.

This transition from trading partnership to European conquest occurred elsewhere. As an integral phase in the European-African connection it can be traced almost as clearly – this time with the British – on the neighbouring Gold Coast and in the forests of Asante. There too a strong new African state would exploit the slaving-musket equation in order to build a zone of security, only to find itself, as European policy shifted towards direct involvement, faced with a power that it could not in the end resist.

8. Asante: The New Battle for the Coast

IMAGINE, for a moment, that the ships of powerful nations had arrived in the Middle Ages, coming from an unknown continent, on the most remote shores of northern Europe. They would have found sparse and unsophisticated peoples, organized in small clans and family groups, who were accustomed to living on the ultimate frontiers of their world and for whom the power and prestige of civilization lay behind them in the hinterland. Such was the situation of the peoples of the Gold Coast seaboard – although the parallel, of course, is not exact – when the Portuguese and other Europeans reached them in the fifteenth and sixteenth centuries.

Most of these small peoples had lived here since times beyond memory; others had entered the coastal plains – a narrow land between the forest and the sea – during the migrations of the Akan in the twelfth century or earlier. They were organized in little units and owed allegiance to more numerous and powerful peoples in the forest hills on their northern skyline. But they wore this allegiance loosely, since there was little tribute they could pay or service they could render.

The peoples of the forest were in a different situation. They too were a mingling of old inhabitants and immigrants from the north. But a complex process of state formation had long been in vigorous growth among them; and this process had culminated many years before the ocean trade began to flourish, in the early states of the Akan and their immediate neighbours. These drew their strength from the efficiency of their organization but also from a thriving trade in gold with the states of the Sudanese grasslands to their north. Asante (Ashanti) and the lands nearby were famous as the source of gold.

It was with the southern outliers of this forest state-system that Europeans eventually made contact: with Akwamu and Akim, Denkyira and Adansi and others. But the contact was slow in making, for the trade and preoccupations of these forest peoples all lay in the north, and they had never looked for profit or peril in the south.

Meanwhile the Europeans landed and built castles with the good will – and to the advantage, since the newcomers paid rent – of the little peoples of the coast itself. One can imagine that the coastal chiefs were delighted with this unexpected source of new importance for themselves: they were now, after all, no longer 'at the back of beyond'. Thus the Portuguese captain who built Elmina Castle, Diogo da Azambuja, had no difficulty in securing the agreement of Casamansa, the local chief, 'a savage man ... yet of good understanding and ... clear judgement'.

Azambuja ran into plenty of difficulties in the course of the work, and once it was done he lost no time in rubbing in the lesson of his new-built strength by burning down Casamansa's village. Quarrels, skirmishes, sieges and reprisals were to be a regular part of the African-European record on this coast for several hundred years. More often than not, though, the mutual interest in trade was strong enough to overcome and always, in the end, to survive such brief affrays. Over the years a partnership evolved and led to the building of some forty European castles on this 400-kilometre reach of undulating cliff between Beyin in the west and Keta in the east – more or less the seaward boundaries of Ghana today. Yet it was invariably an unstable partnership that was subject to sudden interruptions or outbursts of war.

There were two main reasons for this instability: rivalry between Europeans and rivalry between Africans, each fighting for monopoly control of their own side of the trade – the Dutch, for example, against the Portuguese; or Akwamu against Denkyira. This rivalry sharpened on either side as the profits of the gold and slave trade became increasingly apparent to Europeans, and the need for firearms and other European goods made itself increasingly felt among Africans; and in the end, as on the Slave Coast, this dual struggle for monopoly resolved itself into an outright battle between Europeans and Africans, the bloody prelude to colonial rule. But for the most part of the connection here there was no thought of European conquest.

All the Europeans wished for on the coast was to defend themselves against each other and to dominate, so far as was convenient and possible, the little statelets on whose land the European castles were built. In the event it proved easier to dominate each other than to subdue the Africans. One can see this best in the Dutch experience. They were the strongest of the European maritime powers in the seventeenth century and, as such, they took Elmina from the Portuguese, built forts of their own and tried hard to keep out interlopers. They also tried to keep out the inland states who were now challenging, more and more openly, this new-found European power on the coast.

'The better to curb the blacks along the coast and to engross the whole trade,' explains a French report of the late seventeenth century, certainly accurate for the general trend though competitive and therefore unfriendly, 'the Dutch erected small forts at Butri, Shama, Cape Coast, Abomau, Kormantin and Accra, pretending to the blacks that they did it to protect them against the outrages and insults of their neighbouring enemies of the inland country, who used often to attack them.

'Being thus grown powerful, the more to keep down the blacks and prevent their attempting anything against them, [the Dutch] laid duties on their fishery . . . forbade the coastal Africans under severe penalties to hold any correspondence or trade with other Europeans . . . and proceeded to lord it over them absolutely . . . though, on the other hand, they are obliged to pay yearly [taxes] to the native kings for the forts they have there.'

This kind of bullying never worked for long. It offended against the partnership in trade that was fundamental to the whole arrangement. Besides, the inland states were too powerful to be pushed aside. At Accra in the 1680s 'the three European forts have little authority over the blacks, and serve only to secure the trade, the blacks here being of a temper not to suffer anything to be imposed on them by Europeans'. At about this time the important state of Akwamu seized the Danish castle of Christianborg and 'forced the Danes' general to fly to the Dutch to save his life'. Yet Akwamu needed the Danes just as much as the Danes needed Akwamu; and a little later the Danish Government was allowed to buy back its castle for fifty marks of gold and an agreement to forgo any claim to reparations. And this was no isolated case.

This situation persisted along the Gold Coast for decades and even centuries, now with one system of alliances and rivalries in the ascendant, and now with another. Whatever disputes and squabbles might separate the partners for a time – and quarrels were many – they always came together again and patched up their disagreements, so that some kind of peace amongst them generally held firm.

Other pressures were in play among the inland peoples. Between them there was always a natural tension, inevitably resolved in occasional bouts of conquest and absorption, because they were organized in centralizing states which stood in rivalry with one another. But the attractive power of European trade, and afterwards the absolute need for secure access to supplies of guns and ammunition, greatly sharpened these natural tensions until they broke increasingly into wars and invasions. And here too the slaving-musket equation led to a repetition, if in somewhat different terms, of experience on the Slave Coast. This equation may be overstated but it certainly played a part in helping to build and maintain the Asante empire.

Like Dahomey, this powerful and ambitious empire was the product both of African political skills and of the driving pressures of the coastal trade. Unlike Dahomey, Asante was fashioned not into a militarized autocracy but into a militarized confederation under the acknowledged leadership of a single ruler, the Asantehene. It emerged at the end of the seventeenth century – at a time, that is, when scattered units of Akan people in the Asante forest were subject to intensified raiding by their overlords, themselves responding to the increased demand for slaves from the European forts. The immediate overlords of the Akan who came together in the Asante Union were the rulers of Denkyira, then in close alliance with Europeans on the coast.

To assert their independence and meet the increasing threats to their security, the various branches of the Asante had to solve two problems: that of finding a common loyalty, and that of developing a military power. They were successful in solving both these problems thanks to two outstanding men, the one a great military leader and the other a political initiator of remarkable quality; and both must be reckoned among the memorable figures of pre-colonial African history. Osei Tuto led the fight for independence: Okomfo Enokye forged a political alliance into an indissoluble union.

Hitherto the Akan clans and family groups of the central forest zone had recognized a loose relationship with one another, but stood apart, each in its own separateness, in different lineage groups of ancestral loyalty. They had plenty of reasons for standing together, but that was not their habit. Now the habit of standing apart became painfully expensive. Already, in their divided weakness, they were obliged to pay tribute to Denkyira, and the prospect was of heavier tribute as the coastal trade developed. Besides, so long as they were divided, they would never be able to claim a profitable share in this growing business with the coast. They were in much the same position as the Fon of Dahomey: either they submitted to raiding by their more powerful neighbours, or they made themselves strong enough to repel raiders and take a hand in the coastal trade on their own account.

They chose the second course. But first they had to cement their union. They had to find a sense of religious and national community. The traditions of Asante, as relayed by Ward, show how this was done.

'One Friday a great gathering was held at Kumasi; and there Enokye brought down from the sky, with darkness and thunder, and in a thick cloud of white dust, a wooden stool adorned with gold, which floated to earth and alighted gently on Osei Tuto's knees. This stool, Enokye announced, contained the spirit of the whole Ashanti nation, and all its strength and bravery depended on the safety of the stool . . . This was the origin of the famous Sika Agua Kofi, "Friday's Golden Stool", of Ashanti, which in spite of many vicissitudes still survives today with its unifying power unimpaired.'

Okomfo Enokye, comments Ward, 'was a statesman of genius. He succeeded where the Hellenes of old had failed: he brought his people triumphantly through their war of liberation and he held them together afterwards.' By about 1700 Asante had utterly defeated Denkyira, thrown off its yoke of tribute, and broken through to the sea. From now on, if with many setbacks and interruptions, the armies and traders of Asante would scarcely ever lose their hold on the direct route to the coast. It was to their supreme ruler, the Asantehene, that the Dutch at Elmina now had to pay their rent after 1700 (the Dutch 'note of agreement', held previously by Denkyira, having passed into Ashanti keeping) and throughout the eighteenth century this military nation con-

At first the British established diplomatic relations with the Asantehene at his capital of Kumasi in the Asante forest. Then, with the tide of imperialism at its flood, they invaded Asante. After bitter wars and many setbacks they conquered the country. Yet the last act in this transformation of the old slaving partnership into the colonial system was not enacted until 1902, when Asante was incorporated into the British Empire: only fifty-five years, though none could have foreseen it then, before the people of the Asante Union regained their independence as part of the new state of Ghana.

9. The Partnership Cracks

MANY influences were at work in reducing the old connection between equals into one that Europeans would entirely dominate. Not least among these, ironically enough, was the ending of the oversea slave trade.

The ending of the trade was of tremendous significance for both Africans and Europeans. It upset the trading habits of three full centuries, undermined systems of government, disrupted social customs and opened the way for European intervention. But all this has to be seen as a process, a growth, a labour of many years. Britain's legislators might at one stroke declare the trade abolished in 1807, but that was only a beginning. Even if Britain had no longer any interest in slaves, others were differently placed; and these others continued to collect slaves as and when they could and often in large numbers. Not for seventy or eighty years after the British act of abolition would the last slavers creep from West African harbours and defy the risks of British naval arrest on their passage to the Americas. It was during these decades of the nineteenth century that the old equality degenerated, at first slowly and confusedly and then with gathering speed, until Europe had decisively the upper hand.

Two hundred years of slaving had produced along some parts of this littoral, as these pages have tried to show, a society that was specially adjusted to the trade. This society could survive an end to slaving only with considerable adjustment. Abolition did in fact produce a social crisis of more or less severity in all these states; and it was generally the case that European opinion – as in East Africa – mistook this crisis and its accompanying phenomena of insecurity and confusion for a natural inability of Africans to govern themselves in peace and tolerance. This misunderstanding, however easy in the circumstances, had violent results. Flying the banners of 'trusteeship and civilization', European nations now began to interpret the particular effects of the old coastal partnership – on which, of course, they had built much of their own prosperity – as the general and inevitable consequence of 'leaving Africans to themselves'. The real trouble, in terms of that particular argument, was that the Africans had not been left to themselves. They had been drawn into a partnership in exploitation which had far greater wealth-accumulating potential and stimulus for the Europeans than for them. However unwittingly, they had helped the expansion of European systems, and, if indirectly, the enormous widening of the technological 'gap' between Africa and Europe. In their circumstances, they could not abstain from the Atlantic trade, and all the less did they wish to abstain since their own kings and rich merchants gained from it; none the less they had fashioned a rod for their own backs. British and French commercial capitalism developed into industrial capitalism, and, as such, acquired a new drive and dynamism. This was imperialism.

That is part of another story, of one that was to be a repetition of the old duality of motive which had governed Portugal's early relations with the Congo of King Affonso: Christianity, but also profit. King Leopold of the Belgians enshrined the modern version in characteristic words when launching his adventure in the Congo. 'To pierce the darkness shrouding entire populations', he declared, 'that is, if I may venture to say so, a crusade worthy of this century of progress.' He and his soldiers 'pierced the darkness' soon enough; but almost their first action was to declare that all the land and all the products of the land belonged to them; and to this day the peoples of the whole Congo basin bear marks of the fearful consequences that followed. Elsewhere things went differently and better. But generally there arose in new and potent forms the old myth of 'savage Africa', now justifying colonialism as it had previously justified the slave trade:

reinforced, moreover, by the complacent self-congratulation of bourgeois classes who were sure, in the lapped comfort of their joint-stock companies and their new suburban villas, that they were rightly and properly designed to rule the world.

In Africa the matter seemed otherwise. Astonished at Britain's sudden opposition to a trade she had done so much to call into being and extend, African chiefs and rulers at first tried to dissuade their partner from this momentous step. When that failed they had a great deal of trouble on their hands, for much of their trading network relied on the sale of slaves. But after a time, perceiving that the decision was final, they turned to other forms of trade. And it stands as striking proof of the vigour and resilience of these societies that they should so often have achieved the transition to legitimate trade – as non-slaving commerce now began to be called – with clear and rapid success.

They were helped in this by a new demand for soap and lubricating oil in Europe. There was pressing need for vegetable fats that could supplement the insufficient supplies of animal fat. This substitute was found in palm oil, long cultivated in the delta. Baulked of human cargoes, a number of Liverpool merchants asked their captains to load with palm oil instead. Large consignments of delta oil were reaching Liverpool within a few years of the ending of the slave trade. By 1832 a former Liverpool slaving merchant, Tobin, was bringing in some four thousand tons of oil every year; and two years later the whole export of the delta – of the 'Oil Rivers' – was said to be worth half a million pounds sterling. All this oil was produced by the delta 'house rulers' and their like.

Yet slaving continued from the Oil Rivers, especially from the old Portuguese trading stronghold on the Brass estuary. Brazil, Cuba and independent American operators all wanted slaves, and slaves were regularly smuggled out in large quantity despite Britain's long-persisting naval effort.

And it was at this point that the changing nature of the trade became confounded with the rise of imperialism and led, here as elsewhere, to the assertion of political control and afterwards to conquest. One can detect three main steps in the process. First came naval intervention to prevent slaving and protect the interests of European traders, now increasingly turbulent, ambitious, and violently involved in conflict with Africans. Then followed the establishment of consuls with widening powers of political interference. Lastly and with growing need for local revenue, there came the proclamation of a 'right to govern'.

Each step led directly to the next. For if naval patrols succeeded in reducing slave exports they also succeeded, by the same token, in promoting an economic crisis which palm oil would later, but only later, resolve. Yet economic crisis led quickly to political upheaval; and political upheaval called for consular arbitration. And consular arbitration could not be effective, in the end, unless it were backed by force. So in the end the troops were duly sent for.

There were other factors in play. Here in the delta, as on the Gold Coast, Europeans were now of a mind to win control of both sides of the trade: they began trying to dictate prices and credit rates by close combination with each other; and when they ran into African opposition that was too strong for them they regularly called in the British Navy. They were not always successful in getting naval support, but little by little, as the great imperial century moved on, the idea of military intervention in defence of British interests gained currency and even respectability, no matter how disreputable the interests in question might be. Gradually it became clear to powerful and forward-looking merchants that the British Government must sooner or later intervene. And now a new and vital piece of knowledge came to light: in 1830 the Landers finally established that the Oil Rivers were the mouths of the mighty Niger and therefore the high road to the interior.*

Expeditions began pushing inland. The European traders of the delta opposed this, as did many of their African partners, for they saw in European penetration of the hinterland a necessary end to their coastal monopoly. For a time it looked as though the old monopolists would prevail: the expeditions failed. Then came the next point of change. Europe discovered that quinine could defeat malaria; and this proved decisive. On Laird's first disastrous trading expedition up the Niger in 1832 malaria had

*Here I have merely sketched the ways in which the process of the Atlantic slave trade led to the process of colonial enclosure. See especially J. D. Hargreaves, *Prelude to the Partition of West Africa* (London, 1963).

taken such a fearful toll that only nine out of forty-eight Europeans had returned to tell the tale. Baikie's expedition twenty-two years later, making systematic use of quinine, lost not a single life although it went as far as Fuḷani country. Three years after that the British Government subsidized the launching of steamers on the river; and in 1868, with the footfalls of history thundering on the scene, the first British consul in the interior broke out his flag at Lokoja, two hundred and fifty miles from the sea. The colony of Nigeria was in the womb.

Any writer who should wish to explore the impact of colonial conquest on African society and, at the same time, the intricate train of action and reaction which then led to the rise of African nationalism and regained independence, will find a rich and curious field in the history of the delta. Here the records of the transitional years – the second half of the nineteenth century when the old partnership was ending – throw open an amazing gallery of old rogues and new humanitarians, brilliantly enterprising African merchants, desperate slaving captains moored away in forgotten creeks, true-blue British consuls and stubborn chiefs: and all enmeshed in a densely fashioned net of much evil and great good, sober profit and fantastic speculation, wisdom and the wildest folly.

These men and their occupations were quintessentially the outcome of the European-African connection at one of its broadest and most interesting points, and I shall round off this narrative by offering one or two samples of their remarkable quality and experience.

10. Men like Ja Ja: The Last Phase

ONE can easily overlook the positive side of all this commercial enterprise, especially in the delta, by concentrating on the miseries it entailed: it was by doing so that nineteenth-century Europeans came often to the most dismal conclusions about African society. This was rather like seeing the industrial revolution in England uniquely through the sufferings of little children in coal mines and women in basement workshops. The sufferings existed and they undoubtedly condemned the system; but they were not the whole story. Humanity, somehow or other, survives and learns and corrects.

The process of surviving and learning and correcting was extremely difficult for the delta peoples because they were faced, all the while, with the mounting arrogance and pressure of Europeans who were no longer content to accept African equality. Yet the adjustment was attempted; and was achieved, here and there, with outstanding skill. There is no better example of this than the life and work of King Ja Ja of Opobo.

A modern Nigerian historian says that the Igbo people of today regard Ja Ja 'as surely the greatest man produced by their tribe in the last century'; and surely they are right. Ja Ja would have been remarkable in any time and place.

He belonged to that period of the delta partnership when oil had largely displaced slaves, and European penetration had begun. Born into domestic slavery, he was none the less elected while still a young man to be the ruling chief of the Bonny house of Anna Pepple, an old-established trading unit that was famous throughout the African connection. This occurred in 1863 when Ja Ja was forty-two years old. Already a successful merchant, he soon proved his worth by restoring the dilapidated fortunes of the Pepple house. His predecessor in the headship, Alali, had died in great debt, owing European merchants a sum that was variously estimated as lying between ten and fifteen thousand pounds. Within two years of taking over command, Ja Ja had cleared off the whole of this debt and become, for the supercargoes who managed the European side of the business, the most popular of all the Bonny chiefs.

But Ja Ja's methodical enterprise, while arousing the admiration of his European clients, also excited the jealousy of his competitors. His thrusting commercial successes soon led him into trouble with the rival house of Manilla Pepple. Both houses armed for war, which duly came in 1869. Here again one may see the truly international nature of the delta system. For 'while Africans did the fighting', comments Dike, 'the opposing British interests supplied their respective allies with the weapons of war. This armaments race intensified the struggle and widened the area of conflict to the tribal interior. It was certainly the greatest war ever fought in the delta.'

The results were not long in making themselves felt. Ja Ja found himself confronted not only with the armed competition of an African rival but also with the fact of European intervention. Here, as elsewhere, the point was reached where the partnership broke down before a determined British bid to extend their power from West African waters to West African land. Ja Ja met this challenge in his own way. With great foresight, seeing himself outmatched in Bonny itself, he moved in 1870 to Andoni country a few miles to the east and somewhat inland from Bonny; and there he founded a new state, Opobo, of which he became king.

At Opobo he flourished. This country, wrote an eyewitness, 'became under King Ja Ja's firm rule one of the largest exporting centres of palm oil in the delta, and for years King Ja Ja enjoyed a not undeserved popularity amongst the white traders who visited his river'. But it was too good to last. A time came when these traders combined together and cut the price they were willing to pay for Ja Ja's oil. To this monopolist gambit Ja Ja replied in short order with another of his own: he found means of shipping large quantities of oil to England on his own account, and forbade his people to sell more than a part of their produce to the whites.

The reply of the white traders to Ja Ja's independent shipping enterprise was to combine more closely together. They drew up a plan whereby they would equally divide whatever produce came into the river, thus eliminate competition among themselves, and, at the same time, kill Ja Ja's chance of finding a European who was willing to ship his produce.

But Ja Ja out-manoeuvred them again. He had in any case found that the profit on sending his own oil to England was not as large as he liked, 'owing to the length of time it took to get his returns back, namely about three months at the earliest, whilst selling in the river he could turn over his money three or four times during that period.

'He therefore tried several means to break the white men's combination, at last hitting upon the bright idea of offering the whole of the river's trade to one English house . . . His bait took with one of the European traders: the latter could not resist the golden vision of the yellow grease thus displayed before him by the astute Ja Ja, who metaphorically dangled before his eyes hundreds of canoes laden with the coveted palm oil. A bargain was struck, and one fine morning the other white traders in the river woke up to the fact that their combination was at an end, for on their morning spy round the river through their binoculars . . . they saw a fleet of over a hundred canoes round the renegade's wharf, and for nearly two years this trader scooped all the trade.'

Twenty or thirty years earlier Ja Ja would have met with no more than verbal protests for this sovereign act of restriction in his own country: the European supercargoes would have denounced the measure, but thereafter they would have tried to restore peace on the best terms they could. The case was common enough. But now a different spirit reigned among them. They could and did call in the power of their own government. They carried their complaints to Consul Livingstone – the great explorer's not-so-great brother – and Consul Livingstone was more than sympathetic. This marked the beginning of a bitter struggle between the British and Ja Ja that the African was bound, as things now stood, to lose.

For what Ja Ja was really doing was to lay it down that he, and he alone, should decide how the landward side of the oil trade was to be conducted. He claimed and exercised the right to prevent African and European competitors from entering the oil markets under his control, and these were the best in the delta. He barred the way, in Dike's words, 'not only to the Bonny middlemen but also to the invading Europeans . . . [who] found him the greatest impediment to their occupation of eastern Nigeria'. A trial of strength became inevitable. In 1887 the British moved in. Backed by the Navy, Consul Johnston (a great imperial thruster) had Ja Ja seized and taken to Accra on the Gold Coast. There he was tried before Admiral Hunt Grubbe on various charges connected with treaty-breaking but arising, in truth, from Ja Ja's dogged insistence on African sovereignty, and condemned to five years' exile in the West Indies, where he died.

Trial or no trial, Ja Ja was clearly a victim of imperialism. Had he not faced foreign invasion, he might well have realized still wider triumphs and ambitions, and carried the whole of the delta into a new system of law and commerce, social and economic structure, which could have validly confronted the problems of the early twentieth century. For Ja Ja was at home in the widening world of his time. He used techniques of commerce that were no different from those of his clients. He understood the capitalist system at its most intimate heart, there where the tick-tock of money-interest is at work and the crucial factors of marketing are felt and registered; and there is no reason why he should not have developed an economy of cash-production in eastern Nigeria. It can be said of men like Ja Ja – and Ja Ja was by no means unique, among the people of the delta, for energy of mind and enterprise – that they made the very best that could be made of a connection with Europe in which Europe had yet to offer anything that history can record with even modest satisfaction, let alone with pride. For these reasons, men like Ja Ja – and the new techniques for which they stood – were often in a real sense the forerunners and the foundation of modern nationalism.

Yet the success and free-ranging scope of men like these, rapidly and skilfully transforming the old slave markets into palm-oil markets, must be weighed against the social disintegrations that were directly linked with so much of the connection. Great energies went to waste. Much wealth was squandered. Talented men were obliged to work within a framework of possibilities that worked hard against the chance of constructive expansion. As European pressure intensified, this society was shaken to its roots. There spread across it a sense of fatal insecurity. And it was this neurotic condition – felt, as the abundant records show, by almost every man of substance in the delta and in its neighbouring country – that led to the extravagance of autocracy and the gross futility of superstition into which many of these governments fell; and which, in turn, helped to invite British occupation.

One could illustrate this trend with a mass of evidence. It was this same feeling of hopeless doom that ultimately drove the priests and the divine king of Benin out of their wits. It was this that caused the *Oba* in 1897 to refuse a meeting with Consul-General Phillips, replying to Phillips's messenger that 'he had heard of the white men going all over the country and taking the chiefs prisoner, saying, "Now, my friend, we have got you and will keep you" '. Indeed, he must have heard of such things: for the British had already deported King Pepple and King Ja Ja. Why not the *Oba* too? When Phillips persisted in coming up to Benin, he and his party were ambushed and killed. A few months later Benin was occupied by the British Army.

Another case makes the point even more clearly. In 1895 certain chiefs of the Brass city-state were accused of tolerating or even encouraging human sacrifice – known generally, to Europeans of the day, as cannibalism. A useful statement by the Brass chiefs, taken down by Sir Claude Macdonald, then Consul-General in the delta, notes the pressure exerted by the priests for chiefs to 'offer up prisoners' to sacrifice. The statement points out that the Christian chiefs resist this pressure, but they are now in a minority. 'Some years ago the Christian party was much stronger and more powerful than their opponents. Many chiefs who were brought up as Christians have now gone back to fetichism . . . the reason for this being that they had lost faith in the white man's God, who had allowed them to be oppressed, and their trade, their only means of livelihood, to be taken from them without just cause or reason.'

How well grounded were these complaints of European monopoly may be guessed from a report by Sir John Kirk a year later. 'The rules in force', he declared, referring to the sharply monopolist regulations of the newly formed Royal Niger Company, 'are practically prohibiting to native trade, and the Brass men are right in saying that this is so.'

Having broken the power of the African merchants, the European merchants were now determined to exercise all power themselves. And their natural ambition was to force down the buying price of oil, cut out all independent operators on either side, and sell their own goods as dearly as they could. To these African chiefs and traders of the delta it must have seemed that God had indeed turned his back on them, and could now be attracted to their side again only by the most desperate measures.

Even so, the Royal Niger Company found it no easy matter to rule the delta; nor did the British Government later. The delta chiefs fought back, and they fought hard. How and why they fought, and what manner of men they were, may be glimpsed from the case of Ja Ja of Opobo. Or, to offer a contrast, from that of Nana Olumu of Brohemie (Ebrohimi), the last governor of the Benin River.

The story of Chief Nana of Brohemie, a delta settlement not far from the city of Benin, has many aspects that are worthy of note. It makes in fact no bad epitaph to the closing years of the pre-colonial relationship of Africa and Europe. Nana was another of those hard-driving merchants of the delta who had learned how to live with the changing needs of the nineteenth century. He enjoyed good relations with the British in a cautious sort of way, and in 1887 a British vice-consul even went so far as to 'nominate' Nana as the governor of the Benin River. However void of real meaning this nomination may have been, Nana undoubtedly considered himself a sovereign in his own land. What he could not achieve by foresight or persuasion he would certainly, he thought, be justified in carrying through by force. He was a great supporter of trade with Europeans – after all, he depended on it – but a great opposer of European political intervention. He put down powerful barriers to British penetration; and these sooner or later were bound to be felt intolerable. The test of power came in 1894.

Nana won the first round. A British 'punitive expedition' – for such, by now, were the imperialist terms of European presence on the coast – failed to reach him in his stronghold at Brohemie. Consul-General Moor, writing to the Foreign Office from Old Calabar on the last day of August, 1894, told the disagreeable news. Pushing up through dense and tangled swampland, the British force had come at last to the outskirts of Brohemie only to find themselves confronted with a 'most powerful' stockade about three hundred yards long, constructed of hard-wood logs stuck firmly in the ground in rows two or three deep and about eight foot high. The British took this stockade and found inside it twenty-three cannon (Moor calls them heavy cannon), 'loaded, trained and primed': luckily for these much-tried British soldiers, the gunners of Chief Nana had deserted him. 'The charges consisted of 3 lb. balls and tubular bamboo frames filled with broken iron pots.'

Having carried this potentially nasty obstacle, the British then got into a maze of creeks that were difficult to cross. They persevered until they came to Brohemie. But at Brohemie they were met with fire from 'at least thirty or forty cannon . . . in addition to plenty of rifles'. Some of these cannon, they observed, were 'trained directly down the creek so as to render the approach by boats most hazardous, if not impossible'. This was discouraging: what was worse, and finally decisive, was that the British could then find no way of bringing their two seven-pounder field-guns to bear. They had dragged these guns to Brohemie with tremendous difficulty, and now they lacked strength to drag them back again. So they spiked them and retired.

But these were high imperial times. This kind of setback could not be overlooked. A few months later Rear-Admiral Bedford led a naval force up the Benin River and seized Brohemie by sheer weight of metal. And what Bedford discovered inside Brohemie is of no small interest to the general history of the delta, if only because it throws a clear light on the kind of capital accumulation that was made by the leading chiefs and prime merchants of the country.

Reporting to the Admiralty, Bedford said that the defences of Brohemie showed months if not years of preparation, 'and a considerable amount of intelligence . . . in all the arrangements. For instance, the guns were admirably placed to meet any attack from the direction expected . . . and were well and strongly mounted . . .

'Below [Nana's] house was found the magazine, containing 1,500 kegs of powder, which was protected by first double iron-sheeting, then logs of timber three deep, and outside corrugated iron sheets again three deep . . . Nana's house was next visited, where large stores containing munitions of war and trading material in very large quantities were found . . . Scattered about all over the town, and in large quantities, in the stores, were leg and neck irons, also handcuffs, evidently for use in keeping the large number of slaves owned by Chief Nana in order by most severe means . . .'

There were, Bedford continued, a total of one hundred and six cannon from 3-pounder to 32-pounder in size, including 'a large number of 9-pounders, very good-looking cast-iron guns', and stores of powder made up in neat muslin bags and cylinders of split bamboo with iron balls and pieces of scrap iron, enabling rapid fire.

That was one form of capital accumulation. Nana had also contrived another. Bedford found an astonishing quantity of gin. Altogether, he reported, Nana had collected no fewer than 8,300 cases of twelve bottles apiece: a grand total of 99,600 bottles of gin. Well-stoppered, they were – or they would have been without British intervention – a sound and sensible growth investment. It was fair odds that their value would rise steadily in price.

But Nana's story of accumulation, as you see, was written largely in guns and gin. These above all were items that stood witness to the kind of 'development' that Africans had managed to extract from the oversea connection. No doubt there were other and better things available – for example, the first beginnings of modern education by way of missionary endeavour – but these things were marginal or insignificant as yet. And when they did become more readily available, they arrived in a colonial package. Only much later, in the wake of the colonial interlude, was it going to become possible for the oversea connection to have anything to say or give that could help to bring a genuine development to Africa.

And with men like Ja Ja and Nana the case is particularly clear. For they were strongly in favour of progress and modernization. It was precisely their achievements in that direction, as Obaro Ikime has reminded us when writing of Nana*, that brought about their clash with the British and their eventual dispossession by the British. Had they been assisted by the British, rather than dispossessed, they and their kind would surely have developed many new initiatives, and placed the society of the delta on a new productive footing. According to colonialist mythology, they were exactly the kind of men whose modernizing efforts should have been applauded and supported. But according to colonialist reality they were an obstacle to be removed. And removed they were.

* Obaro Ikime, *Merchant Prince of the Niger Delta* (Heinemann, London, 1969).

PART SEVEN

FOUR CENTURIES: A SUMMING UP

Minha Mãe
(as mães negras cujos filhos
partiram)
tu me ensinaste a esperar
como esperaste paciente nas horas difíceis

Mas em mim
a vida matou essa mística esperança

Eu não espero
sou aquele por quem se espera

A Esperança somos nós
os teus filhos . . .
a esperança em busca de vida.

My Mother
(black mothers whose sons depart)
you taught me to wait and hope
as you had learnt in bitter days

But in me
life killed that mystic hope

I am not the one who waits
but the one who is awaited

And we are Hope
your sons . . .
searching for life.

AGOSTINHO NETO

Món pa más que grande
ka na tapa ceú

No fist is big enough
to hide the sky

Peasant saying:
Guinea-Bissau

An End and a Beginning

WITH colonial invasion, the African-European connection entered upon a decisively new phase. Thereafter action and reaction occurred with increasing speed. The first declarations of modern nationalism were heard in West Africa no more than twenty years after European conquest; and the main colonial period in West Africa has lasted little longer than half a century, and not much more elsewhere.

These colonial years were always humiliating, often harsh, sometimes terribly wasteful. But they were relatively few: less than a third of the duration of the major period of the slave trade. They barely spanned three lifetimes. And they led with growing awareness to a new social consciousness, to a political awakening, to a rebirth of African culture and social confidence. This, in the light of imperialist aims, was their supreme irony: but for this as well as for the lesser yet necessary purpose of ending my book, I exclude them from 'the years of trial'.

I have thought of the pre-colonial period as 'the years of trial' because it was then, through those long centuries, that Africa grievously and continuously suffered from a connection with Europe that was neither one thing nor the other: neither the equality that could open wide channels to the outside world, nor the sharp subjection that could provoke and stimulate, however blindly or unintentionally, the rise of African reassertion, political change and economic growth. The years of trial were years of isolation and paralysis wherever the trade with Europe, essentially a trade in slaves, could plant its sterilizing hand.

This is a broad statement, but I think it is broadly true. Of course there were exceptions. A handful of Africans did succeed in reaching the outside world as free men. Yet all but one or two of them were chiefs and the sons of chiefs: men who were in any case committed to the slaving system and without an interest in changing it. Indeed, it was familiar British and French practice to win the friendship of local rulers on the Coast by entertaining their sons in Europe. This was part of the slaving network of alliance, and it often worked exceedingly well.

Some time in the summer of 1750 the British Admiralty received a letter of thanks from the king of Annamaboe on the Gold Coast together with an offer of the labour of twenty thousand men to help the British build a fort on his land. The old man had double cause to be grateful. He had sent one of his sons to England, together with a companion, on a slaving ship whose captain had seized and sold them in the West Indies. But when the story became known in England the youths were released by order of the British Government, which duly paid their ransom. They were brought to England and 'put under the care of the Earl of Halifax, then at the head of the Board of Trade, who had them clothed and educated in a suitable manner'; and they became the talk of the Town.

'There are two black princes of Annamaboe here,' Walpole wrote in his London diary of March 23, 1749, 'who are in fashion at all assemblies, of whom I scarce know any particulars [of their story] . . . though all the women know it and ten times more than belongs to it.' Before returning to Africa the two young men were received by the king and visited Covent Garden where they were greeted by 'a loud clap of applause'. In an aristocratic society it seemed quite logical to applaud a black man who was also a prince, while enslaving his 'subjects' in a manner fit only for beasts. Established attitudes towards white men were not, after all, much different.

Such visitors to Europe could have no more effect on the situation in Africa than the enterprise and exploits of the slaves and ex-slaves in the Americas. It is notable that until the middle of the nineteenth century the only successful relationship between free Africans in Brazil and their old homeland lay within the slaving circuit. Typical was that 'free Negro, born in Brazil' of whom Governor Abson of the British fort at Ouidah was writing in about 1790: Antonio Vaz Coelho, who made several voyages to Ardra on the Slave Coast, where he at last settled and became 'a very respectable trader' – and introduced the idea of mounting swivel-guns on war canoes.

All roads, in those grey years, led to slaving. In a strict sense the European connection was a tragic one for Africa: not, that is, excluding humour and decent hope, love of life or the will to survive – but denying, whenever it came to the matter of choice, any alternative to the death and damnation of the slave trade. This must be one's starting-point in trying to assess the consequences of these four centuries of inter-continental connection.

* * *

How much did Africa suffer from depopulation? Slaving struck other coastal and near-coastal regions than those considered here; yet what was true of the Congo, the East Coast, and the eastern Gulf of Guinea was also true of these other regions. And generally it would seem that depopulation was the least important consequence of the oversea slave trade. For even if we take the number landed alive in the Americas at the top of Curtin's margin of error, or some twelve millions, and add another two millions for those lost on the ocean crossing, and then add half as many again, or seven millions, for those lost before embarkation – and this last figure, I must stress, is the merest guess at the probable maximum figure, having no statistical foundation – we still arrive only at a grand total of twenty-one millions. A huge total, no doubt: but spread over a very long period. And even if we regard the numbers lost before 1650, when the trade got into its stride, as insignificant – which they were not – and place the loss of twenty-one millions in the two centuries of intensive slaving (1650–1850), we still reach a total of some ten millions a century for two centuries. This certainly denotes a crippling loss for those peoples against whom the slave trade struck with especial ferocity, but it does not point to any *general* depopulation on a serious scale.

There was continued loss of people and staggering waste in their use; and at certain times and places this loss and wastage undoubtedly crippled society. Present-day population densities offer some hints. Today in West Africa there is comparatively great density along the coast itself – more than fifty inhabitants to a square mile in many regions – and considerable density in the forest belt. Yet most of the intermediate zone between the forest belt and the Niger grasslands is sparsely peopled: here the density is seldom more than ten to a square mile and is often less than one or two.

Soil and other natural factors go far to explain this variation. But if it is also true that a great number of West African slaves was drawn from this intermediate zone – precisely where peoples lacked strong states of their own – then this relative scarcity of population may have some connection with the slave trade. Colour is lent to this by the fact that the lands of the Mossi in modern Upper Volta are unusually rich in people: there, in the realm of the still surviving Moro Naba of the Mossi, population density once again approaches the level of the coastal regions. And the Mossi were one of the rare peoples of this intermediate zone who successfully defended themselves against slaving.

Yet the evidence for serious depopulation through the trade is far from convincing. Very large numbers of captives were shipped from the forest lands of Nigeria over a very long period; yet these are still among the most densely peopled regions of all Africa. 'If we may judge from nineteenth-century records,' Dike comments, 'over-population was the rule in all sections of the [Igbo] tribe.' Here, at any rate, slaving seems to have had no adverse effect on the birth-and-survival rate. This should not be taken to mean that slaving helped the birthrate but rather that the birthrate in these fertile and favoured areas helped the slave trade: just as, even in remote times, the same high population density in southern Nigeria may have set in motion some of the migratory movements that helped to populate central and southern Africa.

Several peoples of the intermediate zone were raided both from south and north and must have come near extinction. Others suffered less and were able to refill their ranks: from the purely demographic point of view they probably suffered no more than the populations of Italy and Scotland in recent times, when annual average emigration at times equalled or even exceeded the birthrate. This is not to palliate the slaving loss, but merely to conclude that depopulation was seldom a primary social factor of the oversea trade, and even less of the overland trade.

One must look elsewhere for the main impact of this 'new colonial system of slavery which', to quote the *Encyclopaedia Britannica*, 'instead of being the spontaneous outgrowth of social necessities and subserving a temporary need of human development, was politically as well as morally a monstrous aberration'. Whether the slave trade, on which western Europe founded so much of its prosperity, was really an aberration – or whether in fact it merely epitomized the nature of progress in that day and age when, as Marx observed in the face of child labour and factory enslavement, progress resembled 'that hideous pagan idol, who would not drink the nectar but from the skulls of the slain' – is beside the point of this present inquiry. Viewed as a factor in African history, the pre-colonial connection with Europe – essentially, the slave trade – had powerfully degrading consequences for the structure of society. But far-reaching depopulation, we may conclude, was seldom prominent among them.

* * *

The economic evidence is more severe. It cannot yet be absolutely proven that the European connection between 1450 and 1850 was a cause of economic stagnation, or that this stagnation grew worse after slaving became dominant around 1650. For even after the trade got into its stride Africans continued to weave textiles, smelt and forge metals, practise agriculture and carry on the manifold techniques of their daily life. With agriculture, moreover, there was even a gain from European contact, for the ships from South America introduced new and useful crops that became of great importance to Africa: here were the African origins of maize, manioc, pineapples and several other valuable foods.

Yet in spite of an undoubted improvement in food supplies – for the new crops were soon in cultivation by many African peoples – there can be little doubt that on balance the economic effects of the European contact worked steady and decisive damage.

After about 1650, with diminishing exceptions, African production-for-export became a monoculture in human beings. This can be seen to have suffocated economic growth in coastal and near-coastal Africa as surely, and at the same time, as the extension of European production-for-export of consumer goods gave the maritime nations of Europe their long lead in economic development.

The reasons for this suffocation were various. It was obviously an impoverishment to send away the very men and women who would otherwise produce wealth at home. In exporting slaves, African states exported their own capital without any possible return in interest or in the enlargement of their economic system. Slave exports differed radically in this respect from the more or less forced emigration of impoverished men and women from nineteenth-century Europe. Thus the millions who left Britain in those years were able to enter the mainstream of capitalist expansion, and thereby benefit the mother country in many different ways. But the African slaves could contribute nothing except to the wealth of their masters – a wealth that never returned to Africa. Dealers in Africa undoubtedly received payment for the slaves they sold; but the nature of the payment was strictly non-productive. The very conditions of the exchange prevented the kind of capital accumulation that could have led to a more advanced economy. Such 'capital' as the kings and prime merchants could accumulate was in mere baubles or the weapons of war. From an economic standpoint, in short, European slaving may be rightly regarded not only as a prelude to colonialism but also, in itself, as a primitive and particularly destructive form of colonialism: the exchange, that is, of consumer goods for the raw material of slave labour.

Wherever towns grew strong there was, true enough, a shift to cash economies and to new forms of saving and investment. This happened in the great market centres of the Western Sudan, trading across the Sahara, and perhaps still more in the cities of the medieval East Coast that enjoyed contact with India and Arabia. But these developments occurred only where slaving did not dominate the trade. With the partial exception of the delta partnership, the European connection was powerless to reproduce such results – precisely because it was above all a slaving connection.

In face of an ever more pervasive demand for slaves, local industries dwindled or collapsed. Where the only produce that was readily marketable was the producer himself (or herself), handicrafts and cottage industries could not thrive, let alone expand. Cheap European textiles drove out the excellent cloths of the Guinea Coast. Pereira had spoken of these as early as 1506, noting that the Portuguese purchased these cloths and carried them to Europe. Benin was especially famous for its textiles. Yet by 1850 these had fallen to minor importance, although the textile output of Kano in northern Nigeria – produced in an economic system that was far beyond any direct influence of the oversea slave trade, and where the overland slave trade never dominated commerce – flourished and grew at the same time. Dahomey textiles met the same fate as those of Benin, even though Governor Dalzell could write as late as 1789 that Dahomey still manufactured 'very pretty and durable cloths of cotton ... Their dyes stand washing very well, especially the blues, which are inferior to none.' It speaks much for the quality of this manufacture that it could survive at all in face of growing imports of cheap Lancashire cottons.

These local industries declined while chiefs and merchants fattened on the slave trade. Yet here too there was no real expansion of the economic system. For this new trading wealth became increasingly a matter of individual prestige and display. Consider how the king of Bonny responded in 1826 to the offer of a bride by the king of Warri.

'King Pepple having repeatedly sent presents by his canoes to the King of Warri, with whose nation he carries on an immense trade ... [and] the latter hearing of his amazing wealth and extensive connections with the Europeans, offered him his eldest daughter in marriage ... So great and unexpected an offer was received by Pepple with the greatest exultation, and to convince his intended ally how deeply he appreciated the distinguished favour he had conferred upon him, he loaded canoe after canoe with rare and most valuable treasures: English, French, Spanish and Portuguese merchandise were extracted from his warehouses – gold and silver plate – costly silks and exquisitely fine cloths – with embroidered laces and other articles too numerous to mention.'

A glittering display of Pepple's wealth awaited the king of Warri when he eventually brought his daughter for the marriage ceremony. Pepple himself described the scene to a visiting European in graphic 'pidgin' that loses nothing by being left in the original:

'That time I first hear, Warri's canoe come for creek, I fire one gun from my house – then all Bonny fire – plenty powder blow away you no can hear one man speak. I stand for my house – all my house have fine cloth. Roof, walls, all round, he hung with proper fine silks. No possible to look one stick, one mat: all be covered.

'My Queen Father stand for beach. His foot no touch ground. He stand on cloth. All way he walk, he walk for cloth . . . I give Wine, Brandy, plenty puncheon – pass twenty. I give for my people and Warri's. All Bonny glad too much . . . Every man, every woman, for my town, I give cloth – pass one thousand piece I give that day. Pass twenty barrel powder I fire that day.'

There in a nutshell lay the truth about 'capital accumulation' during the high days of the delta trade. Merchants who were also monarchs spent their wealth as traditional rulers must: to glorify their name and reputation and enlarge their power by winning allies from among their peers. The system was stable within its limits; but its limits stopped short of the economic growth that could have led to economic development: to a progressive change, that is, of economic system. And the slave trade continually fortified those limits by enhancing the power of kings and prime merchants, while siphoning off those pressures of population or political dissent which had pressed, elsewhere, towards new development and new systems of production.

After the ending of the slave trade the powerful men of the delta went in for palm-oil production on a large plantation scale: Pepple, like Ja Ja, owed his wealth to oil exports rather than to slaving. Would this new form of production have developed rapidly into a West African capitalism? Perhaps: but it was never given the chance. Pressing on its heels, there followed colonial conquest; and the circumstances of invasion proved even more adverse to economic development than the slave trade. For with invasion came subjection; and this subjection, among other things, meant an end to any African share in the major enterprises of trade or the official administration of trade. One by one, the old trading families and structures were eliminated or elbowed aside by new European monopolies. The latter brought many innovations. Much of the old technological backwardness was swept away. Colonial rule introduced new patterns of economic exchange; coins became widely used for the first time, and banks were established. Overall figures of production rose steadily, whether of cocoa, groundnuts or other crops, and deep mines were sunk wherever worthwhile minerals could be detected. Yet all this expansion, essentially, was no different in its consequences from the expansion of the Atlantic trade during the time of slaving. What was being developed were economies in Europe, not in Africa. The opportunities for the development of an African capitalism, of local systems of capitalism, remained precisely nil: or, rather, they were reduced to nil.

Were these opportunities significantly greater before 1830: before the ending of the last great period of the slave trade in western Africa (it continued somewhat longer, as we have seen, in eastern Africa)? Putting the same question differently, and in spite of what I have said earlier, can one even so perceive some 'development potential' at the African end of the trade? Any answer is bound to be ambiguous, given the extreme diversity of local conditions over a long period.* The trade unquestionably brought gains to kings and ruling groups who were able to gather its profits; yet these were the gains, much more often than not, of a purely personal accumulation of wealth and of privileged access to consumer imports. Here and there, true enough, kings distributed their accumulation in annual hand-outs at festivals such as those that were regularly held in Dahomey among the Fon. But the net effect was no different: it was simply that rather more people collected a bonus.

What economic progress in those days required, given the coming challenge of European imperialism, was the development of local capitalist systems capable of rapid technological advance. And what that required, in turn, was the development of new economic freedoms. But it seems that the reverse occurred, and that the Atlantic trade, far from promoting those kinds of 'free enterprise' which could have broken through the servitudes of tradition, had the effect, instead, of stiffening those servitudes.

Scientific study of the institutions of servitude in pre-colonial Africa was still at an early stage in the late 1970s; but it was

*For an overview in some detail, see Basil Davidson, *Africa in Modern History*, Allen Lane, London, 1978 (U.S. edn, *Let Freedom Come*, Atlantic-Little, Brown, Boston, 1978, chs. 5 and 6).

beginning to get under way.* They were very widely used, had long since given rise to great inequalities of status – which is not, however, the same thing as saying that they had produced sharp stratifications of social class – and were often based on violence and coercion. But they can very seldom be understood as institutions of chattel slavery, the slavery that developed in the Americas. Rather were they institutions of one or other form of what I have called 'wageless labour' – of what Hopkins has called dependent labour as distinct from hired labour. As such they were clearly susceptible of progressive development into forms of wage-paid labour: if, that is, progressive development towards capitalism, or into capitalism, had been in the situation.

With the Atlantic trade dominated or even monopolized by slaving, no such development was in the situation. Another trend was stronger. 'Servitude directly introduced by Europeans', Walter Rodney has argued, 'began to assume an African character': new forms of social oppression, not new economic freedoms, began to take shape. Rodney's evidence is from the western or 'upper' Guinea coast; but it would not be difficult to find it elsewhere as well, for example in Angola. Servitudes probably widened: still more probably, they became more primitive. Nothing like the onset of capitalist economies came out of this. What did come out of it, instead, was the onset of something very like slave economies. That might encourage growth, and at certain points did encourage and even achieve growth; but it could not stimulate development – the movement, that is, out of a less productive system into a more productive system. Again, of course, one has to allow for occasional exceptions as well as for the absolute mysteries of the might-have-been. But on the whole the overall economic impact of the slaving trade is once again seen as negative or as regressive even in the 'best' of cases. In the 'worst' of cases, this impact was simple ruin.

This question of economic gain or loss for Africa during the slave trade epoch has been much argued in recent years, although quite often, or so it appears to me, as a mere reaction against simplistic views of earlier times; and the argument, no doubt,

*For a handily brief summary of work done or in progress, see a review article of Martin Klein's in *Journal of African History*, XIX 4 (1978), pp. 599 ff.

will continue. But the principal conclusions from the evidence that we now have can scarcely be in doubt, no matter what reservations may be urged for this or that exception.

Wealth accumulation from the Great Circuit system, the system of slaving and of plantation-slavery, continuously fed the means of technological and structural development in Europe. To Africa, however, it brought no comparable opportunity or stimulus. And the economic benefits that it did bring to the few in Africa who could profit from the trade were in no way commensurable with the losses that were suffered by the many.

* * *

But it is on the socio-political side that further and probably fuller damage may be found.

Four great phases of political relationship can be traced. Each had profound formative influence. In the beginning, contact was a mere accumulation of points of intercourse, sometimes peaceful though often warlike. The early mariners did little more than burgle or bang on West Africa's back door. Yet even this gave the coastland a new importance to its peoples.

This enhanced importance of the coast had its effect in the sixteenth century. The inhabitants of the new 'frontier of opportunity' quickly adjusted themselves to the business of defending and promoting their interests in oversea trade. This was the second phase, the phase of widening commerce and political alliance.

With the seventeenth century there came the forging of a close-knit partnership between the Europeans and the peoples of the coast. This was no rapid or smoothly worked achievement. It involved a bitter fight for monopolist privilege: between Europeans for monopoly by sea, and between Africans for monopoly on land – and occasionally between allied groups of Europeans and Africans together. Yet in this third phase they evolved with one another a balance of power based on slaving that held good until the nineteenth century. Europeans accepted their restriction to trading from shipboard or from occasional footholds on shore; and Africans settled into a distribution of powers and rights that gave primacy to each strong coastal people in its own region.

Much was promising of a possible or eventual development in some regions during this third phase. Along and behind the Gold

Coast (seaboard of modern Ghana), it looked for a while as though the traditional institutions of servitude were being developed into quasi-capitalist forms. Thrusting entrepreneurs began to carve out profitable near-monopolies. Merchant-princes marched towards the threshold of new systems of production. 'Throughout the seventeenth and eighteenth centuries,' Daaku tells us, 'trading was effecting a near revolution' in the society of the Gold Coast peoples.* But it was a near revolution which failed; while the Gold Coast was anyway very much a special case, because the slaving component in export-import trade here was a good deal smaller than elsewhere. The partnership was thus an unequal one; but still it was a partnership.

There were interruptions. The balance of power kept breaking down on land and by sea. The British fought the French: the Ardras fought the Dahomeyans. Yet the wars were not so frequent as to become a general rule. As often as not there was peace among the partners. The first decisive break occurred in the eighteenth century when inland peoples lost patience with the coastal middlemen and struck through them to direct contact with Europeans, so that Europeans on the Guinea Coast were now faced with expanding African powers for the first time. Hostilities threatened. Wars broke out. But the Africans were too strong to be overawed, much less overthrown. Besides, once their rights were accepted, they were ready to enter the partnership themselves. Provided that Europe was content with equality of rights and respect, slaving could continue.

Then in the nineteenth century, with the fourth phase, the balance shifted again. British and French abolition of the slave trade went hand-in-hand with the rise of a new imperialism. Europeans were no longer content with equality of rights. They wanted domination. Soon they became involved in African politics, intervening by way of alliance with the statelets of the coast against the new powers of the hinterland. Inevitably, industrial Europe triumphed over non-industrial Africa.

Now a review of this changing relationship will show that each

*K. Y. Daaku, *Trade and Politics on the Gold Coast 1600–1720*, Clarendon, Oxford, 1970; and an article of Daaku's in C. Meillassoux (ed.), *The Development of Indigenous Trade and Markets in West Africa* (Oxford, 1971), pp. 168 ff: 'Trade and Trading Patterns of the Akan . . .'

of these phases was linked organically to the next. The slave trade, the crisis of its abolition, colonial invasion: all were aspects of a continuous process. Thus the old coastal partnership – the unique and extraordinary slaving relationship that bound the servitudes and freedoms of Europe and Africa so curiously and inextricably together – paved the way for the colonial system. The one beckoned the other.

This consequence is fairly easily detectable in the dynamics of slaving in respect of African forms of government. Politically – and, generally, economically and culturally as well – the European connection tended to reinforce the conservative aspects of African political organization, and to petrify African politics within traditional forms which grew more brittle and inflexible. One can reasonably say that the whole connection depended for its safety on those who had most to gain from obstructing or discouraging systemic and social change. It boosted the power of traditional rulers. It gave participating chiefs an additional interest in conserving things 'as they were'. And it did more than this.

Aside from bolstering the power of chiefs, slaving also provided a ready means for ridding chiefs of their critics. It was easy to remove the spokesmen of those who suffered most from the system, and who therefore wished to change it. In this respect the powerful men of West Africa behaved no differently from those of Europe: they transported their 'malcontents' and 'trouble-makers' to lands that were safely beyond the sea.

No one can be sure how often this was done. Yet it is not speculation to say that the inland monarchies regularly called in religious sanctions to denounce critics as criminals, and thereby turn them into captives for disposal. Nor is it speculation to say that political opponents in the delta states – where a political society was in budding growth – were given the same treatment. This may be taken as one reason why African revolts against the slaving system seldom occurred at home, but frequently on shipboard and across the seas.

In this elimination of rebels or potential rebels, the chiefs invariably had the backing of their European partners. When the Blood Men of the Old Calabar plantations invaded the town in 1850, records Waddell (and he was there), the apparition of these armed bands from the bush 'so alarmed the ship captains, for their property ashore, that they sent off hastily to Fernando Po, for the consul and a man-of-war'. Like other observers of the African scene, before and since, these captains had misunderstood the evidence of their own eyes. They feared for their property, yet the Blood Men wanted only to protect the lives of slaves. The European traders on the spot were even more upset. 'Talking of these things at King Eyo's table, one of them said: "I would like nothing better than to see the heads of a hundred of these fellows cut off." To that humane sentiment another old trader added: "They ought to be shot down like dogs." '

When nothing happened, because the Blood Men found that there were to be no human sacrifices and accordingly went back the way they had come, 'those who wanted to shoot them and behead them off-hand were ashamed of their panic when the consul and the man-of-war came, and had nothing to do'. Consul Beecroft, backed by his warship, lost no time in arranging matters so as to confirm and defend the *status quo*: 'farm slaves' – that is, the Blood Men – were to be 'forbidden to invade Duke Town armed, combinations for unlawful purposes prohibited, and runaways delivered up on demand'.

Then Waddell adds his most revealing passage. 'Though King Eyo kept silence during the discussion at his table [of the above arrangement between himself and Consul Beecroft] he was not insensible to the danger that might result from a spirit of combination among the slaves; and he sought to prevent its spreading by the old methods of denunciation and terror ...' In other words, since Eyo could no longer rid himself of inconvenient critics, as his predecessors had done, by handing them over to Europeans who regarded not their opinions but only their muscular development, he threatened them with death if they should dare to organize an opposition. And in doing this he could still rely on the backing of a man-of-war and the approval of a British consul. For although Consul Beecroft had obtained from the rulers of Old Calabar the confirmation of an earlier agreement against human sacrifice, the truth was that the Blood Men were the only force that could and did make an end to that practice. Yet Consul Beecroft pledged himself to help King Eyo to frustrate the Blood Men. Once again the built-in defences of the coastal partnership were at work in favour of a conservation that could only, in the long tale of history, cramp and stultify.

African chiefly rule had been – often still was – an efficient and representative form of government. But it suffered increasing perversion. Continued wars and raids on the mainland, Alfred Moloney was writing to the British Lieutenant-Governor of Lagos Colony in 1881, were 'to the personal advantage of a few influential Chiefs on either side who fan the flame to their own benefit, but to the detriment of their country and countrymen'. Moloney may have exaggerated; but there was certainly substance in what he said. Later on, when colonial rule had engulfed the whole of this country and imposed a *Pax Britannica*, chiefs would continue to seek their personal advantage by accommodations with imperial government, and would thereby secure their privileged positions. Apart from some who fought and were defeated, and a few who retired in dignity and said no more, most of the traditional rulers of West Africa accepted imperial Europe as a master who would at least perpetuate their own special prestige or privilege, if at the cost of their actual power; the emirs of Northern Nigeria, thanks to the British doctrine of 'indirect rule', were even successful in expanding both their privilege and their power.

* * *

The reasons for European developmental change between the fifteenth and nineteenth centuries are common knowledge, and they are not in any case my subject here. What I have tried to do is to show, in the light of modern research and analysis, how progress in Europe not only had no comparable development in Africa, but was indeed made possible only at the expense of any such progress in Africa. For it is in this story that one may come to understand why the 'technological gap' between the peoples of Africa and Europe – or, at least, between their leading states and most advanced communities – widened across this period, across these slaving years, from a narrow difference to an abyss; and why colonial conquest could follow so swiftly, and, as it often seemed at the time, almost automatically; and why it became possible for Europeans to regard Africans as being 'primitive', 'without culture', and 'incapable of achieving civilization on their own'. These racist stereotypes have lost much of their poisonous vigour over the past years of African resurgence. It still needs to be remembered that they provided the chief cultural instrument of colonial domination.

Through these four centuries the balance of gain was all one way. In any effective sense there was no creative marriage of cultures, no passage of ideas, no sharing of wealth and achievement. To Europe the trade with Africa was always an enrichment; and this enrichment could and did help Europe into new and more productive forms of society and government. But to Africans the relationship was incapable of carrying through the social and economic changes that were now required: on the contrary, it steered all those societies that it touched into economic or political frustration. The whole connection may be seen, indeed, as another demonstration of the extraordinarily wasteful nature of capital accumulation during the Industrial Revolution in Europe.

The connection worked another evil. It produced among Europeans the mentality of race superiority that helped to hasten colonial conquest, and still lingers like a poison in our midst. They came to believe that the slave trade was none of their contriving but a 'natural' outcome of Africa's indifference to human life. In 1832 the British Government agreed to send an expedition up the Niger 'with Commissioners charged ... to make treaties with the native chiefs for the suppression of this horrible traffic [the slave trade]; and to point out to them the advantages they will derive, if, instead of the wars and aggressions to which it gives rise, they will substitute an innocent and legitimate commerce'. A worthy object, no doubt, but perhaps a trifle hypocritical in view of all that had gone before? Yet we may be fairly sure that it never occurred to those excellent Commissioners, bent on their errand of mercy, to reflect that this disgraceful traffic was a direct and deliberate consequence of centuries of European insistence. Europe, not Africa, had fathered the oversea slave trade; but Europe, in its bland imperial arrogance, had ceased to recognize its monstrous child.

On Africans the mentality of the slaving years has tended to produce a contrary effect: it has sometimes loaded Africans with a sense of inferiority and even, here and there, of guilt and shame;

and this too, in one or other devious form, still persists. 'We, the Europeans', it was afterwards said, 'were certainly wrong to enslave Africans but at least we stopped the trade: while you, the Africans, not only persisted in the trade but perversely enslaved your own people. Can you really believe you are fit to run your own affairs?' This was said regardless of the fact that Europeans had also, in their own time and place, enslaved 'their own people'; and that Africans had in any case no sense of continental unity, while African culture made the concept of 'one's own people' a purely local one. The truth was that Africans had almost never 'enslaved their own people': they had captured other people who happened to live in Africa. In this they were no less 'moral' than the Europeans who had instigated the trade and bought the captives.

Both the one and the other – the pride and the shame, the sense of superiority and the sense of inferiority – are survivals of a past that has long called for resolute burial. But it will not be buried unless the true character and course of the slaving enterprise are understood; and it is the effort to promote this understanding, even within the limits of present historical knowledge, that may, I hope, finally justify these many pages.

For all this, now, should be over and done with. Humanity is too much cluttered and dismayed by the memory of past errors and botches. It is time to learn from them whatever can be learnt and then forget them. People remain. People in Africa, no matter how the habit of those old years might ruin and ravage, held on none the less to their belief in life and in themselves. Thanks to this firm hold, the slave trade passed over them without permanent damage. Today they reassert their equality and unity with the rest of mankind. At last the slaving chain of cause and effect, terminating in colonial subjection, is broken.

One should be careful not to over-stress the accent on 'stagnation' in these years. There was repeated individual effort to meet new situations in new ways. Reassertion took shape here, time and again, in the skill and vigour with which Africans learned new ideas and techniques, or matched their wits against foreign partners and eventual enemies. It was likewise made by all those men in Africa who fought against capture and exile, the overweening power of chiefs, and invasion from abroad.

Clear evidence of this same reassertion of African humanity can be found elsewhere as well. For it was made by all those countless slaves who refused to accept their fate and rose in revolt against their masters, founded free republics in the Americas or died in the attempt. It was proclaimed by the 'mutineers' on board ship, by the nameless heroes of Palmarès, by the revolutionaries of Haiti and the Negro soldiers of Bolivar. Equality: but also, as the records of history so clearly show, unity as well. For these brave men and women were the natural allies and companions of Sharp and Clarkson, Reynal and Grégoire, the Anti-Slavery Society and the Société des Amis des Noirs, not to speak of later times and the pioneers of black liberation in the United States of America and elsewhere. And now, in our own day, the same liberating concepts of equality and unity are once more forged across the world; and all those men and women in Europe who have seen and see the cause of their own further liberation in the liberation of the Africans are welcomed by the lifting voices of a new life in Africa itself: inexhaustible in spite of every set-back, ever-quickened, keen with hope.

A Note to this Edition

WHEN the first *Black Mother* was published, back in 1961, we were pretty much at the beginning of a systematic study of the history of the cultures and populations of Africa, while, in the matter of the Atlantic slave trade and its bearings on those cultures and populations, little or nothing new had been done for a long time. I recalled then, as being true indeed of almost all aspects of these subjects, what G. S. P. Freeman-Grenville had lately said of the condition of East African history: 'we are only at the beginning of its serious study, and there is a vast field of research . . .' I expressed the hope that *Black Mother*, like its predecessor *Old Africa Rediscovered*, would 'play some part in stimulating and inspiring other writers to go further and do better'. Whether or not this hope was made good, and perhaps to some extent it was, the fact remains that slave-trade studies today are much advanced on their situation of 1961.

Even so, a basis for inquiry and synthesis was available; and this basis, as may now be seen, was in most general respects a firm and solid one. The advances since then have been in building a far more detailed and sophisticated structure of cause and effect, scope and size, accuracy of measurement, as well as in placing the whole slave trade into an organically more meaningful perspective within the unfolding development of African and European history. I have taken these advances into account in this new edition, making many changes, some large and many small, while noting at the same time where important scholarly controversies still await definitive answers.

But I have not found that research by many distinguished hands since 1960, when I wrote the first edition, has called for a revision either of the general structure of the book or of the drift and emphasis of the narrative or of its essential conclusions. This is all the more pleasing to record, since the difficulties in making this synthesis were considerable. To begin with, it was necessary to tread new ground in looking at the Atlantic trade from the African rather than from the European point of view: a 'Europe-centred' mooring, in those days, was firmly anchored to the sea-bed of scholarly approaches. The study of African economic history was barely out of its cradle. Financial assistance from academic foundations was hard to find, or simply impossible; and I had greatly to thank the William Cadbury family trust for stepping into the breach. So it was a matter of much encouragement that the book's reception, eventually and indeed continuously by readers in many lands and languages, was and has remained a lively one.

If the first *Black Mother* has deserved its reception, the reason is that I was helped by pioneering figures in modern African historiography, notably K. Onwuka Dike, Thomas Hodgkin, the late Gervase Mathew, Raymond Mauny, Théodore Monod, George Shepperson, and for the Caribbean end of it, Eric Williams; and I should like to repeat my thanks. I also wish once more to record my thanks to the late Lucio Miranda for his help in translating, from sixteenth-century Portuguese, letters from King Affonso to the Kings of Portugal; to the Curator of Rhodes House for allowing me to consult the Morice MS and microfilm of other MSS photographed by the University of Chicago Library from documents in their possession; to the Anti-Slavery Society for permission to consult papers; and to Mario de Andrade for permission to quote the lines by Agostinho Neto, printed in *Antólogia de Poesia Negra de Expressão Portuguesa* (Oswald, Paris, 1958); at the time of writing, it was impossible to reach the poet himself. With this second *Black Mother*, further thanks are due for criticism or advice at various times to J. Ade Ajayi, Christopher Fyfe and Marion Johnson. The book's faults and failings remain of course my own.

As with the first, this new version reaches conclusions which remain to some extent controversial in their emphasis on this or that consequence of the trade, and possibly on certain other matters. But my general picture of the trade's origins, course and overall impact, I would hope, is one that can now win fairly wide agreement. This, and the interest which *Black Mother* happily continues to enjoy as an introduction to its subject, are what, I trust, will justify this new and expanded presentation.

BD

Reading Guide

AN extensive list of sources was useful in the first editions of *Black Mother*, since we were traversing ground which was little known and even less studied. That is no longer the case today. What may now be useful is an introductory guide for (*a*) readers who come to African history through this book, and would like to pursue their interest further; (*b*) readers, but especially students, who are interested specifically in the subject of the trade in captives for enslavement; and (*c*) students, rather than general readers, who require at least a summary of new sources, commentaries and approaches.

Those who have come to African history through this book, and would like to pursue their interest further, should begin with wide views of the subject. In English, for example, they should read J. D. Fage's excellent *A History of Africa* (Hutchinson, London), 1978; or the four-handed work of Philip Curtin, Steven Feierman, Leonard Thompson, and Jan Vansina, *African History* (Little-Brown, Boston), 1978; or my own *Africa in History* (Granada/Paladin, London), repr. 1978. In French they may begin with any one of a number of general histories; most of those available by 1980 omitted North Africa, but a notable exception is R. Cornevin, *Histoire de l'Afrique* (Payot, Paris), 3 vols., of which all were available by 1977. Each of these books has lengthy bibliographics of studies in various disciplines (history, archaeology, anthropology, linguistics, etc.), and related to individual territories, periods, or regions.

Those concerned specifically with the slave trade should make themselves well aware, to begin with, of new studies into the nature of pre-colonial institutions of servitude, relating as these do the whole question of slave-trade origins at the African end of the partnership. Apart from forthcoming work by Professor Fage, 1975 brought *L'Esclavage en Afrique précoloniale*, edited by C. Meillassoux (Maspero, Paris), and 1977 *Slavery in Africa: Historical and Anthropological Perspectives*, edited by S. Miers and I. Kopytoff (Univ. of Wisconsin Press, Madison), each embodying a considerably different approach from the other. Once again, bibliographies available in these two books will carry the student further into a subject where research is still at a relatively early stage, and firm conclusions at an even earlier one.

Secondly, so far as the slave trade itself is concerned, students should turn at once to Philip Curtin's *Atlantic Slave Trade* (Univ. of Wisconsin Press, Madison), 1969. This pathfinding work, as Curtin himself has emphasized, is not the final word on the subject of numbers – see new sources, below – but will remain indispensable. Next, they should read a series of essays (some in French, some in English) in *The Atlantic Slave Trade: New Approaches* (Société Française d'Histoire d'Outre-Mer, Paris), 1976. Thirdly, they should read Roger Anstey's *Atlantic Slave Trade and British Abolition 1760–1810* (Macmillan, London), 1975. It needs to be explained that Anstey's book, being much concerned with the reasons for British abolition, necessarily enters into the controversy set going by Eric Williams in his seminal *Capitalism and Slavery* (new edn, Deutsch, London), 1964, a book which likewise remains indispensable even if certain reservations must now be made about its emphases and conclusions. The debate set going by Williams (whose essential thesis, at least to me, appears to emerge unscathed) goes fruitfully on; but it is peripheral to the subject of *Black Mother* and I accordingly leave its bibliography out of account here.

Peripheral to this subject also, though of enormous importance in its own context, is the study of the impact of the slave trade and enslavement on the Americas. So far as the Caribbean is concerned, the various histories by Eric Williams offer a sound point of departure; but the Latin American bibliography on the subject (a little of which I included in the first *Black Mother*) is now too copious for useful summary here. Students should therefore ask for Latin-Americanist advice, although I still think that relevant works by G. A. Beltran, J. F. King, O. Pi-Sunyer, A. Ramos, R. C. Simonsen, and W. Zelinsky, quite a bit of it to be found in the *Journal of Negro History* over the years, remain of great value. A notable addition bearing on slave imports into Cuba during the Cuban sugar boom which began in 1791, largely because of the French loss of Saint-Domingue (Haiti), is that of Manuel Moreno Fraginals: *El Ingenio: Complejo Económico Social Cubano del Azucár* (Havana), 3 vols., 1978.

In this respect, too, 1975 brought another seminal work by S. L. Engerman and E. Genovese (eds.), *Race and Slavery in the Western Hemisphere: Quantitative Studies* (Princeton). These years also introduced a fruitful debate about the nature of North American institutions of slavery; but this too I leave out of account here. Students interested in this should again ask for specialist advice. I mention here only two good starting-points: J. H. Franklin, *From Slavery to Freedom* (Knopf, New York), 3rd edn., 1967; and D. B. Davis, *The Problem of Slavery in Western Culture* (Cornell, New York), repr. 1969.

Another large aspect of the whole subject is that of the trans-

Saharan and East Coast slave trade; and on this I would advise the student to begin with the three following works: M. Rodinson, *Islam et Capitalisme* (Seuil, Paris), 1966 (now available in English, Penguin, 1977); A. G. B. and H. J. Fisher, *Slavery and Muslim Society in Africa* (Doubleday, New York), 1971; and B. Davidson, 'Slaves or Captives? Some Notes on Fantasy and Fact', in N. I. Huggins, M. Kilson and D. M. Fox (eds.), *Key Issues in the Afro-American Experience* (Harcourt Brace Jovanovich, New York), 1971. This latter volume has valuable essays on several aspects of the slave trade and its consequences; as also does *The Uncommon Market* (New York), 1979.

As to new sources, commentaries and approaches, an exhaustive list would be inappropriate here. On the 'numbers controversy' set going so fruitfully by Curtin (1969), students should begin by reading Anstey (1975, *supra*) and the relevant chapters in Fage (1978, *supra*), and work through the books and papers to which these refer. They should take into account a fairly large number of papers published at one time or another in the *Journal of African History* (whose first year of issue was 1960) and notably, on the numbers controversy, J. E. Inikori, 'Measuring the Atlantic Slave Trade: An Assessment of Curtin and Anstey', in *JAH* xvii, 2 (1976); replies to this critique by Curtin and Anstey in *JAH*, xvii, 4 (1976); and R. Stein, 'Measuring the French Slave Trade, 1713–1792–3', *JAH* xix, 4 (1978). Important new ground in reference to the last was broken in 1978 with the publication under Serge Daget's editing of the monumental work of the late Jean Mettas in the Nantes archives: *Répertoire des Expéditions négrières françaises au XVIIIe Siècle* (Paris), 1978. Here one has many precise details of 1,427 Nantes sailings between 1707 and 1796, and in forty-two per cent of these cases there are figures for slaves carried.

A useful summary of 'where we had got to' by 1965 will be found in a collection of papers edited by C. Fyfe for the Centre of African Studies, University of Edinburgh, *The Transatlantic Slave Trade from West Africa* (Edinburgh), 1966; but much has been done since then, and the student, may I repeat, will profitably work through the *Journal of African History* for important research into various aspects of the subject. The same applies, in French, to the *Cahiers d'Etudes Africaines* and the *Revue Française d'Histoire d'Outre-Mer*. Here I will note only the importance of ideas and findings put forward by Jean Mettas, whose premature death was a painful blow to slave-trade studies as well as to his friends: for example, his '*Honfleur et la Traite des Noirs au XVIIIe siècle*', *Rev. Franc. d'Hist. d'O-M*, LX, 218 (1973), and, of course, the work edited by Daget that is mentioned above.

Generally, an understanding of the impact of the Atlantic trade, in its slaving dimensions as well as in others, has been advanced on almost every front of inquiry by the progress of historiography since the 1950s; and this is especially true, as one would expect from their prime interest in that trade, of the western regions. The pioneering work of K. O. Dike in this field has been taken up and enlarged by African scholars such as I. A. Akinjogbin and K. Y. Daaku, working in the universities of Nigeria and Ghana and elsewhere. Many other scholars have also turned their attention to the subject; and in this respect one may note that studies such as those of D. Birmingham, *Trade and Conflict in Angola (1483–1790)* (Clarendon, Oxford), 1966; W. Rodney, *A History of the Upper Guinea Coast* (Clarendon, Oxford), 1970; A. F. C. Ryder, *Benin and the Europeans, 1485–1897* (Longman, London), 1969; C. W. Newbury, *The Western Slave Coast and Its Rulers* (Clarendon, Oxford), 1961; M. Priestley, *West Africa Trade and Coast Society* (Oxford), 1969, and a number of others provide a ground of factual analysis and perception never available before. Overall syntheses specially designed for secondary-school and first-year university courses are B. Davidson, *History of West Africa 1000–1800* (Longman, London) new revised edn, 1977; and B. Davidson, *East and Central Africa to the Late Nineteenth Century* (Longman, London), 1967. The first of these was written with F. K. Buah and with the advice of J. F. A. Ajayi; and the second with J. E. F. Mhina and with the advice of B. A. Ogot.

It remains to add that the study of African economic history got into its stride during the 1970s, although with an understandable emphasis on the colonial and post-colonial periods. For pre-colonial periods the student should thoroughly digest the first 100 pages of A. G. Hopkins, *An Economic History of West Africa* (Longman, London), 1973; turn to C. Meillassoux (ed.), *The Development of Indigenous Trade and Markets in West Africa* (Oxford), 1971; and then proceed to specialized studies, for example by S. Amin, C. Coquéry-Vidrovitch, P. Hill, E. Terray, C. Wrigley, and others referred to in their bibliographies.

Relevant economic work on other regions of pre-colonial Africa is so far smaller in quantity, reflecting their lesser involvement before the 1830s; but here too the harvest of the last ten or fifteen years is a useful one. From the introductory survey in B. Davidson (1967, *supra*), the student concerned with East African history may pass to the early chapters in R. Oliver and G. Mathew (eds.), *History of East Africa* (Clarendon, Oxford), vol. 1, 1963, although some of these are now somewhat dated; and then to a range of individual studies listed by any competent Africanist library to the credit of E. A. Alpers, C. R. Boxer, A. Isaaman, M. D. D. Newitt and others. These last are concerned especially with Afro-European relations and reactions; but one may emphasize that the student now has available a long list of pathfinding works by East and Central African historians working in the 'pre-European' context, notably those by I. Kimambo, B. A. Ogot and their colleagues in the universities of those regions.

The student will also work through the files of journals other than the *Journal of African History*, and notably the *Journal of the Historical Society of Nigeria*, and *Transactions of the Historical Society of Ghana*, both of which yield new insights into the west coast trade.

BD

Index